D0264669

Oxford Library of Italian Classics

GENERAL EDITOR: ARCHIBALD COLQUHOUN

ALESSANDRO MANZONI

The Column of Infamy

PREFACED BY

CESARE BECCARIA'S

Of Crimes and Punishments

ALESSANDRO MANZONI

The Column of Infamy

PREFACED BY

CESARE BECCARIA'S

Of Crimes and Punishments

Translated by
Fr. KENELM FOSTER, O.P.
and
JANE GRIGSON

With an Introduction by
A. P. d'ENTRÈVES
Professor of Political Theory in the
University of Turin

London
OXFORD UNIVERSITY PRESS
NEW YORK   TORONTO

1964

Oxford University Press, Amen House, London E.C.4

GLASGOW NEW YORK TORONTO MELBOURNE WELLINGTON
BOMBAY CALCUTTA MADRAS KARACHI LAHORE DACCA
CAPE TOWN SALISBURY NAIROBI IBADAN ACCRA
KUALA LUMPUR HONG KONG

English translation and Introduction
© Oxford University Press 1964

Printed in Great Britain by
Richard Clay and Company Ltd.,
Bungay, Suffolk

CONTENTS

OF CRIMES AND PUNISHMENTS

THE COLUMN OF INFAMY

INTRODUCTION

by A. P. d'Entrèves

IN the days, still fresh in our memory, when a tide of 'recurrent barbarism' (as Vico would have called it) swept over the sunny fields of Europe and did not leave the Italian orchards untouched, we used to ask ourselves the question: how could such things have happened? Was there any possibility of redress? In those days we Italians remembered our ancient traditions and heritage. We turned to our classics. We found in them a message of encouragement and hope. Among these classics, two books were especially topical, and these are here presented to the English reader.[1]

Close bonds link the authors of these two books. They were both born, and both died, in Milan. They were closely related: Cesare Beccaria's daughter, the remarkable Donna Giulia, was the mother of Alessandro Manzoni. They were both members of that Lombard aristocracy which, under the enlightened rule of the Habsburgs, contributed so much to the rebirth of their country. They bear, if not actually a physical likeness, many similarities in temperament and character. Both took an active part in the intellectual life of their native city. Both left a mark in Italian letters. But there is another deeper bond between the two works here published. Both are burning denunciations of human folly, pleas for the cause of humanity and justice. They are classics, indeed landmarks, in the never-ending battle against cruelty, intolerance, oppression. Few documents in Italian literature could be chosen as better illustrations of that

---

[1] It is significant that the two books were both reprinted in popular editions in Italy during the last war (Manzoni, *Storia della colonna infame*, a cura di G. Vigorelli, Biblioteca Universale Bompiani, 1942; Beccaria, *Dei delitti e delle pene*, a cura di P. Calamandrei, Collezione in Ventiquattresimo, 1945). The late Professor Calamandrei's Preface to Beccaria is particularly moving, coming as it does from the pen of a leading figure in the Italian resistance.

happy combination of warmth and balance, of gentleness and clear-sightedness, that are typical of the best Italian minds.

Yet once the parallel and similarities are stressed, the differences remain, and should not be overlooked. They are differences in style and purpose. They are also differences in reputation and destiny. Beccaria's *Dei delitti e delle pene* is a work of world-wide impact and success. Manzoni's *Storia della colonna infame* is better known to the specialist than to the general reader. The first is a manifesto, an appeal addressed to all mankind; the second, an offshoot from, almost a footnote to, another and greater work. More than a generation divides the grandson from the grandfather: 'two centuries, in arms against each other',[2] provide the different setting as well as the different inspiration of the two books. To compare and contrast them is a fascinating experience. It opens up most stimulating perspectives into that fateful period in Italian history which is usually known as the *Risorgimento*.

Historians, both Italian and foreign, are now generally agreed in extending the *Risorgimento* from the short span of the actual wars which brought about the unification of Italy, to a much wider period, about a century (1763–1861), which marks, as it were, the second 'renaissance' of the country. In that renaissance, a more and more important part is now being conceded to the period that immediately preceded the French Revolution. Italy, in the second half of the eighteenth century, enjoyed a period of peace such as she had not enjoyed for many centuries. Still divided into several petty states, the country as a whole was governed by independent or semi-independent rulers. More important, these rulers were for the most part 'enlightened despots'. Nowhere in Europe did enlightened autocracy find a better testing ground than here. And nowhere perhaps better than in Lombardy—a Habsburg dominion enjoying considerable autonomy—was the benefit of long overdue reforms more apparent.

The story of the resurrection of Lombardy with the transition from Spanish to Austrian rule is a wonderful story, and

---

[2] '. . . *due secoli | l'un contro l'altro armato* . . .' (Manzoni, *Il cinque maggio*).

one which Italian historians, whatever their patriotic feelings, have never been reluctant to tell. Milan and her province were one of the richest areas in Europe. They had been immensely prosperous in the days of the Visconti and the Sforza. Every reader of Manzoni's *I promessi sposi* ('The Betrothed') has the picture of two centuries later clearly before his eyes. But now, if only for the benefit of a vast and distant Empire, Lombardy was set on her feet again. The good empress Maria Theresa carried out her reforms slowly and methodically. Her successor, Joseph II, the crowned revolutionary, would let nothing stand in his way. But these reforms would never have been so successful had there not been, on the side of the Italians, willingness to collaborate with their northern rulers. At a time when nationalism had not yet sown the seeds of bitter hostility, the government in Vienna could count on the loyal and even enthusiastic support of the intellectual élite in Milan, which had among its members such men as Pietro and Alessandro Verri, Gianrinaldo Carli, Paolo Frisi, Cesare Beccaria.

Most of these men were the scions of old families; they belonged to what we would call today the upper class. But unlike what happened in other parts of the peninsula, the Lombard aristocracy had never severed itself from active participation in business and administration. The best among them were not ensnared by the idle and gilded life which Parini so aptly derided in his satirical poem, *Il giorno*. They were full of the new ideas of the day and eager to contribute to their triumph. In the early seventeen-sixties, the French *philosophes* had many ardent disciples among them. Their little group had founded a kind of literary club, *l'Accademia dei Pugni*. Shortly after, they started publishing a paper, *Il Caffè*. It took as its model the British *Spectator*. It appeared regularly, every ten days, from 1 June 1764 to the end of May 1766. In that very summer, 1764, *Dei delitti e delle pene* had just appeared in print. Its author, hitherto unknown, was soon to become one of the best-known writers in Europe.

Cesare Beccaria was barely twenty-five when he began, in

March 1763, to write the small book that was to bring him fame. He was inspired and prompted to the task by Pietro Verri, a much stronger and more ambitious character, ten years his senior. The book itself, as Beccaria's latest biographer has remarked,[3] is a typical product of that 'internal dialogue' which went on within the enlightened circles of the eighteenth century. But this does not abate in any way its originality and novelty. The wind of reform was blowing in all directions. But one field, which was in need of reform more than any other, had not yet been tackled: that of criminal legislation. The great Montesquieu himself—one of Beccaria's acknowledged sources—had been strangely reticent on that matter. In the very year when Beccaria was composing his treatise, Voltaire was involved in the *affaire Calas,* too busy with horrible details to find time for a discussion of principles. Surely Beccaria was right when, after pointing out the immense progress of the age, the 'fruits we owe to this enlightened century', he added:

> But how very few men have examined and set themselves against the cruelty of punishments, and the irregularity of criminal procedure, a part of legislation so fundamental and so neglected through most of Europe. How few have blotted out, by a return to commonly-accepted principles, those errors which have accumulated through the centuries, or have attempted at least to curb, with the force of accepted truth, the unbridled advance of ill-directed power, which until our day has exhibited nothing but one long example of cold, legalized barbarity.[4]

The 'general principles' which should be resorted to, in order to reform criminal law, were, according to Beccaria, few and simple. They could all be summed up in one single principle, which Beccaria had discovered in Helvétius and in turn handed over to Bentham. What should be borne in mind was that laws had one ground and purpose only: 'the greatest happiness of the greatest number'. 'O my master,' so Bentham was one day to address Beccaria,

[3] F. Venturi, *Illuministi italiani,* Vol. III (*La letteratura italiana, storia e esti,* Vol. 46, III, 1958), p. 6.

[4] See p. 12.

first evangelist of Reason, you who have raised your Italy so far above England and I would add above France, were it not that Helvétius, without writing on the subject of laws, had already assisted you. . . . You who have made so many useful excursions into the path of utility, what is there left for us to do?—Never to turn aside from that path.[5]

To follow that path was difficult enough in England. On the Continent it might well have seemed an almost desperate enterprise. For, in Italy, law in general and criminal law in particular was hallowed by its traditional association with ancient Roman law. It needed all the iconoclastic fury of youth, all the revolutionary enthusiasm of the enlightened zealot, to declare flatly, as Beccaria did in the opening sentences of his book:

Certain residues of the laws of a race of conquerors in times long past, compiled by order of an emperor who ruled in Constantinople twelve centuries ago, later intermingled with Lombard usages, and eventually gathered into ill-digested tomes by obscure commentators who spoke only for themselves—such go to form the body of traditional opinion which passes for law in the greater part of Europe today. . . . These laws—this debris of barbarous times, are examined in this book in so far as they have a bearing on criminal procedure.[6]

Nothing could, in Beccaria's eyes, be saved of the old edifice. It had to be pulled down for a new one to take its place: a formidable task, and one which needed a revolution to achieve it. We are apt to forget it, for we live in that new edifice and take its amenities for granted. The fact remains that most of the changes which Beccaria advocated are now law in all civilized countries.[7] As for the death penalty, which survives in England and elsewhere but has long been discontinued in

[5] Quoted by Halévy, *The Growth of Philosophic Radicalism*, Ch. 1.

[6] See p. 6.

[7] They are, to mention only the most important, the 'certainty' of law, the respect of the principle *nulla poena sine lege*, the adoption of clear and simple rules of procedure, the guarantees which were to be secured in the 5th Amendment, the very notion of punishment as a measure of safety and prevention, not of expiation and revenge.

Beccaria's native country, neither Koestler nor Camus has been able to find more cogent arguments for its abolition than those stated in Chapter XVI of *Dei delitti e delle pene*. The book came in the right place and at the right moment. To follow up its quick and startling success is to follow the progress of the cause of penal reform in Europe as well as across the Atlantic. It was more than a success; it was a triumph. Actually the book, in the end, completely overshadowed the author, whose almost pathological shyness, sensitivity, and indolence made him shrink more and more from the limelight in which he had been cast unexpectedly and almost against his will.

But it is with the man behind the book that we ought to concern ourselves if we are to understand the subtle and complex relationship between the famous author of *Dei delitti e delle pene* and his no less famous grandson. To read Beccaria's work as an autobiography, rather than as a treatise on law, is the only way to penetrate his inmost feelings and convictions, indeed his almost religious faith—if this be not too strong a word for an outlook formed in an age that equated religion with bigotry. To be sure, Beccaria's style lacks the lashing irony of Voltaire, the prophetic assurance of Rousseau, the analytic precision of Bentham. There is, it must be admitted, a propensity to 'calculation', and it is this which probably contributed to endear him so much to Bentham. He seems at times to conceive of moral and legal problems as a matter of abstract, almost mathematical, reckoning. He was a born logician, and he knew how to press his argument with the utmost clarity and coherence. But coherence and clarity are not the main or the only reason for the eloquence of Beccaria's plea. What makes some of his pages so forceful is the warmth of emotion that pervades them, his capacity for feeling with victims of injustice, with the defenceless and the oppressed. It is more than the usual eighteenth-century *sensiblerie*; it is also something very different from the rationalist vindication of the rights of man.

If it were my sole merit to be the first to make much clearer to Italy those things which other nations have dared to put into writing

and now into practice, I should consider myself happy. But if, by
upholding the rights of man and the rights of invincible truth, I
should help also to rescue from the pains and anguish of death some
hapless victim of tyranny and ignorance, which are equally fateful,
then the thanks and the tears of that one innocent man, in the
transports of his joy, would console me for the contempt of all men.[8]

The man who wrote these words was a passionate believer in
human equality and dignity. There is an anticipation of Kant
in his famous line: 'Liberty vanishes whenever the law, in
certain cases, allows a man to cease to be a *person,* and to
become a *thing.*'[9] There is also an unmistakable adherence to
the Christian heritage which, unlike most of his fellow
philosophes, and notwithstanding his early revolt against an
'éducation fanatique',[10] he never really renounced.

This, I submit, is the invisible link which unites the 'free-
thinking' author of *Dei delitti e delle pene* with the devout
author of *I promessi sposi.* If nothing else, they have this in
common: that they deliberately espouse—they, born aristocrats
as they were—the cause of the underdog, the meek, the lowly.
The dominating theme of Manzoni's great novel is a plea for
the 'unfortunate victims' of prejudice and oppression: but it is
cast in the key of the Sermon on the Mount rather than in that
of the *Social Contract.* Manzoni's path seems indeed to have
been exactly the reverse of that of his great forebear; but it
led to very much the same conclusions. He was brought up in
unbelief, or at any rate in a world that was almost entirely de-
christianized; he returned to the fold of the Church on the tide
of the great wave of romantic nostalgia for the old religion.
What to the earlier generation had appeared as an age-long,
almost inexplicable imposture, suddenly revealed to the new its
unparalleled treasures, its kernel of truth and wisdom. But, as
far as Italy was concerned, the transition was effected without
the hatred and bitterness that accompanied it in other
countries. Manzoni's conversion is extremely significant in

[8] See p. 13.
[9] See p. 67.
[10] *Letter to the Abbé Morellet* of 26 January 1766, in Venturi, p. 202.

this respect. It was the capital event in his career as a writer. It was also a capital event in Italian spiritual history.

The first decades of the nineteenth century were marked all over Europe by a return to the old order. It was a period of restoration and conservatism. But the restoration in Italy was something very different from that in the rest of Europe. For one thing, it was not the old order that was restored in the peninsula after 1814. It was the hegemony of a foreign power. Furthermore, as a great and unfortunate Milanese patriot put it, pleading in vain with the British for a more sympathetic appraisal of the Italian cause: the Italians were no longer the same; but neither were the Austrians.[11] Awakened patriotic feeling made the 'fatherly government' of the Habsburgs intolerable; in fact, it had ceased to be fatherly at all. On the other hand, the revulsion against eighteenth-century rationalism was also a reaction against the predominance which French thought had long exercised over the intellectual élites of the country. Romanticism thus meant to the Italians a blend of religion, patriotism, and liberalism: and Manzoni was the standard-bearer of Italian Romanticism. He never felt that he had to renounce the ideals of liberty in which he had been reared and which ran, as it were, in his blood. Like many Italian patriots of the early nineteenth century, he saw those ideals at work in the Christian tradition of Italy, in the struggles of the medieval Church against the foreign invaders, in its efforts to curb the arrogance of Emperors and Kings. Conversion certainly did not turn Manzoni into a reactionary. Rather, it gave a new value, a new dimension, to his literary and political views. In the words of another distinguished Catholic writer of the period: 'the spirit so intimately religious as well as liberal which pervaded Manzoni's works was a determining factor for Italian public opinion. It was this spirit which contributed . . . to draw many Catholics to liberalism and many liberals to Catholicism'.[12]

Nowhere in Manzoni's work is this combination of the old

---

[11] Federico Confalonieri, *Carteggio*, Vol. I, pp. 135–137.

[12] Cesare Balbo, *Sommario della storia d'Italia*, Appendice.

and the new, this continuity between the eighteenth- and the nineteenth-century belief in the dignity of man, more apparent than in the short essay on the *Colonna infame*. In fact, the essay can be read almost as a postscript to Beccaria's work, as the greatest homage of the grandson to his grandfather. Manzoni always cherished the memory of his great forebear. He was proud of him, not only because of his fame, but because of the cause he had championed. Beccaria's genius, Manzoni pointed out, had turned paradoxes into commonsense.[13] In our essay here, he expressly refers, with one of his characteristic understatements, to 'that little book' *(quel libriccino)* which produced such world-wide consequences.[14] He obviously considered the author of *Dei delitti e delle pene* as one of the greatest benefactors of mankind. And it is in fact one of the practices of Roman criminal law which Beccaria had most vehemently denounced—the use of torture—that provides the main topic of the *Colonna infame*.

The reason for Manzoni's concern with criminal law was apparently quite incidental. In writing his 'Milanese tale of the seventeenth century', *I promessi sposi,* Manzoni had found himself overwhelmed by the details he had patiently and learnedly collected about life in Milan under Spanish rule, and about the great plague of 1630. He could never make up his mind how far to curtail these details in deference to his critics (the most prominent of them was Goethe) who found them too lengthy and cumbersome for a novel. Moreover, ever since the first draft, besides the meticulous historical setting, Manzoni had found himself saddled with two more or less self-sufficient 'stories within the story'. One was the tale of the Nun of Monza, with all its piquant details: a tale of lust and murder. The other was that of the trial and execution of the

[13] *Appendice storica sulla Colonna infame* (first draft of 1823) in *Tutte le opere*, a cura di A. Chiari e F. Ghisalberti, 1954, Vol. II, t.3°, p. 683. This passage was dropped in the final edition of the essay. But, as late as 1868, Manzoni still found an opportunity of paying a tribute to Beccaria as the 'wise and courageous' reformer of criminal law (*Appendice alla Relazione sulla lingua*, in *Opere varie*, a cura di M. Barbi e F. Ghisalberti, 1943, p. 845).

[14] See p. 134.

untori, the unfortunate men who had been suspected of spreading the plague and had confessed, under torture, to having done so: a typical tale of witch-hunt and judicial murder. The episode of the Nun of Monza, which is still prominent in the first draft of the novel, was mercilessly pruned down in the second. The author found the love story as a whole incompatible with his moral views about the novel. He suppressed most of it with a stroke of the pen, with what has been called the greatest understatement in world literature: *'la sventurata rispose'.*[15] The gruesome tale of the *untori* he deliberately reserved for separate publication. The *Storia della colonna infame* was published as a sequel to the revised and final edition of the novel in 1842. At the end of Chapter XXXII of *The Betrothed,* Manzoni expressly refers to it as 'another book', written for a purpose quite different from that of the novel.

What then were Manzoni's intentions in dealing in a separate work with a question of criminal law, and precisely with one which had been given a prominent place in Beccaria's *Dei delitti e delle pene?* To the reader who has just perused Beccaria's chapter on torture, Manzoni's essay will no doubt appear as different as history is from political theory, as bare facts are from their evaluation. But Manzoni does not only tell us a story, and a terrifying one at that. He is bent on pointing a moral, and the moral is exactly the same as that outlined in Beccaria's reflections. Torture was not only a monstrous survival of cruel and barbarous ages, a premium given to the strong over the weak, a substitute for the real task of justice, which is to ascertain the truth. It was also a violation of the dignity of man, a denial of the right of everyone to be presumed innocent until he is proved guilty. All that Manzoni does is to shift the indictment of torture from the plane of principles and logic, which Beccaria had chosen, to the stage itself where the horrible drama was enacted. And it is on this plane that he encounters a problem which is to him the greatest problem of all: that of human responsibility. If the laws of the

[15] 'The wretched woman replied.' (*The Betrothed,* tr. by Archibald Colquhoun, Ch. X. Revised edition, Everyman's Library, 1962.)

seventeenth century allowed and even recommended the use of torture, how could the judges of that time be blamed for using it, let alone for the absurd miscarriage of justice which it entailed?

Here is the point where Beccaria and Manzoni part company; but in order to appreciate fully the difference of their approach, mention must be made of a work which Manzoni had in mind together with Beccaria's. Its author was Pietro Verri. We have already met him. Verri had been the leader of the little group to which Beccaria had belonged in his youth. He had filled important posts in the administration of Lombardy. He had acquired a great reputation as an expert on finance, and his writings on political economy are said to compare favourably with those of Adam Smith, his great contemporary. But Verri had never been able to overcome the frustration of seeing his friend Beccaria reap the glory of a book which he was convinced he had inspired himself. In the years 1776–77 he composed a short *Essay on Torture*.[16] The immediate occasion of it was the fact that the complete abolition of torture decreed by Maria Theresa for her dominions had been opposed, in part at any rate, by the Senate, the governing body of Milan. But Verri's real concern is revealed from the very first sentences. He wanted to write on the subject of torture something different from, and possibly better than, what Beccaria and 'many other men of intellect and heart' had written.[17] 'They, for the most part, take their start from the highest principles of legislation, which only a few deep thinkers understand.' Verri on the contrary believed that one should put oneself on a level with the reader; that, rather than announcing in prophetic tones a truth which no one would heed, one should make use of facts and common-sense to shock and convince public opinion. What was needed to clinch the argument against torture was a practical

---

[16] *Osservazioni sulla tortura e singolarmente sugli effetti che produsse all'occasione delle unzioni malefiche alle quali si attribuì la peste che devastò Milano l'anno MDCXXX.* The essay was published posthumously in 1804.

[17] N. Valeri, *Pietro Verri*, Milan, 1937, p. 205.

B

demonstration of its consequences, the account of what really could and did happen. Such an account Verri had found. It was a story which should have weighed heavily on the memory and conscience of every decent Milanese. It was the story of the trial of the *untori* at the time of the great 'black death'—the same which Manzoni was later to unearth again when he started writing *I promessi sposi*.

Verri's *Osservazioni sulla tortura* certainly carry conviction. His account of the drab realities of the 'inquisitorial process' as it was practised according to Roman criminal law is even more shattering than Beccaria's strictures on its absurdities and contradictions. But by introducing us to the actors on the stage, by giving us, as it were, a living specimen of that 'process', Verri was bound to focus attention not only on the laws, but on the men who accepted and applied them. How could respectable judges, people who had lived only a century and a half ago in your own town, under the same sky, have committed the crime of condemning innocent men to a horrible death on flimsy evidence extorted in agony? Verri's explanation was in keeping with his enlightened creed. The fault was not with the men, but with the age: an age which did not yet have the benefit of light and reason; which was full of ignorance, error, and superstition; and was therefore bound to run amuck when hit by such a 'public disaster' as the plague. On all such occasions, wrote Verri, 'human weakness is always led to suspect extravagant causes, instead of seeing in them the result of the natural course of physical laws'. The monstrous trials were the inevitable outcome of panic and of absurd legislation: when laws and law-books, the legacy of a cruel past, were worshipped for the sake of their antiquity instead of being submitted to the judgement of Reason and Truth. It was, in fact, impossible that dark ages should not have bred dark deeds. There was an inner logic in what had happened.

Now this is precisely the attitude to history which Manzoni takes to task. His is a downright attack on what Sir Isaiah Berlin has so aptly described as the doubtful and dangerous dogma of historical inevitability. Though the essay on *La colonna infame* centres on a problem of criminal justice, Manzoni is not concerned with the same question which Beccaria had raised: what is the ultimate justification of punishment? He does not share his grandfather's view that all will be clear and easy once the principle of utility is accepted.[18] He is concerned with another problem, the one raised by Verri: the problem of laws that were bad and of men who were wrong in applying them. He deals with one issue alone, with a particular and glaring example of injustice. But that particular issue raises for him another and broader one: are men responsible for what they do, or are they merely the pawns of mysterious, impersonal forces? Is all that happens in history inevitable? Manzoni pleads for a closer look at what actually happens when an error is indulged in, when an injustice is committed. His is the concern of the Christian to reserve moral judgement, to provide, if not an answer, at least some ground of hope when iniquity seems to triumph, when the forces of evil are let loose. But why add more? Manzoni has put all this so well himself that it is hardly necessary, indeed almost impertinent, to paraphrase his words. They are the words that offered us comfort in the days to which I referred at the beginning, the days when everything, even hope, seemed lost.

If we regard a complex series of cruelties inflicted by man on man merely as the effect of times and circumstances, the horror and pity we feel is accompanied by a sense of discouragement, by a sort of despair. We seem to see human nature driven irresistibly to evil by forces beyond its control, caught in the toils of some evil and exhausting dream which it can neither throw off nor even become clearly conscious of. And so the indignation that spontaneously springs up in us against the men who did such things begins itself to appear unreasonable, even while, at the same time, we feel it to be noble and religious. Our horror remains, but the deed itself seems to have lost its guilt; and our mind, seeking the true culprit, the right object for its revulsion, is dismayed to find itself hesitating between two alternatives, equally blasphemous and insane: a denial,

[18] See p. 126. Manzoni's arguments against Utilitarianism are developed at length in an Appendix to the second edition of his *Osservazioni sulla morale cattolica* ('Del sistema che fonda la morale sull'utilità').

or an indictment, of Providence. But if, on a closer examination of
the facts, we are able to discern an injustice which those who committed it could themselves have recognized; a violation of rules
which they themselves accepted; an acting in clean contradiction to
principles not only admitted in that age but also evidently respected,
in similar circumstances, by the very men who acted in this way—
then we can with relief conclude that if these men did not know
what they were doing it was because they did not choose to know,
and that theirs was the kind of ignorance which men adopt and
discard as they please; not an excuse for crime, but itself a crime;
and that such things as they did may indeed be suffered, but not
done, under compulsion.[19]

These words seem to hold good not only for the judges who,
applying the existing laws, sentenced *untori* and witches to
torture and death in the past. They hold good also for other
more recent, legalized murders, for the officials who invoked
superior orders for again resorting to torture and for spreading
death on a scale hitherto unknown. No wonder that we feel
Manzoni nearer to us than Beccaria. Manzoni does not share
the optimism of the eighteenth century any longer. He is aware
that the great question is not so much, or not only, one of
reforming laws and institutions but of strengthening man
against the evil tendencies which he carries within himself.
Manzoni was willing to admit that the perversion of justice
which he had come across could be attributed to 'prevailing
ignorance' and to 'a barbarous legal system'. But, he pointed
out, 'bad institutions do not function automatically'. . . . 'The
real and effective cause of what was done [was] a passionate
perversion of the human heart.'

Thus there seem to be two morals that Manzoni draws from
his re-examination of the story of the Column of Infamy. The
first is that we should never be smug and self-righteous because
our laws are better and our institutions more enlightened than
those of the past. The real causes of the crimes that were committed in the name of those laws and institutions, Manzoni
warns us at the very beginning of his essay, 'are not, un-

[19] See p. 107.

fortunately, confined to a particular age'. And in a letter to a friend in France, written shortly after the publication of the essay, he explained that even though he had been dealing with 'an isolated event, with little bearing upon the great facts of history', with 'obscure actors, both those who had power and those who were without defence', with 'a misconception which is now apparent to anyone', with 'institutions, against which we no longer have to fight'; yet he had formed the conviction that 'underlying it all, there was still one point which bore upon the ever-present dangers that menace the human race, upon its highest as well as its most material interests, upon the perpetual struggle of mankind on earth'.[20] There is a prophetic ring in these words. We have learnt from bitter experience that Manzoni was right, that those dangers are indeed ever present.

But there is another moral in Manzoni's little essay, and it is in keeping with his whole career as a writer, with those deep convictions which make him a 'moralist' in the best sense of the word. It is the same moral that pervades his great novel, where the artist fully displays his ability at unravelling the secret recesses of the human heart. It is the moral which flows from the very core of Christianity: that men are responsible, not irresponsible beings; that the source of good and evil is not outside, but inside man. The Christian may never plead in his defence that he was ordered to commit a crime: there can be no shifting of responsibility; each and every decision we take is our own. The judges who condemned those innocent men were not the victims of a system, instruments of a corrupt society, of a dark and barbarous age. They were themselves corrupt, inasmuch as they betrayed their proper and only duty, which was that of seeking the truth, not of resting content with confessions extorted by violence. There was nothing inevitable in that monstrous miscarriage of justice. There is nothing inevitable in history, for it is men who make history, not history men.

[20] Letter to the Comte de Circourt, 14 January 1843, in *Epistolario*, a cura di G. Sforza, Milano, 1882–83, Vol. II, pp. 89–91. See p. 99 below.

No wonder that the pundits of historical inevitability—they called themselves 'historicists' in Italy—should have attacked Manzoni so sharply. Pointing to a few inaccuracies in Manzoni's narrative, they accuse him of having purposely painted a distorted picture of the condition of Italy during the Baroque age.[21] More particularly—and there is some ground for this criticism too—they denounce Manzoni's implacable rigorism, the 'casuistry' with which he indicts and prosecutes the protagonists of an old and forgotten drama, retrieving them, as it were, from oblivion to hold them up to the execration of posterity.[22] The answer to such strictures can be found only if we read Manzoni's essay in the context of his whole work. *The Column of Infamy* is not simply a footnote to the novel, a story within a story, a side-glance at the background with which Manzoni had grown familiar in the preparation of his novel. It is no more a piece of history than it is a plea for reform. Rather, it is a meditation on the human predicament, a fragment of that ideal *traité de l'homme* which haunted Manzoni all his life. The story of the Column of Infamy, when Manzoni wrote it, was well-nigh forgotten, and perhaps not even worth telling again. The point—as a recent and most sensitive critic has admirably put it—is that, to a Christian, 'time does not really matter. Blood unjustly shed will cry out for vengeance until the consummation of time.'[23]

[21] F. Nicolini, *Peste e untori nei 'Promessi sposi' e nella realtà storica*, Bari, 1937 (Chapter IV deals at length with the *Storia della colonna infame*).

[22] B. Croce, *Alessandro Manzoni. Saggi e discussioni*, 4th ed., Bari, 1952.

[23] G. Alberti, *Alessandro Manzoni, Introduzione allo studio della sua vita e delle sue opere*, Milan, 1964, p. 291.

Cesare Beccaria

OF CRIMES AND PUNISHMENTS

translated by Jane Grigson

PREFACE

CESARE, MARCHESE BONESANA BECCARIA was born on
15 March 1738, of an old aristocratic family, and educated by
the Jesuits at Parma. Having taken, in 1760, a degree in law
at the university of Pavia, he quarrelled with his father over
the choice of a wife, and at about the same time was, as he put
it, 'converted' to philosophy, which then meant the humanitarian rationalism of the French Encyclopaedists. His versatile
mind was attracted to both jurisprudence and economics, but
humanitarian feeling combined with the influence of Montesquieu and Rousseau to draw him first to the subject of the
reform of criminal law. The result was the bold and powerful
little work, *Dei delitti e delle pene,* which Beccaria began early
in 1763 and finished in less than a year. It came out at Leghorn
in 1764 and made an extraordinary impression. Beccaria found
himself a European figure, hailed by the leaders of the movement for reform as a new champion of reason and humanity.
From Paris D'Alembert wrote to P. Frisi: 'Ce livre, quoique
d'un petit volume, suffit pour assurer à son auteur une réputa-
tion immortelle. Que de philosophie, que de vérité, que de
logique, de précision et en même temps de sentiment et
d'humanité dans son ouvrage!' By the end of 1765 a French
translation was in print and an English one followed in 1767,
by which time Voltaire had already written and published
(anonymously) his *Commentaire* on the work. Meanwhile from
the conservative side there came, in 1765, Fachinei's violent
attack on Beccaria as a revolutionary and a heretic; and then
the official disapprobation of the Church when, in January
1766, *Dei delitti e delle pene* was placed on the Roman Index.

In October 1766 Beccaria went to Paris in response to
flattering invitations from the *philosophes,* but he was tempera-
mentally unable to enjoy celebrity and in December fled back

to Milan. The one thing he desired, he wrote to Verri, was to be left alone, left to himself. As F. Venturi remarks, there is something in all this that reminds one of Jean-Jacques Rousseau, and indeed Beccaria and Rousseau had more than a little in common. But the Italian was not of the stuff that revolutionaries are made of, and it is curious to observe that it was the Austrian government in Lombardy which saved Beccaria, temporarily, from the lethargy that always threatened to engulf him, by offering him a newly founded chair of political economy at Milan, as part of a plan for enlisting the support of progressive thinkers in an official project of administrative reform. Beccaria accepted and lectured for two years (1769–71) on 'elements of public economy'. Meanwhile Catherine II had tried, and failed, to draw him to St. Petersburg. In 1770 he brought out an interesting study of literary style, which was immediately translated into French but did not enhance his reputation in Paris ('un ouvrage sur le style,' commented Diderot, 'où il n'y a pas de style'). In April 1771 he was appointed to the Supremo Consiglio di Economia for the province of Lombardy, but this final mark of official esteem virtually coincided with the end of his brief career as a writer. He sank slowly into a melancholy lassitude. A work he had planned on the development of civilization, and which might have been a masterpiece, petered out in a few scattered *pensieri*. He died on 28 November 1794.

By his first marriage—the love-match with Teresa Blasco which occasioned the rupture with his father mentioned above —Beccaria had two daughters, of whom the elder, Giulia, was to be the mother of Alessandro Manzoni.

BIBLIOGRAPHICAL NOTE

The standard edition of Beccaria's works is by Sergio Romagnoli, *C. B. Opere,* Florence, Sansoni, 2 vols., 1958. The *Dei delitti* is also printed in its entirety (along with extracts from other works of B.) in *Illuministi italiani,* Vol. III ('Riformatori Lombardi, Piemontesi e Toscani'), edited, with an ample introduction, by Franco Venturi, Milan, Ricciardi, 1958. The last English translation was by J. A. Farrer, *Crimes and Punishments,* London, 1880. This volume contains a long introductory essay by the translator, chiefly concerned with the influence of B.'s treatise on legislation, particularly in Great Britain.

Of biographical and critical studies the following should be noted: E. Landry, *C.B., Scritti e lettere inediti,* Milan, 1910; C. A. Vianello, *La giovinezza di Parini, Verri e Beccaria,* Milan, 1933, and *La vita e l'opera di C. Beccaria,* Milan, 1938; C. Cantú, *Beccaria e il diritto penale,* Florence, 1862; C. Phillipson, *Three Criminal Law Reformers: Beccaria, Bentham, Romilly,* London, 1923; M. T. Maestro, *Voltaire and Beccaria as Reformers of Criminal Law,* New York, Columbia University Press, 1942.

The text used for the present translation of *Dei delitti e delle pene* is that published by Rizzoli, Milan, for the 'Biblioteca Universale', no. 123, 1950, identical, except for some punctuation, with the edition by S. Romagnoli mentioned above.

KENELM FOSTER

TO THE READER

In rebus quibuscumque difficilioribus non expectandum, ut quis simul et serat et metat, sed praeparatione opus est, ut per gradus maturescant.[1]

BACON

CERTAIN residues of the laws of a race of conquerors in times long past, compiled by order of an emperor who ruled in Constantinople twelve centuries ago,[2] later intermingled with Lombard usages, and eventually gathered into ill-digested tomes by obscure commentators who spoke only for themselves—such go to form the body of traditional opinion which passes for law in the greater part of Europe today. It is as pernicious as it is prevalent that a view put forward by Carzov, or an ancient custom to which Caro happened to allude, or some torture proposed with irate satisfaction by Farinacci,[3] should now be laws blandly accepted by those who ought to be abashed by the responsibility of governing the lives and fortunes of human beings. These laws—this debris of barbarous times, are examined in this book in so far as they have a bearing on criminal procedure. The author, in making bold to draw the attention of those charged with public welfare to the confusion of such laws, does so in a manner unlikely to attract a reader who is impatient and unlettered. The open-minded search for truth, the independence from popular opinion with which this book is written, are results of the gentle and enlightened government under which the author lives. The great monarchs, benefactors of humanity, at present ruling, like to see truths

---

[1] In all matters, particularly difficult ones, no one should expect to reap and sow at the same time, but should see the need of preparation so that they gradually reach maturity.

[2] Justinian's *Corpus Iuris.*

[3] All eminent sixteenth- and seventeenth-century jurists. [Tr.]

laid bare by an obscure philosopher. Their vigour, though not their fanaticism, is aroused only by those who reject reason and menace order and industry. Present confusions of law, as anyone must realize who examines all their circumstances, are a bitter comment and reproof against past ages, not against this one and its legislators.

So let anyone who wishes to honour me by his criticism begin by a true understanding of this book's purpose; a purpose that, far from diminishing legitimate authority, should serve to increase it, if opinions have more effect on men than power, and if that authority is justified in all eyes by its gentleness and humanity. Criticisms[4] published against this book have been based on misunderstanding and confused ideas, and they oblige me to interrupt for a moment my arguments, addressed to enlightened readers, in order to try to put a stop once and for all to errors due to timid zeal or calumnies due to malice.

There are three sources from which derive the moral and political principles that regulate mankind: revelation, natural law, and the artificial conventions of society. The first is in no way comparable to the others in its chief purpose; but all three are similar in that they all tend towards happiness in this mortal life. To consider the permutations of the third is not to exclude any permutations in the first two; quite the contrary, for those first two, though divine and immutable, have been confused in innumerable ways by the fault of men, by false religions and arbitrary notions of vice and virtue thrown up by corrupt minds. Thus it seems necessary to examine, separately from any other consideration, what has come about by purely human contrivance, been declared or presumed as of common necessity and utility. This concept of common necessity and utility is in fact one to which every faction and system of morals must necessarily adhere; for it will always be considered praiseworthy to urge the recalcitrant and incredulous to conform to the principles that drive men to live together in society.

Thus three classes of vice and virtue can be distinguished:

[4] By Fra' Fachinei, in a booklet *Note ed osservazioni sul libro intitolato 'Dei delitti e delle pene'*, published in 1764. [Tr.]

the religious, the natural, and the political. These three should never be in contradiction between each other. But not all the consequences and duties which result from one result from the others. Not all that is exacted by revelation is exacted by natural law; nor all that is exacted by natural law exacted by purely social law. But it is most important to distinguish the results of the latter contract, that is of the pacts, tacit or expressed, made by man, because these are the limitations of the power that can legitimately be exercised by man on man without a special mandate from the Supreme Being. The concept of political virtue, therefore, can unhesitatingly be called variable. The concept of natural virtue would always be clear and obvious were it not obscured by men's follies and passions. The concept of religious virtue is always one and constant because it has been revealed directly by God, and preserved by him.

Thus it would be an error to attribute to a person discussing social covenants and their consequences any principles contrary to natural law or to revelation, because the latter would not enter into discussion. It would equally be an error for one discussing, say, the possibility of a state of struggle existing before a state of society, to take this in the sense that Hobbes did; that is of no previous duty or obligation having existed, instead of taking this state of struggle as something born of the corruption of human nature and of the lack of any express penalty. It would be an error to blame a writer who is considering the emanations of the social contract for not admitting their existence before he admits that of the contract itself.

Divine justice and natural justice are of their essence constant and unchangeable, because a relationship between two objects that remain the same is itself always the same. But human justice, or rather political justice, being no more than a relationship between the actions and the variations of society, can vary in proportion as those actions become useful or necessary to society; nor is this variation easily discernible except by those who analyse the complicated and very changeable interconnexions of civic interests. As soon as these principles, which are essentially distinct, become confused, there is no hope of any more clear reasoning on matters of public administration. It is for theologians to establish the confines of the just and the unjust, the intrinsic evil or goodness of an action. It is for the man in public life to establish the relationship between political justice and injustice, between what is useful and what is harmful to society. Neither can ever jeopardize the other, as each sees that purely political virtue must cede to the immutable virtue coming from God.

Anyone, I repeat, who wishes to honour me by his criticism should therefore not begin by supposing that I harbour principles destructive either to virtue or to religion, for I have now shown that such are not my principles; and instead of making me out to be either seditious or unbelieving, let him try to prove me a bad logician or a superficial observer of public affairs; let him not tremble with alarm at every proposition of mine that sustains the interests of humanity; let him show me the advantages of traditional practice. I have given public testimony of both my religion and my submission to my sovereign in the reply to Fra' Fachinei's 'Notes and Observations'. It would be superfluous to reply to other writings of the kind. But anyone who writes about my book with the decency proper to honest men, and with an intelligence that dispenses with my proving first principles of whatever character they may be, will find me not only one ready to reply, but a pacific lover of truth.

1. INTRODUCTION

MANKIND in general leaves the regiment of its most important affairs to the day-to-day prudence or discretion of those whose interests set them against the most far-seeing laws— laws which by nature universalize the benefits of life and resist that force by which these benefits tend to become concentrated in a few hands, accumulating on the one side the utmost of power and felicity, on the other all weakness and misery. It is thus only after they have picked their way through a thousand errors in matters essential to their life and liberty, only after they are weary of suffering evils, that men, able to stand no more, can be induced to remedy the disorders which oppress them, and recognize the most palpable truths which, precisely because they are simple, escape the common mind, unaccustomed as it is to the analysis of things, and taking its impressions, in a rigid way, more from tradition than from inquiry.

If we open our histories, we shall see that laws which are, or should be, pacts between free men, have for the most part been only the instrument of the passions of the few, or the product of an accidental and temporary need; they have never been dictated by a cool scrutineer of human nature, able to condense to one particular the activities of a multitude of men, and consider them from this point of view: *the greatest happiness of the greatest number*. Happy those rare nations who, instead of waiting for human changes and vicissitudes to proceed at their sluggish pace from the extremities of evil to the first steps in goodness, have hastened the stages in between with good laws. Worthy, too, of men's gratitude that philosopher who, from the despised obscurity of his study, had the courage to sow widely the first seeds of useful truths, fruitless for so long.

We are now aware of the right relationship between sovereign and subject, between nation and nation; trade has been quickened in the light of philosophic truths disseminated by the printing-press; and there has been kindled between the nations a tacit war of industry, altogether more humane, and more worthy of rational beings. Such are the fruits we owe to this enlightened century. But how very few men have examined and set themselves against the cruelty of punishments and the irregularity of criminal procedure, a part of legislation so fundamental and so neglected through most of Europe. How few have blotted out, by a return to commonly-accepted principles, those errors which have accumulated through the centuries, or have attempted at least to curb, with the force of accepted truth, the unbridled advance of ill-directed power, which until our day has exhibited nothing but one long example of cold, legalized barbarity. Yet the groans of the weak, sacrificed to cruel ignorance and wealthy indifference; the barbarous tortures, multiplied with prodigal and useless severity for crimes either illusory or unproved; the filth and horrors of a prison, augmented by that most cruel tormenter of the wretched, uncertainty, ought surely to have struck home to those magisterial persons who guide the opinions of mankind.

The immortal President de Montesquieu has touched briefly on this matter; truth, which is indivisible, has compelled me to follow in the shining path of this great man; but thoughtful men, for whom I write, will know how to distinguish his steps from mine. I shall be happy if, like him, I also can earn, in secret, the thanks of reason's obscure and pacific followers, if I too can inspire that sweet tremor with which feeling spirits respond to those who uphold the cause of humanity.

At this point order should lead us to examine, and distinguish between, the different kinds of crime, and the ways in which they are punished. Crimes and punishments, however, vary so much in their nature according to the differing circumstances of the age and the country, that this would involve us in too great an immensity of tiresome detail. Enough if I indicate the most general principles, and the commonest and most ruinous errors, disabusing in that way no less those who would introduce anarchy, out of a wrong conception of the love of freedom, than those others who would so willingly reduce mankind to the regularity of the cloister.

What punishment is best suited to a given crime? Is death a punishment which is really *useful,* and *necessary* for the security and good order of society? Are torture and instruments of torture *just,* and do they attain the *ends* propounded by law? What is the best way of preventing crimes? Are the same penalties always equally useful? What influence have they on social custom? These are the problems which ought to be solved with a precision so geometric that it cannot be overcome by mists of sophistry, seductive eloquence, or timidity and doubt.

If it were my sole merit to be the first to make much clearer to Italy those things which other nations have dared to put into writing and now into practice, I should consider myself happy. But if, by upholding the rights of man and the rights of invincible truth, I should help also to rescue from the pains and anguish of death some hapless victim of tyranny and ignorance, which are equally fateful, then the thanks and the tears of that one innocent man, in the transports of his joy, would console me for the contempt of all men.

2. THE ORIGIN OF PUNISHMENTS. THE RIGHT TO PUNISH

No lasting advantage can be expected from political morality, unless that morality is founded upon the ineffaceable sentiments of mankind. Any law deviating from these sentiments will always meet a contrary force, which will defeat it in the end, just as the smallest of forces, if continuously exerted, defeats any violent motion imparted to a mass.

Let us consult the human heart, for it is there that we shall find the fundamental principles of the true sovereign right to punish crimes.

No man ever freely gave up a portion of his individual liberty for the public good; such an illusion is to be found only in romances. Were it possible, all of us would prefer the covenants which bind others not to bind ourselves. Every man acts as if he were the centre of all the permutations of the globe. It was the multiplication of the human race, inconsiderable in itself, yet producing needs which ever outstripped the resources of nature in its barren and neglected state, that caused the union of the first savages. These first societies gave rise inescapably to other societies opposed to them; and in this way the state of war was transferred from individuals to nations.

Laws are the conditions of that fellowship which unites men, hitherto independent and separate, once they have tired of living in a perpetual state of war and of enjoying a liberty rendered useless by the uncertainty of its preservation. They will sacrifice a portion of this liberty so that they may enjoy the rest of it in security and peace. The sum of all these portions of liberty sacrificed for each individual's benefit constitutes the sovereignty of a nation; the sovereign is the lawful depositary and administrator of these portions of liberty. But to constitute this deposit was not enough: it had to be defended from the private encroachment of each individual man, since the individual always tries not just to take back from this common store his own contribution, but to purloin that contributed by others. Palpable motive forces were therefore needed, sufficient to dissuade the arbitrary spirit of the individual from plunging society's laws once again into primitive chaos. These palpable motive forces are the punishments ordained against breakers of the law. I say 'palpable motive forces' because experience shows that the majority of men adopt no stable principles of conduct, and only evade that universal principle of dissolution, which is to be observed both in the moral and the physical world, if there exist motive forces which make an immediate impress on the senses and present themselves continually to the mind in such a way as to counterbalance the strong effect of passions whose bias is opposed to the general good. Eloquence, declamation, even the most sublime truths, have not been enough to curb passions for any length of time when excited by the lively impact of present objects.

Since then it was necessity which compelled men to yield

portions of their individual liberty, it is certain that the portion each man was willing to add to the common stock was the smallest possible—only as much, that is to say, as would induce others to defend the whole. The right to punish is the sum of these smallest possible portions. Anything above that sum is abuse, and not justice; a fact, but certainly not a right.[1]

Punishments which go beyond the need of preserving the common store or deposit of public safety are in their nature unjust. The juster the punishments, the more sacred and inviolable the security and the greater the liberty which the sovereign preserves for his subjects.

3. CONSEQUENCES

THE first consequence of these principles is that laws alone can decree punishments for crime, and this authority can reside only in the legislator who represents society as a whole united by a social contract. No magistrate (himself a part of society) may with justice ordain punishments for another member of the same society. A punishment increased beyond the limit fixed by the laws is another punishment added to the just one; it follows that a magistrate cannot, on whatever pretext of zeal or the public good, increase the punishment already decreed against an offending citizen.

The second consequence is that the sovereign, who represents society itself, can only make general laws which are binding on

---

[1] Observe that the word *right* does not contradict the word *force*. *Right* is rather a modification of *force*—i.e. the modification most useful to the greater number. And by *justice* I mean nothing else than the bond required to unite private interests without which they would disperse into the old state of insociability.

We must guard against attaching the idea of something concrete to this word justice, as if it were a physical force or an actual being: it is a simple form of concept about mankind, and one which has immense influence upon the happiness of individuals. Still less do I refer to that other kind of justice which emanates from God, and whose immediate connexion is with the rewards and punishments of the life to come.

all members, but he certainly cannot judge whether anyone has violated the social contract; if he did the nation would be divided into two parts, one represented by the sovereign, who asserts that the contract has been violated, and the other by the accused, who denies it. Therefore it is necessary that a third party should judge the truth of the matter. Hence the need of the magistrate, whose decisions admit of no appeal and consist merely of simple confirmation or negation of particular facts.

The third consequence is that, when extreme severity of punishments (though not immediately opposed to the public good and to the same purpose of preventing crime) can be shown to be useless, then in this case, too, such severity would not only be contrary to the kindly virtues born of an enlightened reason which would rather govern happy men than a herd of timidly cruel slaves, but would also contradict justice and the nature of the social contract itself.

4. INTERPRETATION OF THE LAW

A FOURTH consequence is that authority to interpret penal laws cannot rest with criminal judges, precisely because they are not makers of law. Judges have not received laws from our forefathers as one receives a family tradition or a testament that allows posterity no other option than to fulfil its conditions. Laws come to them from living society, or from the sovereign who is that society's representative as well as the lawful depositary of the present state of the will of the people. They do not receive laws as if these were obligatory under an ancient oath[1] (such an oath, binding wills which did not exist when it

---

[1] If every individual member is bound to society, society is equally bound to every individual member by a contract binding by its nature on both parties. This obligation, which descends from the throne to the hovel and binds equally the greatest and the most miserable of men, means exactly this: that it is in all men's interest for agreements beneficial to the greatest number to be observed.

The word *obligation* is one of those words more frequently used in morals than in any other science and which are the symbolic abbreviations of a

was sworn, would be null and void, and also iniquitous, since it would reduce men from the status of a society to the status of a herd). But they receive them as the outcome of an oath, implied or expressed, which all living subjects have sworn with a united will to their sovereign, in order to restrain and control the ferment of private interests. This is the actual and physical authority of the laws.

Who then can legitimately interpret laws? The sovereign, in other words the depositary of all that now results from the will of the people? Or the judge, whose sole business is to discover whether or not a man has acted against them?

In every criminal case the judge should reach a perfect syllogism. The major premiss should be the general law, the minor premiss whether the action does or does not conform to the law; the conclusion should be either release or punishment. If a judge is compelled to make, or makes of his own free will, even two syllogisms, he opens the door to uncertainty.

Nothing is more dangerous than the common axiom that we should 'consult the spirit of the law'. This is to allow the dyke of law to be breached by the torrent of opinion—a truth which to me seems irrefutable, though it may appear a paradox to vulgar minds who are more impressed by an immediate modicum of disorder than by the remote disasters which follow when a false principle is allowed to take root in a nation. Our knowledge and all our ideas are connected reciprocally. The more complex they are, the more numerous will be the paths which lead both to and away from them. Every man looks at things in his own way, every man thinks differently at different times. 'The spirit of the law' will therefore depend upon the good or bad logic of the judge, upon his good or his bad digestion; it will depend on the degree of violence in his emotions, upon the feebleness of the sufferer in the case, upon the relations between the judge and the victim,

---

process of reasoning and not of a single idea. Search for an idea corresponding to this word 'obligation' and you will not find it. Reason about it, and you will understand and be understood.

or on all those minutiae of circumstance which alter the look of everything in the fluctuations of the human mind. Hence we might observe a citizen's fate changing many times in his progress from court to court, we might see wretches' lives victimized by the false reasoning or the good or bad humour of a judge, who thinks that the law is rightly interpreted by the vague outcome of all the confused series of notions which move his mind. Or we might see the same crime punished differently by the same court at different times, because the court has consulted, not the constant and fixed voice of the law, but an instability of errant interpretation.

Any momentary disorder caused by the rigorous observance of the letter of a penal law is nothing compared to the disorders which follow from interpreting a law. Such a passing inconvenience calls for the change in legal wording necessary to remove the uncertainty; but such an easy remedy hinders that fatal freedom of debate, which is the source of arbitrary and venal disputes. When a fixed code of laws, which he has to follow to the letter, leaves the judge no other duty than that of examining the actions of the citizen and determining whether they conform or not to the written law; when a norm of justice and injustice, equally binding upon the actions of the unlearned and the philosophic citizen, is a matter, not of controversy, but of fact; then citizens will no longer be exposed to the petty tyrannical actions of many men, which become all the more cruel as the distance between victimizer and victim decreases, and which are deadlier than the tyrannical actions of a single man, in as much as the despotism of many men can be corrected only by the despotism of one man, whose cruelty is proportioned, not to his power, but to the obstacles in his path. Under a fixed code of law citizens acquire that personal security which is just, because it is the purpose for which men join together in society; which is useful, because it enables them to calculate the exact consequences of misdoing. True, they will also acquire a spirit of independence, but not such as to overthrow laws or to resist supreme magistrates; the men they resist will be those who have dared to dignify by the sacred name of virtue the feeble surrendering to their own caprices, interests, and opinions.

These principles will give no pleasure to those who have taken upon themselves the right to hand on to their inferiors the blows of tyranny they have received from their superiors. I myself should have everything to fear if the spirit of tyranny and the spirit of culture ever went hand in hand.

5. THE OBSCURITY OF LAWS

IF interpretation of laws is an evil, their obscurity will evidently be another, since that will demand interpretation too; and it will be worse if laws are written in a language which the people do not understand,[1] which forces them to depend on a very few men and makes them unable to judge the chance of liberty for themselves; such a language transforms a sacred and public book into one which is in effect personal and private. The greater the number of people who understand the sacred code of laws and have it by them, the fewer will be the number of crimes committed; since one cannot doubt that ignorance and uncertainty of penalties help the strong urge of passion. What must we think of mankind when we reflect that obscurity of law is the inveterate custom of a large part of cultivated and enlightened Europe?

One consequence of these last thoughts is that without written laws a society can never achieve a fixed form of government, in which power is vested in all rather than some, and in which laws can neither be altered except by the general will nor corrupted as they pass through the mob of private interests. Experience and reason have made us see that human tradition diminishes in power to convince and satisfy the further it recedes from its origins. If there is no enduring monument of the social contract, how can laws resist the inevitable force of time and of the passions?

From this we observe how great is the usefulness of printing,

[1] I.e. in Latin, as was general up to Beccaria's day. [Tr.]

which makes the public and not a mere handful of men the depository of law; and to what a degree the gloomy spirit of cabal and intrigue has been dissipated in the face of enlightened sciences, which are apparently despised, yet in reality feared by its partisans. This is why we see in Europe a diminution of those terrible crimes which brought groans from our ancestors, and made them in turn either tyrant or slave. Those who know the history of our own and the two or three previous centuries will be able to see how the most gentle of human virtues—humanity, charity, and toleration of human error—have sprung from the lap of luxury and soft living. They will see, too, what were the effects of 'ancient simplicity and good faith', so called: humanity groaning under implacable superstition; the greed and ambition of a few, staining with human blood the coffers of gold and the thrones of kings; treachery in secret, slaughter in public; every nobleman a tyrant to the people; the servants of the truths of the Gospel polluting with blood hands which day by day touched the God of gentleness—such are not the work of this enlightened century, which some men call corrupt.

6. OF IMPRISONMENT

ONE error, as common as it is contrary to the proper end of society (the consciousness of personal security) is to allow a magistrate to become arbitrary executor of the laws, able to send a citizen to jail, to take away the liberty of a personal enemy on frivolous pretexts, or to leave a friend unpunished despite the strongest proofs of his guilt. Imprisonment differs from every other kind of punishment, because it must of necessity precede the decision of the court; but this distinctive character does not deprive it of the other essential, that it is only law which can determine the cases in which punishment is deserved.[1] The law must therefore indicate what evidence is required to justify the detention of an accused man, his sub-

[1] A principle first laid down in Magna Charta (1215). [Tr.]

mission to examination, and his punishment. Common report, flight, extra-judicial confession, the confession of an accomplice, threats and inveterate hostility against an offended party, the circumstances of a crime, and similar evidence, are proofs enough to justify detention. But these proofs must be established by law and not by the judges; whose decisions always run counter to political liberty if they fail to apply, in a specific way, a general maxim of the public code. The more punishments are moderated, the more squalor and starvation are banished from prisons, the more compassion and humanity penetrate their gates of iron and take charge of the hardened and unrelenting servants of justice, the slighter will be the evidence on which a man may properly be detained under the law.

A man accused of a crime, put in prison, and then acquitted, should be freed of any mark of infamy. How many Romans, accused of the gravest crimes and then found innocent, were venerated by the people and honoured with magistracies! In our day very different circumstances attend the acquittal of an innocent man. Why? Because under our present criminal system the idea of strength and power seems to prevail in people's minds over the idea of justice; because accused and convicted are thrown together into the same dark hole; because prison is less a holding of the person of the accused than a punishment; and because that internal force which is the guardian of the laws, and that external force which is the defender of throne and nation, have become divorced when they should be united. If they were, the former would be combined in a common reliance upon law with the judicial authority, while remaining independent of that authority for its immediate power; and the infamy and disgrace, which like all public sentiments are apportioned less to the thing itself than the appearance of the thing, would disappear in the glory which always goes with the pomp and circumstance of soldiers on parade; of which there is proof in the fact that military imprisonment is popularly held to be less of a disgrace than civil imprisonment. But then in customs and in legislation, which are always more than a century behind the actual

goodness and enlightenment of a nation, we still retain the barbarous stamp and ferocious ideas of those hunters of the north
from whom we descend.[2]

7. EVIDENCE AND FORMS OF JUDGEMENT

THERE is a general theorem which is most useful for weighing
up the certainty of a fact, the strength of the evidence for a
crime, for example.

When the proofs of a fact depend only on one another, that
is to say when the various pieces of evidence stand together or
not at all, then the more proofs are advanced the less probable
that fact will be, because the possibilities of error in the
antecedent proofs increase the likelihood of error in the subsequent ones. When the proofs of a fact all depend equally on
a single proof their number neither increases nor lessens the
probability of the fact, because their whole strength rests upon
the strength of that one proof alone. When the proofs are
mutually independent, in other words when the items of
evidence stand up by themselves, then the more of them there
are the greater the probability of the fact, as the fallaciousness
of one item does not invalidate another. I speak of 'probability'
in the matter of crimes, though crimes should be proved before
they are punished. The paradox, however, will vanish if one
considers that moral certitude, strictly speaking, can be no
more than a probability—but one of such a kind as to be called
a certainty, seeing that every man of common sense must
acquiesce in it by a force of habit which arises from the need
to act and which precedes all speculation.

The proofs of a crime can be distinguished as perfect and
imperfect. We call perfect those proofs which exclude all
possibility of a man's innocence: we call imperfect those by
which it is not excluded. Only one perfect proof is required for

[2] The Lombards. [Tr.]

a condemnation. Of imperfect proofs as many are required as will form one perfect proof; in other words, although each proof of this second kind taken by itself does not establish a man's guilt, agreement between such proofs on the same matter makes his innocence impossible. Note that imperfect proofs which an accused fails to answer, though he is given the chance to do so, become perfect proofs. But this moral certitude in the matter of proof is one more easily felt than exactly defined. For that reason I believe the best law to be one which assigns to the chief judge a jury chosen by lot rather than selected; ignorance, which judges by feeling, being in this case more dependable than knowledge which judges by opinion. Where laws are clear and precise, the duty of a judge consists only in the verification of fact. If ability and dexterity are required, and if the presentation of the outcome demands clarity and precision, nothing more is needed in judging the outcome than ordinary, simple good sense; which is less fallible than the knowledge of a judge whose habit is to wish men guilty, and who reduces everything to an artificial system borrowed from his own studies. Happy the nation whose laws are not a science! A very useful law is that by which a man should be judged by his equals, since where a citizen's life and liberty are involved, feelings inspired by inequality should have no voice. In such proceedings no part should be played either by that superiority with which the man of fortune regards the unfortunate or by that scorn with which the inferior regards his superior. But when the crime is an offence against a third party, half the judges should be social equals of the accused, half the social equals of the injured party. Thus by establishing a balance of every private interest, which affects the way things appear to us whether we will or no, the only voices heard are those of truth and law. It also accords with justice that the accused should to some degree be able to exclude any judge he suspects; though if this is allowed and he persists in his objections, he will appear to be condemning himself. Proceedings and proofs of guilt alike should be public, so that informed opinion, which is perhaps the only cement of society, can impose restraints on brute force and the passions; and so that the people may say, we are not slaves, and we are defended; this feeling inspires courage, and is worth as much as taxes to a sovereign who knows his own real interest. I shall not go into other details and precautions which demand similar underlying principles. Had it been necessary to tell the whole story, I should have said nothing.

8. OF WITNESSES

IT is an important point in all good legislation to determine exactly the credibility of witnesses and the proofs of guilt. Every rational being, in other words everyone who is capable of connected thought and whose sentiments conform to those of the rest of mankind, can give evidence. The true measure of his credibility must be the interest which he has in speaking, or not speaking, the truth; whence it would seem pointless to reject women on the ground of their weakness; puerile to treat condemned men, because they are dead in law, as if they were dead in fact, and inconsistent to make much of the infamy of the infamous, when none of these have an interest in lying.

Rendering null and void the evidence of a guilty man who is already condemned is one of those notable abuses of grammar which have had no inconsiderable effect upon human affairs. He is *dead in law,* say the peripatetic masters of jurisprudence, and a *dead* man is incapable of any action. To uphold this vain metaphor, many victims have been sacrificed; and it has often been quite seriously asked whether truth ought not to give way to judicial formulas. Provided that the deposition of a condemned criminal does not go so far as to hold up the course of justice, why, even after sentence, in consideration of the criminal's extreme misery and in the interests of truth, should a period not be allowed during which he can produce new evidence that may change the nature of the case, and so be able to clear himself or others in a new trial? Formality and ceremony are necessary in the administration of justice because they leave nothing to the arbitrary conduct of the administrators, because they give the public the idea of a justice which is not violently confused and self-interested, but stable and regular; and because, men being slaves of habit and imitation, their feelings make more impression on them than reasoned argument. But formality and ceremony can never, without great danger, be arranged by law in such a manner as to do injury to the truth, though by reason of being either too simple or too complex the truth does need such outward show to make it acceptable to popular ignorance.

The credibility therefore of a witness must diminish in proportion to the hatred, friendship, or close relationship which subsists between himself and the accused. More than one witness is essential, because so long as the witness says one thing and the defendant another there can be no certainty, and the right, which everyone has, to be believed innocent, carries the day. The credibility of a witness also diminishes as the atrociousness of the crime[1] and the improbability of the

---

[1] According to the criminal lawyers, the credibility of a witness increases as the atrociousness of the crime increases. The wording of this cast-iron axiom is at once extremely cruel and foolish: *In atrocissimis leviores coniecturae sufficiunt, et licet judici jura transgredi.* Translate this into the vulgar tongue, and Europeans will have a clear view of one out of the many equally irrational dictates which, almost without realizing it, they allow to govern their lives: *In the most atrocious crimes* (that is to say in the crimes of the least probability), *the slightest conjectures are enough, and the judge may go beyond the limits of the law.* Absurd legal practices are often the product of fears, which are the principal source of human contradiction. Alarmed by the condemnation of some innocent man, lawmakers (nothing else really than lawyers whom chance has armed with authority to decide about everything and has changed from corrupt self-seeking scribblers into the arbiters and legislators of the fortunes of man) have loaded jurisprudence with a surplus of formalities and exceptions, which would seat anarchy unchecked upon the throne of justice, if we were to take exact account of all of them. Then, alarmed by some particularly atrocious crime which was also difficult to prove, they decided that they now had to get round the very formalities and exceptions they themselves had established. So between a dictatorial impatience and a feminine timidity, they have transformed the gravity of trials into a species of game in which the chief figures are trickery and chance.

circumstances increase. This applies for example to witchcraft and acts of unmotivated cruelty. In cases of witchcraft it is more likely that most men should lie—since ignorance, delusion, hatred, and desire to persecute so easily combine—than that one man should exercise a power which God has either taken away from created beings or else never given them. It is the same in cases of unmotivated cruelty, since a man's cruel actions are proportioned only to self-interest, hatred, or imaginary fears. Man, properly speaking, indulges in no super-fluity of emotion: his emotions are always proportionate to the impressions made upon his senses. In the same way the credibility of a witness is sometimes diminished by his member-ship of some private society the ways and principles of which are not well known or are not those of public life. Such a witness is actuated not only by his own passions, but by those of other men.

Finally, the credibility of a witness is almost nil when the crime is a spoken one; because the tone of voice, the gestures, everything he saw before and after, the different ideas which men attach to the same words, alter and modify the words a man actually uses so much that it is almost impossible to repeat them exactly as he spoke them. Moreover, extraordinary acts of violence, which are the real crimes, leave their traces behind in a multitude of circumstances and consequences; the more circumstances adduced in evidence, the more the accused man's opportunities of clearing himself. But words only remain in the often deceived and for the most part unreliable memory of those who hear them. For that reason it is a great deal more easy to calumniate a man's words than his actions.

9. SECRET ACCUSATIONS

AMONG the evident yet time-honoured abuses, made necessary in many countries by the weakness of the constitution, must be counted the custom of levelling secret accusations.[1] It renders men false and withdrawn. Everyone who sees an informer in another man, sees an enemy. Men therefore get used to masking what they really feel, and from this habit of hiding it from others they come to hide it eventually from themselves. Wretched are those driven to such a pass! Without clear and fixed principles to steer by, they toss to and fro, lost and wandering in a vast sea of opinions. Always occupied in saving themselves from monstrous threats, for them one moment is always rendered bitter by the uncertainty of the next. Deprived of the lasting pleasures of peace and security, the few moments of happiness scattered here and there in their sad lives and devoured in hurry and confusion, are scarcely enough to console them for their existence. Out of men such as these how are we to make brave soldiers who will defend their king and country? How are we to find among them magistrates above corruption, who shall be able, with eloquence inspired by liberty and patriotism, to sustain and enlarge the true interests of their sovereign and to take to his throne not only the tribute, but the love and blessings of men of every class, and bring back, alike to mansion and to hovel, peace and security and that diligent hope of bettering one's lot which is the useful leaven, the very life of a country?

Who can defend himself from slanders which are secure inside tyranny's strongest armour, secrecy? What kind of government can be hoped for when the ruler scents an enemy in every subject and is constrained to destroy each man's tranquillity so that he may secure the tranquillity of the state? What are the motives used to justify secret accusation and punishment?

[1] The allusion is particularly to the Republic of Venice. [Tr.]

D

Public welfare? The protection and maintenance of the existing form of government? It is a strange constitution surely in which he who has force and public opinion (which is stronger than force) on his side, has to be afraid of every citizen!

Immunity of the accuser? In that case the laws do not protect him adequately—and are we to suppose subjects stronger than their sovereign?

Saving the informer's reputation? Then we are to authorize injurious reports, if they are made in secret, and punish them, if they are made openly!

The character of the crime? If acts which harm no one, or even acts useful to the public, are called crimes, then the charges and the proceedings can never be secret enough! But can there be crimes, that is to say public offences, which it is not at the same time in everyone's interest to make into a public example!

I respect all governments, and speak of no governments in particular. The nature of the circumstances could make one suppose that the abolition of an evil inherent in a country's system might spell the country's complete ruin. But if I had to dictate new laws in some deserted corner of the universe, then with all posterity before my eyes, my hand would tremble, before I allowed a custom such as this of secret accusations!

It has already been remarked by Montesquieu[2] that public accusations accord more with a republic, whose citizens should desire the public good above all things, than with a monarchy in which the very nature of the government so much weakens that sentiment, making it best to appoint commissioners to bring accusations in the public name against those who break the law. But every government, whether a republic or a monarchy, should visit on the false informer that punishment which would have been inflicted on the man he informed against.

[2] *L'Esprit des lois*, VI, 8:XII, 23.

10. SUGGESTIVE INTERROGATION.
DEPOSITIONS

Our laws forbid, in a trial, interrogation of the kind known as *suggestive*; that is (according to the professors of law) interrogation which asks questions about the particular instead of the general circumstances of a crime; interrogations, in other words, which, having an immediate connexion with the crime, *suggest* an immediate answer to the accused. Interrogations, according to criminal lawyers, ought as it were to envelop the facts of a case spirally, but never go to them in straight lines. The motives behind this method are either not to *suggest* to the accused an answer which faces him squarely with the charge, or the thought perhaps that it is against nature for a man to accuse himself. Whichever explanation is right, the law contradicts itself in a remarkable way by forbidding suggestive interrogations and yet authorizing torture; for what interrogation can be more *suggestive* than pain? That first motive would apply equally to torture, since to a robust man the pain will *suggest* an obstinate silence, whereby he exchanges the greater for the lesser punishment; and to the weak man it will *suggest* confession, whereby he frees himself from the torture of the moment which for the time being affects him more than the pain to come. It is evident that the second motive would also apply in case of torture, because if a *special* interrogation makes a guilty man confess against his natural right, his sufferings under torture will make him confess all the more easily. However, men are governed less by the actual difference in things themselves than by the different names they give to them.

Finally, a man who obstinately refuses to reply to interrogation deserves a punishment, which should be fixed by law and be of the severest kind; since men cannot be allowed to escape in that way from the necessity of furnishing a public example. This punishment is not necessary when it is beyond all doubt that a man has committed a given crime, in which case, the other proofs being sufficient to establish his guilt, there is no more point in interrogation than there is in confession. This is the more usual situation, since we find by experience that in most trials the accused plead not guilty.

11. OF OATHS

THERE is a contradiction between the laws and the natural sentiments of mankind in the matter of oaths, which are required of a criminal to make him tell the truth, when it is in his greater interest to lie; as if a man could really swear an oath to contribute to his own destruction, and as if religion were not silent in most men while self-interest has its say. The experience of all time has made it clear that no other of the precious gifts of heaven is more frequently abused than religion. Is there any reason why criminals should respect it, when it has been so often profaned by those reckoned the wisest of men? For most men the motives which religion opposes to the surge of fear, and to the love of life, are too weak because too remote from their senses. The affairs of Heaven are governed by laws altogether differing from those governing the affairs of men. Why use them to compromise each other? Why place men in the terrible contradiction of offending against God or else concurring in their own destruction? The law which insists on such an oath in fact orders a man either to be a bad Christian, or a martyr. Bit by bit the oath becomes a mere formality, destroying in this way the strength of religious sentiment which is for most men the one and only pledge of honesty. How useless oaths are has been shown by experience, for every judge will be my witness that no oath has ever made a guilty man tell the truth. Reason shows this too, by declaring useless, and consequently dangerous, every law which is opposed to the natural sentiments of man. The fate of such laws is the fate of embankments set directly across the flow of a river; they are either immediately pushed over and swept away, or a whirlpool set in motion by themselves eats away at them and imperceptibly undermines them.

12. OF TORTURE

THE torture of an accused man while the case against him is being prepared is a cruelty consecrated by long usage among the majority of nations, its purpose being to make him confess to the crime, or clarify his contradictory statements, or discover his accomplices, or purge him in some metaphysical and incomprehensible way of infamy, or finally to bring to light other crimes which he may have committed but of which he is not accused.

A man cannot be called *guilty* until he has been sentenced by the judge; nor can society deprive him of public protection until it has been proved that he has violated the pacts which accord him that privilege. What right, then, but one of force empowers the judge to inflict punishment on a citizen while his guilt or his innocence remains in doubt? This is no new dilemma: the crime is either certain, or uncertain: if uncertain, no other punishment is appropriate than the one established by law, torture being pointless, just as a guilty man's confession would be pointless; if uncertain, it is wrong to torture an innocent man, since by law a man is innocent until proved guilty.

What is the political end of punishment? To intimidate others. But how should we judge the torture, private and in secret, inflicted by the tyranny of custom upon guilty and innocent alike? It is important that no divulged crime should go unpunished; but there is no point in revealing who committed a crime which itself continues to be buried in darkness. The civil point of punishing an evil already committed and beyond repair is that if such action were not taken others might be encouraged with a hope of going unpunished. If it is true that more men, whether from fear or virtue, respect the law than break it, then the risk of torturing an innocent man should be deemed all the greater, since other things being equal, he too is less likely to have broken the law than to have respected it.

I would say also that requiring a man to be accused and accuser at one and the same time, and requiring pain to be the crucible of truth as if truth could be judged in the nerves and muscles of some poor wretch, reveals only a desire to confound the known relationship of things.

The law which ordains torture is a law which says: 'Man, resist pain; and if nature has created in you an inextinguishable self-love, if she has given you an inalienable right of self-preservation, I now create in you a totally opposite emotion: an heroic hatred of yourself; and I command you to incriminate yourself by telling the truth even while they tear your muscles and dislocate your bones.'

This infamous crucible of truth is an enduring monument of that ancient and barbarous system of law which held that ordeal by fire and boiling water, and the uncertain outcome of trial by combat, were the 'judgements of God'—as if the links of that eternal chain which lies deep in the First Cause could be disarranged and disconnected from moment to moment, to suit the frivolous works of man! The only difference between torture and ordeal by fire or boiling water is that the issue of the one seems to depend on the will of the accused, and of the other on a purely physical and irrelevant fact; but this difference is apparent and not real. One is as free now to tell the truth, in between convulsions and tearings of the flesh, as one was in those days to escape, without trickery, from the natural effects of fire and boiling water. Every act of our will is always proportionate to the strength of the impression which gave rise to it; and every man's sensibility has its limits. The impression made by pain can therefore increase to such a degree that it entirely possesses a man under torture and leaves him no liberty but to choose the shortest way out of his present situation and so escape the pain. Thus the response of the man under torture is no less inevitable than the effect of fire and water. Thus the innocent man who is sensitive to pain will declare himself guilty because he believes this will put an end to his torment. So the very means which, it is claimed, will distinguish between innocence and guilt, in fact destroys all difference between them.

Torture is the certain way of letting sturdy criminals go free and condemning those who are innocent but weak. Here you see the fatal drawback of this pretended criterion of truth —a criterion worthy only of cannibals—which the ancient Romans, barbarous as they were in many ways, reserved only for slaves, who were thus the victims of their masters' ferocious and over-lauded virtue. Of two men equally innocent or equally guilty, the one who is robust and physically brave will be acquitted, the one who is feeble and fearful will be condemned, in virtue precisely of this train of reasoning: 'As judge I had to find you guilty of such and such a crime; you, the stronger one, have been able to withstand the pain, so I acquit you; you, the weaker one, have given way to pain, so I condemn you. I feel that the confession wrung from you by torture has little force, but I shall torture you again if you do not confirm what you have now admitted.'

The outcome of torture, then, is a matter of temperament and of calculation; it varies with each man according to his physical strength and response to pain. By this method a mathematician could solve the following problem better than a judge: 'Given the strength of muscles and the sensibility of nerves of an innocent man, find the amount of pain required to make him confess that he has committed a given crime.'

The purpose of examining an accused man is to find out the truth; but if it is difficult to discover the truth from the appearance, gestures, and countenance of a man in normal composure, how much more difficult will it be to discover it on a face where the signs that generally reveal the truth despite a man have all of them been altered by pain and convulsion! Violence confounds and obliterates those minute differences between things which enable us at times to know truth from falsehood.

A strange consequence, which necessarily derives from the use of torture, is that the innocent man is placed in a worse situation than the guilty. Both are tortured, but the former has every chance stacked against him: if he confesses to the crime, he is condemned; if he is declared innocent, he has suffered an undeserved punishment. But the guilty man's situation is in his favour. If he stands up firmly to torture, he is acquitted as if he were innocent, and he will have undergone a lesser punishment instead of a greater one. So the innocent man always loses by torture, while the guilty man stands to gain.

In the end this truth is felt, though confusedly, even by those who reject it. A confession made under torture is not valid unless it is subsequently confirmed by oath; and if he does not confirm his guilt, the accused man is tortured again. Some doctors of law—and some countries—allow the infamous *petitio principii* to be repeated only three times; other countries and authorities leave it to the judge's discretion.

It would be superfluous to throw even more light on this subject by citing examples of innocent men who have confessed themselves guilty under torture. Every nation, every age, could cite its own. But men neither change nor draw conclusions. Every man, who lifts his thoughts above the merest needs of life, runs at some time to the arms of Nature who calls him to herself in a voice secret and unclear; but habit, that tyrant of the mind, dismays him and thrusts him back.

The second motive of torture is to resolve contradictions in the evidence of a supposedly guilty man—as if the fear of punishment, the uncertainty of the verdict, the pomp and majesty of the judge, and the ignorant state of guilty and innocent alike, were not enough to make it probable that innocent as well as guilty would fall into contradiction—the innocent man out of fear, the guilty man from an endeavour to shield himself; as if, too, self-contradictions, common among men in tranquillity, were not multiplied in the turbulent mind of a man all absorbed in the thought of saving himself from imminent peril!

Torture, too, is employed to discover whether a man is guilty of other crimes than the one he is charged with. The reasoning goes like this: 'You are guilty of one crime, so perhaps you are guilty of a hundred more. This doubt disturbs me, I want to employ my criterion of the truth to make sure: the law tortures you, because you are guilty, because you may be guilty, and because I want you to be guilty.'

Another purpose of torture is to make a criminal reveal the accomplices of his crime. But if we have proved that torture is a bad method of discovering the truth, how can it be employed to find out who the accomplices were, which is one of the truths to be discovered? As well suppose that a man who accuses himself is not even more likely to accuse others! And is it just to torture one man for the crimes of others? Will his accomplices not be revealed by interrogating witnesses, by interrogating the accused, by weighing the evidence, and from the crime itself—in short, by all those means which should have been employed to discover whether the accused man did or did not commit the crime? Accomplices generally flee the moment their companion has been apprehended. Uncertainty and fear in themselves condemn accomplices to exile and deliver their country from the danger of more crimes, while the punishment carried out on the guilty man achieves its one sole purpose, which is to deter other men by fear from another such crime.

Yet another of the ridiculous motives for torture is that it purges a man of infamy. In other words, a man judged infamous by law must confirm his own deposition by having his bones dislocated. This abuse ought not to be tolerated in the eighteenth century. The belief is this: that pain, which is a physical sensation, purges infamy, which is a purely moral denunciation. Is pain perhaps a crucible, infamy perhaps a substance mixed and impure? But infamy is a sentiment, subject neither to laws nor reason but only to public opinion. Torture itself inflicts a genuine infamy on its victim. So by this method infamy is purged by inflicting infamy.

It is not difficult to discover the origin of this ridiculous law since the very absurdities indulged in by an entire nation always relate in some way or another to ideas which that nation respects and holds in common. The practice seems to have had its origin in the religious and spiritual motives which exert so much influence on human thought in all countries and all ages: an infallible dogma assures us that the blemishes due to human frailty, which have not deserved the everlasting wrath of the Supreme Being, must be purged by an incomprehensible fire. Now infamy is a civil blemish, so if pain and fire can remove blemishes incorporeal and spiritual, why should the agonies of torture not be efficacious in removing that civil blemish which is infamy? I believe that the confession of an accused man, which some courts insist upon as necessary to condemnation, originated in a not dissimilar way, seeing that in the mysterious tribunal of penance a necessary part of the sacrament is the confession of those who have sinned. Thus do mankind abuse the surest light of Revelation; and since it is that light alone which exists in times of ignorance, submissive man has recourse to it upon every occasion, applying it in the most absurd and far-fetched ways.

These truths were already recognized by the lawmakers of Rome, who inflicted torture only upon their slaves, whom they deprived of all corporate existence; they are accepted in England, the glory of whose literature, the superiority of whose commerce and wealth, and therefore of power, added to her examples of virtue and courage, allow us no doubt of the excellence of her laws. Torture has been abolished in Sweden, abolished too by one of the wisest monarchs of Europe,[1] who, by bringing philosophy to the throne and making himself the legislative friend of his subjects, has rendered them equal and free in their dependence upon the laws, which is the sole liberty and equality that rational men can demand in our present state of things. Torture is not considered necessary in military law, though armies, for the most part composed of the dregs of each country, might be held on that account to be more in need of it than any other class of men. Strange, if one forgets for a moment the tyrannical power of custom, that

[1] Frederick II of Prussia. [Tr.]

law and peace should have to learn from minds hardened in blood and slaughter, the most humane methods of adjudication.

13. PROCEEDINGS AND PRESCRIPTIONS

As soon as the evidence has been prepared and the certainty of the crime established, the accused man must be allowed the necessary time and means to prepare his defence. But the time must be short, so as not to be prejudicial to that promptitude of punishment which we have seen to be one of the most effective curbs upon crime.

Such shortness of time might appear in conflict with a love of humanity, if that love is wrongly understood. Doubt will vanish if we consider that every defect in law increases the danger to the innocent.

But the law should fix a certain space of time both for preparing the defence of the accused and preparing the case against him; if the time for preparing evidence were left to the judge to decide, then it would be the judge who laid down the law. When it comes to really atrocious crimes of the kind which are not quickly forgotten, there should be no prescriptive period allowed in favour of an accused man, if he should have taken to flight, once the crime has been established. But in cases of minor, less sensational crimes, it is right to allow a prescriptive period, which will cut short a citizen's uncertainty of his own fate; because the long period in which he goes without punishment will not be a bad example to others, seeing that his crimes are not generally known, and that the period will allow him a chance of amending his ways.

It will be enough if I do no more than indicate these principles, since it is possible to set precise limits for a particular system of law and in particular social circumstances; I shall only add that where a nation has discovered the usefulness of

moderate punishments, then laws which increase or decrease
the times of prescription and preparation of the case according
to the gravity of the crime, and which count voluntary exile
or imprisonment before trial as part of the sentence, will
establish a simple and restricted category of mild punishments
for a large number of crimes.

However, the times in question should not be increased in
exact proportion to the atrocity of the crime, seeing that the
likelihood of crimes is in inverse ratio to their atrocity. So the
time for inquiry into the crime ought sometimes to be decreased, and the time of prescription increased; which may
seem to contradict what I have just said—namely, that equal
punishments may be given for unequal crimes, if the period
of detention or of prescription before sentence is reckoned as
punishment.

To explain my idea to the reader, I shall distinguish two
classes of crime. The first includes all crimes of atrocity, beginning with homicide and comprehending all the extremer
villainies; the second includes the lesser crimes. This distinction
has its basis in man's nature. The safeguarding of the individual
human life is a natural right; the safeguarding of property is a
social right. The motives which drive a man beyond the natural
sentiment of compassion are very much fewer than the motives
which drive a man through a natural longing for fortune, to
violate a right which he finds not in his heart but in the conventions of society.

The extreme divergence in probability between these two
classes of crime requires that they be regulated by different
principles. In crimes of atrocity, because they are less frequent
and because in such crimes the probability of the accused
man's innocence increases, the time allowed for inquiry should
be decreased; and the prescriptive period should be increased,
because only a definite verdict of innocent or guilty puts an
end to the flattering hope that crimes may go unpunished, the
harm of which increases with the atrocity of the crime. Minor
crimes diminish the probability of an accused man's innocence,
so the time allowed for inquiry into them ought to be in-

creased; and since they diminish the harm caused by that impunity, the prescriptive period should be decreased.

Distinguishing in this way two classes of crime would be inadmissible if the harm which comes from crimes not being punished were to decrease in proportion to the increasing probability of the crime. We should reflect that an accused man, who has been found neither innocent nor guilty and has been set free for lack of evidence, can be subjected to new imprisonment and new examination for the same crime if new legal evidence is adduced against him, provided that the prescriptive period laid down for his crime has not been exceeded.

Such at least appears the best way of defending the security and liberty of the subject, it being all too easy to favour the one at the expense of the other, until these two blessings, which are the inalienable patrimony of every citizen to be enjoyed equally by them all, are in danger of becoming the defenceless prey, in the one case of tyranny open or unavowed, in the other of lawlessness and disorder of the mob.

There exist some crimes which are at the same time common in society, and difficult to prove. As difficulty of proof goes hand in hand with probability of innocence, one need not in these cases make so much of the dangers of impunity, the frequency of such crimes depending upon causes other than the risk of punishment; for which reasons the period of investigation and the period of prescription should equally be curtailed. Yet cases of adultery and pederasty, which are not easy to prove, are the very ones, on received principle, in which tyrannical presumptions of *quasi-proof* and *half-proof* are admitted (as if a man could be *half-innocent,* or *half-guilty,* in other words, *half-punishable* or *half-acquittable*); in which, too, torture exercises its cruel power over the person of the accused, over the witnesses, and even the whole family of an unhappy man, according to the coldly iniquitous teaching of some learned men who presume to offer rule and precept to the judiciary.

In view of these principles, it will seem strange to those who do not reflect that reason has hardly ever been the lawgiver of nations, that the most atrocious, the most obscure, or most illusory crimes, in other words the crimes most unlikely to be committed, should be the ones proved by conjecture, on the weakest and most equivocal evidence; as if the law and the bench were interested not in searching out the truth, but merely in discovering a crime; as if the danger of condemning an innocent man were not the greater, when his innocence is more probable than his guilt.

Most men lack that vigour required no less for the greatest crimes than for the greatest virtues; each appears to co-exist with the other more in those nations sustained by energetic governments and passions both conspiring to the public good, than in nations depending upon their size or the unremitting excellence of their laws. In the latter, enfeebled passions seem better fitted to maintain than to improve the form of government. From which an important consequence may be deduced, that great crimes in a nation are not always proof of its decay.

14. ATTEMPTED CRIMES, ACCOMPLICES, EXEMPTION FROM PENALTY

BECAUSE intentions are not punishable by law, it does not follow that a criminal act merely begun with some deed which shows the will to complete it, does not also deserve punishment, even if a lighter punishment than would have been incurred by the completed crime. The importance of preventing an attempted crime justifies a penalty: but since attempt and completion may be separated by an interval, there is room for a change of heart if heavier penalties are retained for crimes brought to a conclusion. The same may be said when there are several accomplices in a crime, not all of whom were its immediate perpetrators; but for a different reason. When several men join together in a risky venture, the greater the risk the more they try to share it equally between them; on which account it is very difficult for them to find one of their number willing to perform the actual deed, the perpetrator running more risk than his confederates. The only exception is a case in which the perpetrator is given an agreed reward; punishment should then be the same for the accomplices and for the man who has been rewarded for his greater risk. Such reflections may seem too metaphysical to those who have not reflected that it is best if laws encourage as few motives as possible for agreement between comrades in crime.

Some courts make an offer of impunity to an accomplice in a serious crime if he reveals who his companions were. This expedient has its disadvantages and advantages. The disadvantages are: that society thereby authorizes treachery, an offence detestable even among criminals; society being damaged less by courageous than by cowardly crimes, since courage is a rare quality requiring only a beneficent guiding power to turn it to the public good, whereas cowardice is more common, more catching, always more self-centred. Moreover a court displays its own irresolution and the weakness of the law, when it calls for the help of someone who has broken that law.

The advantages of such an offer of impunity are that it prevents serious crime, and that it has an intimidating effect on the populace, inasmuch as the results are known and the agents unknown. Moreover, it helps to show that the man who breaks his faith legally, that is publicly, is likely also to break it privately.

In my opinion, a general law promising impunity to an accomplice who gives information about any crime at all would be preferable to a specific declaration in a particular case, since the fear of exposure common, in that event, to all the accomplices would prevent their association in crime; the court would not make criminals audacious by showing in a particular case that their help was called for. Such a law however should couple impunity for the informer with banishment. . . . But why torment myself in a vain effort to expunge that remorse I feel for thus authorizing the law, the inviolable, monumental basis of public confidence and man's morality, to dissimulate and to betray? Imagine the example to the nation if the promise of impunity were not kept, if, through learned quibbles, that man who had responded to the invitation of the law were dragged to punishment, in defiance of public pledges!

Such instances are not few among the nations, and for that reason neither are those men few who in a nation see no more than a complex machine, the parts of which are set in motion at their own pleasure by the more dexterous and the more powerful. Frigid and insensible to all that is the delight of spirits at once tender and sublime, such men excite, as they need them, either the gentlest of emotions or the fiercest of passions, playing upon the minds of men as musicians play upon their instruments.

15.   MILDNESS OF PUNISHMENT

FROM the simple consideration of the truths expounded so far, it is evident that the purpose of punishments is neither to torture and afflict a sentient creature nor to undo a crime already done. Can the man who, far from acting on passionate impulse, is charged with moderating the private passions of man, harbour, in the body politic, such useless cruelty, such an instrument of frenzy and fanaticism, or of the weakness of tyranny? Can one suppose that the shrieks of some poor wretch will call back out of ever-advancing time actions already consummated?

The aim, then, of punishment can only be to prevent the criminal committing new crimes against his countrymen, and to keep others from doing likewise. Punishments, therefore, and the method of inflicting them, should be chosen in due proportion to the crime, so as to make the most efficacious and most lasting impression on the minds of men, and the least painful of impressions on the body of the criminal. Can one read history without horror and disgust at the useless barbarity of the tortures so coldly invented and inflicted by men who were reckoned wise? Must one not shudder at the sight of thousands of unhappy men reduced by misery, either willed or tolerated by the law (which has always favoured the few and outraged the many), to a desperate state of nature? The sight of thousands accused of impossible crimes, fabricated by fearfulness and ignorance, or guilty of nothing except loyalty to their own principles, whom men endowed with the same senses, and so with the same passions, have lacerated with the premeditated, protracted formalities of torture, making them a blithe show for a fanatical populace?

For a punishment to be efficacious, it is enough that the disadvantage of the punishment should exceed the advantage anticipated from the crime; in which excess should be calculated the certainty of punishment and the loss of the expected benefit. Everything beyond this, accordingly, is superfluous, and therefore tyrannical. Men regulate their conduct in response to the repeated action of the disadvantages they know, not of the disadvantages they do not know. If we take two nations, in which the scale of crime and the scale of punishment are in due proportion to each other, and if in one the heaviest punishment is perpetual servitude and in the other the wheel, I say that the one will have as much fear of its maximum penalty as the other; and that if for some reason the heavier maximum penalty of the second nation were to be transferred to the first nation, by the same reasoning this maximum penalty could be increased, and passing imperceptibly from the wheel to more protracted and more studied forms of torture, would arrive at the ultimate refinements of a science in which tyranny is all too expert.

As punishments become more cruel, men's minds, adjusting themselves like fluids to the level of surrounding objects, become increasingly hardened; and human emotion has such an always lively force that after a hundred years of cruel punishment of that kind the wheel would seem only as terrifying as the prison had been earlier on.

The worse the ill that confronts them, the more men are

E

driven to evade it. The very savagery of a punishment has this effect, and to avoid the penalty for the one crime they have already committed, men commit other crimes. Countries and times in which punishments have been most savage have always been those of the bloodiest and most inhuman acts, inasmuch as the spirit of ferocity which guided the hand of the lawgiver also guided the hand of the parricide and the cutthroat; dictated iron laws upon the throne for savage and slavish spirits to obey; and in darkness and privacy moved men to slaughter one tyrant and install another.

Two other grievous consequences derive from cruelty of punishment, contrary to that very purpose of preventing crime. One is that cruelty makes it difficult to maintain the necessary proportion between the crime and the punishment, for however much an ingenious cruelty may have multiplied and diversified the modes of punishment, still these cannot exceed that ultimate of force which human physique and sensibility are capable of enduring. When this extreme has been reached it is impossible to find, for more damaging and more atrocious crimes, penalties correspondingly greater such as are required to prevent those crimes. The other consequence is that atrocity in punishment breeds impunity. Men are hedged within certain bounds, whether of good and evil; and a spectacle too atrocious for mankind can result only from a passing frenzy; and can never partake of a settled system, proper to law. If the laws are indeed cruel, either they are altered or they occasion a fatal tendency not to punish.

I end with this reflection, that the weight of punishment should be relative to the condition of the nation itself. Stronger and more palpable impress must be made upon the hardened minds of a people who have barely emerged from a state of savagery. A thunderbolt is required to subdue a ferocious lion which walks off at the touch of a bullet. But as men's minds become gentler from living in a state of society, so their sensibility increases; and with that increase there must be diminution in the severity of punishment, if a constant relation is to be maintained between object and feeling.

16. OF CAPITAL PUNISHMENT

THIS useless prodigality of punishment, which has never made men better, drives me to ask whether death can be inflicted either usefully or justly in a well-organized state. By what right do men take it upon themselves to slaughter other men? Certainly it cannot be that right which gives birth to sovereignty and law; which are nothing but the sum of the smallest portions of each man's personal liberty, representing the public will, which is the aggregate of individual wills. But who has ever been willing to give other men authority to kill him? How can the least possible sacrifice of each individual's liberty ever be equated with the greatest of all good things, that is with human life itself? And were it possible, how would it accord with that other principle, that a man is not master of his own life and death? Which he must be, if he has been able to give that right to others, or to the whole of society.

The penalty of death is not therefore a *right*—I have shown that it cannot be—but a war of the nation against a citizen; because it has been judged necessary or useful to destroy him. But if I shall demonstrate that his death is neither useful nor necessary, I shall have won the cause of humanity.

The death of a citizen can only be thought necessary for two reasons. First, that although he has been deprived of liberty, he still has such connexions and such power that the safety of the nation is endangered; and that he can provoke by his existence a revolution dangerous to the settled form of government. The death of such a citizen, then, becomes necessary when a nation is regaining or losing its freedom, or in a period of anarchy, when disorder takes the place of law. But under the calm rule of law, under a form of government which unites the suffrages of the nation, which is secured within and without both by its strength and (perhaps more efficacious than strength itself) by public opinion, in which supreme command is vested only in the true sovereign, in which wealth purchases pleasure but not power, I see no need to destroy a citizen, unless his death be the only true way of keeping other men from crime; which is the second reason for believing that the penalty of death can be just or necessary.

Though the experience of all the ages, in which the supreme penalty has never yet deterred a resolute man from offending against society, though the example of the citizens of Rome, though the twenty years of the reign of the Empress Elizabeth of Russia in which she set so illustrious a precedent to the fathers of her people, worth as much to them as many conquests bought with the blood of their sons, have none of them convinced mankind, suspicious always of the voice of reason, believing always in the voice of authority, it will be sufficient, if you would learn the truth of my assertion, simply to consult the nature of man.

It is not intensity of pain which most greatly affects the mind, but its continuance; since human sensibility is more easily and permanently influenced by very small but repeated impressions than by a strong yet transient impact. The power of habit is universal in every living creature; and just as habit helps man to walk and talk and satisfy his needs, so it takes a steady repetition of blows to impress moral ideas upon his mind. It is not the terrible but transient spectacle of a criminal's execution, but the long sustained example of a man's loss of liberty, of a man paying for his offence to society by labours resembling those of a beast of burden, which is the most powerful brake upon crime. 'If we do such misdeeds,' we say to ourselves, 'we shall be reduced to the same endless state of wretchedness.' This is efficacious, because the thought occurs to us over and over again; and it is much more powerful than the notion of death, which is always obscurely in sight on man's horizon.

The penalty of death makes an impression which for all its strength cannot counterbalance that rapid forgetfulness, which is natural to man even in his most essential affairs, and which his passions only accelerate. The general rule is that violent passions take men by surprise, but only for a short while, on which account they may effect those revolutions which make either Persians or Spartans of the common man; whereas the impressions made under a free and tranquil government should be many rather than strong.

The penalty of death becomes for most men a spectacle, and for a few an object of compassion mingled with indignation, one or other of these sentiments occupying the spectator's mind to the exclusion of that salutary dread which the law pretends to inspire. But in moderate and continuous punishment the latter is the dominant feeling, because it is the only one. The limit which the lawmaker should affix to the rigour of punishment ought therefore to be determined by the point at which compassion begins to prevail over other sentiments in the spectator's mind, the spectator feeling that the punishment is being inflicted on himself rather than on the criminal. To be just, a punishment must not exceed that degree of intensity which will deter other men from crime. Now there is no one who, on reflection, would choose the total, permanent loss of his individual liberty, no matter what advantages a crime might bring him. It follows that the severity of a sentence of imprisonment for life, substituted for the penalty of death, would be as likely to deflect the most determined spirit—indeed I should think it more likely to do so. A great many men contemplate death with a steady, tranquil gaze; some out of fanaticism, some out of vanity, which attends us again and again to the very edge of the grave, some out of a last desperate effort to free themselves from life and misery; but neither fanaticism nor vanity can subsist among the fetters and the chains, under the rod, or under the yoke, or in the iron cage, where the desperate man rather begins than ends his misery.

Our spirit offers more resistance to violence and to extreme but transient pain than to time and perpetual affliction; since it is able to concentrate wholly for one moment upon withstanding the former, while its vigour and elasticity will not suffice to resist the long and repeated action of the latter. When the penalty is death, every example which its application gives to a nation presupposes a crime. When the penalty is imprisonment for life, each single crime affords a multiplicity of enduring examples. Also if it is important that men should frequently be shown the power of the law, then exactions of the death penalty must follow quickly one upon another; which supposes a frequency of crime; which means that the punishment, if it is to be effective, must not make all the impression on men that it ought to make; which is to say that it should at the same time be effective and ineffective. Should it be said that imprisonment for life is as painful as death, and on that account equally cruel, I should reply that if one could add together all the unhappy moments of imprisonment, it would perhaps be more painful than death; but such moments are spread over a whole lifetime, while death exerts its whole force in a single moment; there is also this advantage to imprisonment for life, that it terrifies the man who sees it more than the man who suffers it, since the former contemplates the whole sum of the moments of unhappiness, while the latter is distracted by the unhappiness of the present moment from the moments to come. All evils increase in the imagination; whereas the man who suffers finds compensations and consolations which onlookers, who set their own sensitivity in place of the hardened spirit of the criminal, would neither guess nor credit.

Let us consider the approximate reasoning of a thief or a murderer, whose counterpoise to breaking the law is no more than the gallows or the wheel (I am aware that self-analysis of the feelings is an art to be acquired only by education. But it does not follow, because a thief cannot clearly express his principles, that he has no principles to act by). 'What are these laws,' he would ask, 'which I have to respect, and which leave such a gulf between myself and the rich man? He denies me the penny I seek from him, and excuses himself by exhorting me to hard work, which he knows nothing about. Who made these laws? Men of wealth and power who have never deigned to visit the squalid huts of the poor, and have never had to share out a mouldy loaf of bread, to the innocent outcry of their starving children and the sobbing of their wives. Let us break these ties which are disastrous to most men, and advantageous to a few idle tyrants: let us attack injustice where it begins. I shall return to my natural state of independence, I shall live free and happy for a while with the fruits of my courage and my labour. Perhaps there will be a day of suffering and regret; but that will not last long, and for one day's distress I shall have had many years of freedom and pleasure. King of some few others like myself, I shall correct the errors of fortune, and I shall see those tyrants tremble and turn pale in the presence of one whom, in their days of insolence and splendour, they treated as less than their horses or their dogs.' Religion then enters into the mind of the ruffian, who puts everything to bad use, and by offering him an easy repentance and a more or less certain prospect of eternal felicity, greatly diminishes for him the terror of the ultimate tragedy.

But the man who sees before him a prospect of year upon year, or even a whole lifetime, of servitude and suffering, in sight of his fellow citizens with whom he lives in freedom and sociability, slave of those laws by which he was protected, usefully compares all this with the uncertainty of the outcome of his crimes, and the shortness of the time in which he may enjoy their fruits. The constant example of those whom he actually sees as victims of their own inadvertence makes upon him an impression far stronger than the spectacle of a punishment which hardens him more than it reforms him.

The penalty of death is ineffectual because of the barbarity of the example it gives to men. If the passions, or the necessity of war, have taught the spilling of human blood, the law, which is the moderator of the conduct of men, ought not to augment so cruel an example, made all the more grievous, the more legalized death is inflicted with deliberation and formality. To me it appears absurd that the laws, which are the expression of the public will, which detest and punish murder, should themselves commit murder; and, to deter citizens from killing, should ordain a killing in public. What are the true and most effectual laws? Surely those compacts and conditions which all men are willing to observe and to propound, when private interest, normally so much heard, stays silent or coincides with the public interest. What are every man's feelings about the punishment of death? We may read them in the signs of indignation and contempt with which everyone regards the executioner, who is no more than the innocent translator of the public will, a good citizen who contributes to the public welfare, an instrument as necessary to public safety at home as brave soldiers are to public safety abroad. Wherein then lies the source of this contradiction? And why is this feeling—in defiance of reason—indelible among men? Because men, in their heart of hearts, where, above all, they preserve intact the fundamentals of their nature, have always believed that life should be at the mercy of none save that Necessity which rules the universe with its iron sceptre. What are men to think when they look on the wise magistrates and the solemn priests of justice, who with tranquil indifference have a criminal dragged with slow ceremony to his death; or when they see a judge, with unfeeling coldness and perhaps a secret self-satisfaction in his own power, walk past a poor creature who writhes in his last anguish and awaits the fatal blow, on his way to enjoy the comforts and the pleasures of life? 'Ah,' they say, 'these laws are nothing but the pretexts of force; and the cruel, premeditated formalities of justice are no more than a conventional language for immolating with greater security, as it were, victims destined to be sacrificed to the insatiable idol of despotism. Murder, which they preach to us as so terrible a misdeed, we see them employing coolly and without aversion. Let us take advantage of their example. Violent death seemed horrifying to us when they described it, but we see it is the affair of a moment. How much less terrible it will be to a man who is not expecting it, and so is spared almost all of its pain?'

Such are the fatal paralogisms, which if not clearly, then confusedly, dispose to crime those men acted upon, as we have seen, more by the abuse of religion than by religion itself.

If it is objected that in almost all ages and almost all nations some crimes have been punished by death, I shall reply that the objection vanishes in the face of truth, which triumphs over all prescription; that the history of mankind appears a vast sea of errors, among which there float a few confused truths, each one far from the next. Human sacrifices were common to almost every nation; and who would dare to excuse them? That very few societies, and only for a very brief time, have forborne to inflict death, is more favourable than contrary to my case; since it accords with the fate of all great truths, which endure for no longer than a flash, compared with that long dark night in which mankind is enveloped. Not yet have we come to that happy enoch in which truth, as error heretofore, shall be the portion of the majority of men; from which universal decree those truths alone have so far been exempt which the Infinite Wisdom has been pleased to distinguish from the rest by Revelation.

The voice of a single philosopher is too weak to overcome the tumult and the cries of so great a multitude whose guide is the blindness of habit. But the few wise men scattered across the face of the earth will echo my words in their innermost hearts; and if Truth, among the crowd of obstacles between herself and a monarch, manages in spite of him to penetrate to his throne, then tell him she comes with the secret desires of all mankind; tell him that before his face the bloody fame of conquerors will fall silent; and that a just posterity will elevate his peaceful trophies even above those of the Tituses, the Antonines, and the Trajans.

How happy mankind would be if laws were being laid down for the first time, now that we see restored to the thrones of Europe benevolent monarchs who encourage the virtues of peace, of science, and of art, fathers of their people, citizens who wear the crown, the increase of whose authority constitutes the happiness of their subjects, since it frees them from that intermediary despotism, the more cruel because the less secure, by which the always sincere desires of the people, which are always lucky if they can reach the throne, have come to be suppressed. If, I say, they allow the ancient laws to continue, it is because of the infinite difficulty of revealing error beneath the venerated rust of ages; which is a reason why enlightened citizens should long even more ardently for the continued increase of the authority of such rulers.

17. BANISHMENT AND CONFISCATION

EVERYONE who disturbs the public peace, everyone who will not obey the laws, in other words the conditions by which men afford each other mutual support and defence, should be excluded from society, that is, should be banished.

It would seem that punishment should be inflicted on those men who are accused of an atrocious crime which cannot be brought home to them in spite of the great probability of their guilt. But such cases require a statute as little arbitrary and as precise as can be devised: it would condemn to banishment a man who has placed his country in the fatal dilemma of either going in fear of him or injuring him, though it should leave him the sacred right of proving his innocence. It follows that the reasons for banishing a citizen should be stronger than the reasons for banishing a foreigner; likewise for banishing a first offender, in contrast to a man who has often offended.

But should a man who has been banished and excluded for all time from the society of which he was a member be deprived also of his property? Such a question can be looked at in different ways. The loss of one's goods is a severer penalty than that of banishment: there ought therefore to be some cases in which, proportionately to the crime, a man should lose the whole or part of his property, or none at all. The whole of a man's property should be forfeit when the banishment ordained by law is such as to sever all ties between society and the delinquent citizen. In such a case the citizen is dead, and only the man remains; the consequences, so far as the body politic is concerned, should be the same as the consequences of natural death. It would seem then to follow that the property taken from the guilty man should pass to his lawful heirs rather than to the prince, inasmuch as death and such a banishment are the same thing in regard to the body politic. But it is not this subtlety which emboldens me to disapprove of the confiscation of property. If some have maintained that confiscation is a bridle upon acts of revenge and private oppression, they have not considered that though a punishment may have a good result, it is not on that account always just; to be just a punishment must be necessary; and an effectual injustice must never be tolerated by a lawgiver who wishes to close every door to the watchfulness of tyranny, which flatters with the prospects of momentary advantage and the good fortune of few in high places, while scorning the ruin that follows and the tears of multitudes of the humble.

Confiscation puts a price upon the head of the weak, causes the innocent to suffer the pains of the guilty, and places those same innocent persons in the desperate strait of resorting to crime. What more melancholy spectacle than to see a family dragged down to infamy and wretchedness by the crimes of the head of the house, which their subjection to him ordained by law made them unable to prevent, even had there been a way of doing so.

18. DISGRACE

DISGRACE is a sign of public disapprobation, which deprives the guilty man of the goodwill of the public, the confidence of his country, and that almost fraternal bond which community inspires. It is not within the arbitrament of the law. Therefore it is essential that the disgrace which the law inflicts should be the same as that which arises from the relationship of things; the same as that which is dictated by morality, whether universal morality or particular morality which depends upon particular systems and lays down the law for vulgar opinion or for this or that nation. If the one kind of disgrace differs from the other, either men will no longer venerate the law or else notions of morality and probity will vanish in spite of wordy harangues which are powerless against facts. Whoever applies the word disgraceful to actions which in themselves are unimportant, diminishes the disgracefulness of actions which really merit that name.

Painful bodily punishment should never be given for crimes which, having their source in pride, find in the actuality of pain both their glory and their nourishment. Ridicule and disgrace agree better with such crimes, inasmuch as these employ the onlooker's pride to curb the fanatic's pride, and hold so fast that truth itself can only be free of them by slow and dogged effort. Thus by setting force against force, and opinion against opinion, the wise legislator destroys that surprised admiration occasioned in the crowd by a false principle, the plausible consequences of which are apt to veil from the common man the absurdity of its origin.

The penalty of disgrace should neither be too often inflicted, nor allowed to fall on too many persons at one time; because in the one case the real and too frequent effects of matters of opinion weaken the force of that opinion, and in the other the disgracing of many resolves itself into the disgracing of none.

Here then is the way to avoid confounding the relationship of things and their immutable nature, which, free from the limitations of time and incessantly at work, upsets every narrow rule and regulation which is apart from it. The pleasurable and tasteful arts are not alone in having for their universal principle the faithful imitation of nature; the political art itself, if it is to be true and durable, is subject as well to this general maxim, since it is none other than the art of directing in a better way, and in a common direction, the immutable sentiments of man.

19. PROMPTITUDE OF PUNISHMENT

THE more prompt the punishment and the sooner it follows the crime, the more just it will be and the more effective. I say the more just, because the guilty man will thereby be spared the useless and harrowing torments of uncertainty, which grow with the vigour of the imagination and the feeling of his own weakness; the more just, because deprivation of liberty, in itself a punishment, should not precede sentence beyond the requirements of necessity.

Custody, then, is simply the holding of a citizen until he can be judged; and this custody, which is essentially unpleasant, should last as short a time as possible, and should be as little harsh as possible. This short period should be measured both by the length of time necessary for preparing the case, and by the prior rights of those who are already awaiting trial. Confinement should be strict enough only to prevent flight or concealment of the proofs of crime. The trial itself should be over in the shortest possible time. What contrast more cruel than the indolence of a judge and the anguish of the accused? Or the convenience and pleasures of an unfeeling magistrate set against the tears and wretchedness of a prisoner? In general the weight of punishment and the consequences of a crime should have the greatest possible effect on others and an effect as little harsh as possible on the sufferer, since the only just society is one based upon the infallible principle that men's purpose in coming together was to subject themselves to as few evils as possible.

I have said that promptness of punishment is more effective, because the shorter the time between punishment and misdeed, the stronger and more durable in the human spirit is the association of these two ideas of *crime* and *punishment*; so that they come insensibly to be considered, one as cause, the other as necessary and unfailing consequence. It has been shown that the association of ideas is the cement of the whole structure of the human intellect, without which pleasure and pain would be isolated sensations devoid of effect. The more men lose touch with general ideas and universal principles, the more commonplace they become, the more they act by their immediate everyday associations, to the neglect of associations remoter and more complex, which are of service only to men who are passionately dedicated to the pursuit of one object; the light of their attention shines clearly upon that one object alone, leaving all others in darkness. Such associations are equally of service to more elevated minds, which have acquired the habit of running quickly over many objects at once, and which are skilled in weighing, one against the other, many partial opinions, so that the result—in other words their course of action—is less perilous and unsure.

The proximity of crime and punishment is therefore of the greatest importance, if we desire that in clumsy, commonplace minds, the seductive picture of the rewards of crime be followed at once by the associated idea of punishment. Long delay can only have the effect of separating these two ideas more and more; and any impression made by the chastisement of crime will be made less as chastisement than as spectacle, and only after the horror of a particular crime, which would have served to reinforce the idea of punishment, has weakened in the minds of the spectators.

Another principle serves admirably to bring still closer the important connexion between the misdeed and the punishment: wherever possible, punishment should conform to the nature of the crime. This analogy points the proper contrast between the impulse to a crime and the repercussions which follow from its punishment; the latter, that is, distracts the mind and directs it to a course altogether different from that into which it is enticed by the seductive idea of breaking the law.

Persons convicted of lesser crimes are usually either punished in the obscurity of a prison or else deported, so that by a long and almost wholly pointless slavery they may set an example to nations they have never offended.

Since the worst crimes are not those which men resolve upon in a flash, the public punishment of a grave misdeed will generally seem a thing foreign and unlikely to most of the onlookers; but the public punishment of lighter crimes, since they are less remote, will make an impression upon the mind, which while deterring it from such crimes will also influence it against greater ones. Punishments should be properly related to one another and to crimes not only in their force, but also in the way they are carried out.

20. CERTAINTY AND INEVITABILITY OF PUNISHMENT. PARDONS

ONE of the greatest checks upon crime is not the cruelty of punishment but its inevitability. Consequently the vigilance of magistrates, and the inexorable severity of a judge, if it is to be a useful virtue, must go hand in hand with a mild system of laws. The certainty of being punished, however lightly, always makes a stronger impression than the fear of another worse punishment, associated with a hope that it will not be inflicted; for even the least of ills, when inescapable, will always terrify men's minds; and hope, that celestial gift which so often takes the place of everything, will always thrust away the thought of greater ills, especially if it is increased by the impunity often accorded by greed or weakness.

Some men escape punishment for a minor crime because the offended party forgives them: such an action conforms with mercy and humanity, but is contrary to the public good; as if a private citizen, by his forgiveness, could do away with the need of an example in the same way that he can remit the damages due for an offence. The right to punish rests not with an individual, but with all citizens or with the sovereign. The individual can renounce only his share of that right, he cannot annul that of others.

In proportion as punishments become milder, the need for

clemency and pardon diminishes. Happy that nation in which
they should be grievous! It follows that clemency, a virtue
which for a sovereign has sometimes been no more than an
appendix to all the duties of his throne, should be excluded
from a perfect legal system in which punishments are mild
and methods of adjudication regular and quick. This will seem
a hard truth to anyone who lives amid the disorder of a penal
system in which pardon and mercy are necessarily proportioned to the absurdity of laws and the appalling severity of
sentences. Pardon is the fairest prerogative of the throne, it is
the most desirable attribute of sovereignty, and it is a tacit
disapproval by the beneficent dispensers of public happiness
of a code, which, with all its imperfections, has on its side the
prejudice of ages, a voluminous and imposing apparatus of
endless commentary, the weighty paraphernalia of eternal formalities, and the adherence of the most insinuating and the
least alarming of the half-educated. But let it be considered
that clemency is the virtue of the maker and not of the administrator of the law; that it should shine in the code and not in
particular judgements; that showing men that crimes may be
pardoned or that punishment is not their inevitable consequence, encourages the hope of impunity, and creates the belief
that sentences which go unremitted when remission is possible,
are violent acts of force rather than emanations of justice.
What shall be said, then, when a prince grants a pardon, that
is a public immunity, to an individual, and when his private
act of unenlightened beneficence amounts to a public decree of
exemption from penalty?

So let the laws be inexorable, and also those who administer
them in particular cases; but let the lawmaker be gentle,
lenient, and humane. Let him be a wise architect who makes
his edifice rise upon a foundation of self-respect, and let the
public interest be the outcome of the interests of every individual; and he will not be constrained by partial laws and
clamorous remedies to separate at every point public from
private good, or to build a false image of public safety on fear
and distrust. Let the deep and feeling philosopher leave

men, his brothers, to enjoy in peace that little portion of happiness which the vast system established by the First Cause, by him *who is,* lets them enjoy in this corner of the universe.

21. PLACES OF ASYLUM

THERE remain two questions for me to examine, first whether places of asylum are just, also whether agreement between nations to extradite each other's criminals is useful or not.

Within the borders of a country there should be no place independent of its laws.[1] Their power should follow every citizen as a body is followed by its shadow. Between impunity and asylum there is next to no difference; and as the effect of punishment depends more upon its certainty than its severity, places of asylum invite to crime more than punishments influence against it. To multiply such places of asylum is to create so many small sovereignties; because where laws have no say, new laws may be made contrary to the common law, which in turn will lead to a spirit contrary to that of the whole body of society. History shows that places of asylum are the source of great revolutions both in states and in the opinions of mankind. Some have maintained that a crime—an action, that is, contrary to law—can be punished no matter where it was committed; as if being a subject were indelible, in other words synonymous with, or indeed worse than, being a slave; as if a man could be subject to one kingdom while living in another, and as if his actions could be subordinated without contradiction to two sovereigns and two codes which often contradict each other. Likewise some people believe that a cruel act done, for instance, at Constantinople could be punished in Paris, for the abstract reason that a man who offends humanity deserves to be universally execrated and have all humanity against him; as if judges were avengers of human sensibility, and not of the pacts which

---

[1] The ancient right of Sanctuary lasted in Italy until the nineteenth century. [Tr.]

F

bind men one to another. The place for punishment is the place of crime; there alone, and nowhere else, are men compelled to injure an individual in order to prevent injury to the public. A scoundrel, but one who has not broken the pacts of a society he does not belong to, may be feared and on that account exiled and excluded by the superior force of that society; but he may not be punished by the formal processes of law, which avenges the pacts but does not exact vengeance for the intrinsic malice of actions.

But whether a reciprocal agreement to extradite each other's criminals is useful remains a question I would not venture to decide, until laws are better suited to the needs of humanity, until punishments are milder, and, dependence upon caprice and opinion being done away with, security is achieved for both oppressed innocence and hated virtue; until under the impact of universal reason (which brings ever closer the interests of throne and subject) tyranny exists nowhere but in the vast plains of Asia, though the conviction that no span of earth could be found where true crimes go unpunished might prove a means most efficacious in preventing them.

22. OF SETTING A PRICE UPON MEN'S HEADS

THE other question to be answered is, whether it be useful to set a price upon the head of a known criminal, so putting a weapon into the hand of every citizen and turning him into an executioner. The criminal is either outside the borders or within them: in the first case, the sovereign encourages citizens to commit a crime and expose themselves to punishment, since he thus does injury to other countries and usurps their authority while authorizing the other nations to do the same to himself. If the criminal has not fled, the sovereign, by setting a price, displays his own weakness. One who already has power to defend himself does not seek to buy it. Moreover, such an edict upsets every notion of morality and virtue, which are apt to vanish from the human mind at the least puff of wind. At one moment the laws invite to treachery, at another they punish it. With one hand the lawmaker tightens the bonds of family, of kindred, of friendship; and with the other he rewards those who break them, and those who hold them in contempt; always contradicting himself, at one moment he invites trust between the suspicious souls of men, at the next sows distrust in every heart. Instead of preventing one crime he gives birth to a hundred. Such are the expedients of weak nations, whose laws are no more than hasty repairs to a building already ruinous and crumbling at every point. The more light shines in a nation, the more necessary are good faith and mutual confidence, and the more they tend to identify themselves with sound policy. Trickery, cabal, dark and devious ways are thus more easily foreseen, and a common sensibility abates the sensibility of each individual.

The very centuries of ignorance, in which public morality compelled men to obey private morality, provide lessons and experience for the centuries of enlightenment. But laws which reward betrayal incite a clandestine war and sow mutual mistrust among citizens, work against that most necessary meeting between morality and policy, which could bring happiness to men, peace to the nations, and to the world a somewhat longer interval of tranquillity and rest from the evils which trample upon it.

23. PROPORTION BETWEEN CRIMES AND PUNISHMENTS

It is to the common interest both that crimes should not be committed and also that they should be rare in proportion to the evil they inflict upon society. Therefore the obstacles to crimes should be stronger according to the degree in which those crimes are contrary to the public good, and the degree of incentive which causes them. For that reason a proportion must be established between crimes and punishments.

If pleasure and pain are the moving powers of sentient beings, if the Invisible Legislator has decreed reward and punishment to be among the motives which impel men to their sublimest deeds, the inexact distribution of these motives must give rise to a contradiction as little noticed as it is common—the punishment of crimes which have been caused by punishment. If equal punishment is decreed for two crimes which do not cause equal offence to society, there will be no stronger obstacle to prevent the committing of the more serious crime when it brings the greater advantage.

Whoever sees that the same penalty of death is laid down, for example, for the man who kills a pheasant, the man who murders another man, or the man who falsifies an important document, will draw no distinction between these crimes; this destroys those moral sentiments, which are the work of many centuries and the result of much spilling of blood, which have been produced so slowly and painfully in the human mind; their birth, we may believe, having depended upon the help of the sublimest of motives and the gravest of formal observance.

It is impossible to prevent all the disorders which arise in the universal conflict of human passions. They increase at the compound rate of the population and the intertwinement of private interests, which cannot be geometrically directed in the public interest. For mathematical exactitude we must, in political arithmetic, substitute the calculation of probability. A glance at history will show how disorders increase with the frontiers of empire; and national sentiment declining in the same proportion, the impulse to crime increases with the increase of the individual's interest in these same disorders; for which reason the need to aggravate punishment always increases.

The force, like the force of gravity, which compels us to our own well-being, can be checked only by measure of the obstacles opposed to it. Its effects are the confused series of human actions. If these clash and impede one another, then punishments, which I would call *political obstacles*, prevent their bad effects without doing away with their compelling cause, which is the sensibility inseparable from man; and the lawmaker acts the part of the skilful architect, whose business it is to counteract the ruinating course of gravity and cause the interaction of all that contributes to the strength of his building.

When we allow that men must form societies, when we allow that the very clash of their private interests must result in pacts between them, we discover in disorders a scale; at the top, all those that are immediately destructive of society, at the bottom, the smallest injustices which can be done to the private individuals who form that society. Between these extremes are comprised all those actions opposed to the public welfare which we call crimes, and which diminish, by imperceptible degrees, from highest to lowest. Were geometry adaptable to the infinite and obscure combinations of the actions of men, doubtless there would be a corresponding scale of punishments, which would descend from the severest to the lightest; if we had an exact and universal scale of crimes and punishments, we should have an acceptable and general measure of the degrees of tyranny and liberty in the various nations, of their stock of humanity, or the reverse. But the wise legislator will be content to indicate the chief divisions on the scale without upsetting its order and inflicting punishments of the lowest degree for crimes of the first degree.

24. THE MEASURE OF CRIMES

WE have seen that the true measure of crimes is *the injury done to society*. This is one of those palpable truths which, though we need neither quadrant nor telescope to discover them, and though they are obvious to the most mediocre intellect, have yet, through a marvellous combination of circumstances, been clearly recognized only by a few thinkers in every nation and in every age. But Asiatic ideas, passions in the trappings of authority and power, have, most often by insensible thrusts, occasionally by violent assaults upon the timorous credulity of mankind, dissipated those simple notions; these seem to have been part of the first philosophy of infant societies; and the enlightenment of this present century of ours may lead us back to them, though with that greater surety which may now be given by accurate analysis, much dismal experience, and the very obstacles themselves.

They were in error who believed the true measure of crimes to be the intention of those who commit them. Intention depends on the way objects actually impress a man, and on the previous disposition of his mind; which in all men, and in each individual, vary with the rapid succession of ideas, passions, and circumstances. If intention were the measure we should need not only a separate code for each citizen, but a new law for each criminal act. Sometimes with the best of intentions men do the greatest harm to society; at other times, with the wickedest of intentions, they do it the greatest good.

Others measure crime more by the rank of the injured party than by the importance of the crime in regard to the public good. If this were the true measure, a single irreverence to the Supreme Being ought to be punished more ferociously than the assassination of a monarch; the superiority of his nature compensating infinitely for the difference in the offence.

Finally there are some who think that crimes should be measured by the gravity of the sin they involve. The fallaciousness of this view will be obvious to anyone who examines with impartiality the true relationship between man and man, and between man and God. The first is an equal relationship. Necessity alone, out of the conflict of men's passions and the opposition of their interests, has given rise to the idea of *public utility,* which is the basis of human justice. The relationship between man and God is one of dependence on a perfect Being and a creator, who has reserved to himself alone the right to be lawgiver and judge at the same time, because he alone can be both without impropriety. If he has ordained eternal punishment to such as disobey his omnipotence, what insect will dare take the place of divine justice, will desire to avenge that Being who is sufficient unto himself, upon whom things can make no impression of pleasure or of pain, and who, alone of all beings, acts without being acted upon? The gravity of sin depends upon the inscrutable wickedness of the heart. No finite being can know it without revelation. How then can it furnish a standard for the punishment of crimes? Men in that case would be able to punish when God pardons, and pardon when God punishes. If men can be in contradiction to the Almighty when they offend, they can be so too when they punish.

25. DIVISION OF PUNISHMENTS

SOME crimes are immediately destructive of society, or of its representative: some are offences against the private security of a citizen, in regard to his life, his goods, or his honour: others, again, are acts contrary to that which each man is under obligation to do or not to do, in view of the public good.

Any act which falls outside the above-mentioned limits can be called a *crime,* and can be punished as such, only by those who find it in their own interests to give it that name. Unsureness about these limits has produced in nations a morality which contradicts their lawgiving, indeed actual laws which are mutually exclusive, a multitude of laws which expose the wisest of men to the severest of penalties. *Vice* and *virtue* have in this way been reduced to words of vague and fluctuating meaning, and their very existence being made uncertain, lethargy and a fatal somnolence supervene in the body politic. The opinion that every individual citizen must be allowed to do anything which is not contrary to the laws without fear of any inconvenience other than that which arises from the act itself, this is a dogma of politics which the people should believe in, which chief magistrates should proclaim, and which should be upheld by the incorruptible protection of the laws; a sacred dogma, without which there can be no lawful society; a just recompense for our sacrifice of that total liberty of action, common to all sentient beings, and limited only by its own power. This dogma shapes the free and vigorous spirit, and the enlightened mind; it renders men virtuous, but with that virtue which knows how to resist fear, and not with that supple prudence fit only for those whose existence is at once precarious and uncertain.

Whoever turns a philosophic eye on to the history of nations and their codes of law, will almost always find that the meaning of *vice* and *virtue,* of *good citizen* and *guilty man* changes with the revolution of the ages, not in accord with the changes which occur in a country's circumstances—and so are always in conformity with the common interest—but in accord with the passions and errors which move the different legislators. He will very often observe that the passions of one age are the basis of the morality of future ages; that the strong passions born of fanaticism and enthusiasm are weakened and so to say eroded by time (which reduces all physical and moral phenomena to an equilibrium) until gradually they change into the prudence of another age, and a useful instrument for the strong and the clever. In this way our most obscure ideas of honour and virtue have come into being; obscure, because they change with the revolution of time which makes the name survive the thing, because they change too with rivers and with mountains, which are very often the boundaries not only of our physical but of our moral geography.

26. CRIMES OF HIGH TREASON

OF the first degree, the greatest because the most destructive, are the crimes known as *lèse-majesté*. Only tyranny and ignorance, which confound the clearest words and ideas, can apply this name—and so the severest punishments—to crimes of a different nature; thus making men, as in a thousand other instances, the victims of a word. Every crime, however private, is hurtful to society; but every crime does not attempt its immediate destruction. Moral actions, as well as physical ones, have their own limited sphere of activity, and are differently circumscribed, like all motions of nature, by time and by space;

and only a quibbling interpretation—the common philosophy of servitude—can therefore confound that which eternal truth has distinguished by immutable report.

27. CRIMES AGAINST THE SECURITY OF THE INDIVIDUAL. ACTS OF VIOLENCE. PUNISHMENT OF NOBLES

AFTER crimes of high treason come crimes against the security of the private citizen. The right of security being the primary purpose of every lawful association, violation of that right, which belongs to each citizen, cannot escape the infliction of some of the heaviest penalties established by law.

Of these crimes some are attempts against a man's person, others against his property. The former ought infallibly to be rewarded with corporal punishment.

Attempts, then, upon the security and liberty of citizens are to be classed as major crimes; among them fall not only murders and robbery by the commonalty, but also by grandees and magistrates, whose influence spreads farther and with more effect, destroying in those who are under them all notions of justice and duty, and substituting the notion that might is right, which in the end proves equally dangerous to those who act by it and those who suffer from it.

Neither the great nor the rich ought to be able to pay money for attempts against the weak and the poor; or wealth, which under protection of law accrues as the reward of industry, becomes the nutriment of despotism. Liberty vanishes whenever the law, in certain cases, allows a man to cease to be a *person,* and to become a *thing*; then one sees the powerful devoting their whole efforts to discovering which of all the possible combinations of civil life are legally to their own advantage. This discovery is the magic secret which changes citizens into beasts of burden, and in the hands of the strong it is the chain that binds the actions of the heedless and the weak. It is why in some governments which have all the appearance of liberty, tyranny lies concealed or else insinuates itself, unnoticed, into some corner which the legislator has overlooked, and where insensibly it swells and grows strong. Men usually oppose the firmest of dykes to open despotism, but fail to see the insect which imperceptibly nibbles through the dyke, opening a way (more certain because more hidden) for the invading flood.

How then should we punish the crimes of noblemen when their privileges are so great a part of the law of nations? I shall not examine here this hereditary distinction between noblemen and commoners, I shall not ask whether it serves a good purpose in government, or is necessary to a monarchy; whether a nobility is in fact an intermediate power which limits the excesses of the two extremes, or whether it does not form a class which, a slave to itself and to others, confines all the circulation of credit and expectation to one very narrow round, like those fruitful and pleasant oases which are scattered among the vast and sandy wastes of Arabia; nor, supposing it to be true that inequality is inevitable, or useful to society, shall I ask whether inequality between classes is really preferable to inequality between individuals; whether it should really be confined to one part of the body politic and not circulate through the whole; and whether it should be perpetuated rather than incessantly destroyed and reborn. I shall confine myself to the sole question of how people of that high rank should be punished, with the assertion that punishments should be the same for the greatest as for the least of citizens. Every distinction, whether of honour or of wealth, if it is to be lawful, supposes an anterior quality based upon the law which regards all subjects as equally dependent upon itself. We should suppose men to have said, when they renounced their natural state of individual despotism: 'The greatest honour shall go to the hardest worker, and his fame shall shine out among his successors. The man who is happiest and most honoured shall hope for more; but let him fear no less than other men to violate those pacts by which he is raised above them.' It is true that such decrees did not emanate from a parliament of the whole human race. None the less they have their being in the fixed relationship of things; they do not destroy those benefits which are supposed to derive from a nobility; they prevent its drawbacks; and they make the laws a force to be reckoned with by closing every path to impunity. To those who say that the same punishment inflicted on a nobleman and a commoner is not really the same because of the difference in their upbringing, and because of the disgrace such punishment spreads through an illustrious family, I shall answer that punishment is measured, not by the sensibility of the guilty man but by the injury done to society, which is all the greater when he has been society's favourite; that equality of punishment cannot be other than extrinsic, since it is in fact different for each individual; that such disgrace as falls upon the innocent family of a guilty man can be removed by public demonstrations of a sovereign's goodwill towards them. This formal display, we all know, supplies the place of reason in the admiring credulity of the crowd.

28. INJURIES TO HONOUR

PERSONAL injuries against a man's honour, against, in other words, that fair share of esteem which the citizen has a right to expect from his fellows, should be punished with disgrace.

There is a remarkable contradiction between the civil laws, those jealous custodians above all of the person and the goods of every citizen, and the laws of *honour,* as it is called, which sets opinion above everything else. *Honour* is one of those words around which long and brilliant discussion has raged without attaching to it any firm or stable definition. How miserable a state for the human mind, that it has a clearer, more immediate cognizance of the most distant and least important details of the movements of heavenly bodies, than of the close and highly important notions of morality, which are always in flux and confusion as they are buffeted by the winds of passion, and as ignorance is guided to receive and transmit them! But this seeming paradox will disappear, if we consider that just as objects are always blurred when seen too close to the eyes, so too close a view of moral ideas easily muddles the many simple ideas of which they are composed, to the confusion of those dividing lines which the geometric spirit requires when it would measure the phenomena of human sensibility. Then it will seem less of a marvel to the impartial inquirer into human affairs, who will have suspected that there is perhaps no need of such a paraphernalia of morality, and of so many restrictions, in order to make men happy and secure.

This *honour,* then, is one of those complex ideas which are an aggregate, not only of simple ideas, but of ideas equally complicated, which in their various occurrences in the mind now admit, and now exclude, some of their constituent elements; preserving only a few ideas in common, just as a number of complex algebraical qualities admit a common divisor. To find this common divisor of the various ideas which men have formed of *honour,* we must glance quickly at the origins of society. The first laws and the first magistrates were born of the need to remedy disorders caused by each individual's physical despotism: this was the founding aim of society; and it is this primal aim, in reality or in appearance, which has always governed every code of laws, even ones destructive of that aim. But association between men and increase of knowledge gave birth to an infinite series of mutual activities and requirements, which could never be satisfied by either the providence of law or the immediate power of the individual. From this epoch began the despotism of opinion, which was the sole means of obtaining from others those benefits, and averting those evils, for which the law was unable to make provision. And it is opinion which torments both wise and foolish; which has caused the appearance of virtue to be esteemed above virtue itself; which to its own end makes a missionary even of a rascal. Hence men's esteem has become not merely useful, but essential, if one is not to fall below the common level. Hence, if the ambitious man woos it because it is of use to him, if the vain man begs for it as evidence of his worth, the man of honour is seen to demand it as a necessity. This *honour* a multitude of men make a condition of their very existence. Brought to birth after the creation of society, it could not be added to man's common deposit of surrendered liberty, and is rather a sudden reversion to the natural state of man, a momentary withdrawal of a citizen from those laws which in this situation fail to give him adequate defence.

Hence, both in the extreme of political liberty and in the extreme of subordination, ideas of honour vanish or are utterly confused with other ideas; since in the first case the despotism of law makes it pointless to look for the esteem of others, and in the second case the despotism of men, by nullifying civil existence, reduces everyone to a personality at once precarious and momentary. Honour therefore is one of the basic principles of those monarchies which are a diminished despotism; in them it has the same effect as revolutions in despotic states, causing a momentary return to the state of nature and reminding a master of man's aboriginal equality.

29. OF DUELLING

FROM this need of being esteemed by others came private duelling, which originated in nothing else but the anarchy of law. Duels are said to have been unknown to antiquity, perhaps because the ancients did not come suspicious and armed into their temples or theatres or the company of their friends; or perhaps because duelling was an everyday spectacle served up to the people by enslaved and debased gladiators, so that free men disdained to be thought, or called, gladiators who fought in private. Edicts of death against those who take part in a duel have been used in vain to extirpate this custom, which is founded on what some men fear more than they fear death; for if the man of honour is deprived of the esteem of others, he sees himself either as someone exposed to a mere solitary existence, a state which no social creature can endure, or to

becoming a target for insult and defamation, the constant repetition of which weighs more with him than the risk of punishment. What is it that makes duels less frequent with ordinary
folk than with the great? Not simply that the poor go unarmed, but that they depend on other men's esteem less than
the men of rank, who on that account regard their fellows with
more suspicion and jealousy.

It may be useful to repeat at this point what others have
written, that the most effective way of preventing this crime is to
punish the aggressor—that is to say, the man who starts the
duel—and to declare innocent the man who, for no fault of his
own, has been forced to defend what existing laws do not secure
to him, that is to say the opinion entertained of him by others.

30. ROBBERY

ROBBERY unaccompanied by violence should be punished by
a fine. The man who seeks to enrich himself with another man's
property should be made poor by the loss of his own. But since
this is generally the crime of the wretched and the desperate, of
that unhappy portion of mankind deprived by the rights of
property—terrible and perhaps unnecessary rights—of all but
their barest existence; and since fines increase the number of
criminals over and above the number of crimes, take bread
from the mouths of the innocent and hand it over to villains,
the most opportune punishment for robbery without violence is
the one kind of subjection which can be called just: the temporary subjection, that is to say, of the criminal's labour and
person to society, so that by this complete personal subordination he may repair the despotic and unjust encroachment he
has made upon the social compact.

When robbery is combined with violence, the punishment
should likewise be a combination of the corporal and the
servile. Other writers before myself have pointed to the obvious
confusion which arises if we fail to distinguish between punish-

ment for robbery with violence and punishment for robbery by fraud, thus absurdly equating a large sum of money with a human life. These two kinds of theft are crimes of a different nature; and to politics we may most certainly apply the axiom of mathematics: that heterogeneous quantities are separated by infinity. But it is never superfluous to repeat what has seldom been acted upon. The political, more than any other machine, preserves its conceived motion, and is slowest to acquire a new one.

31. SMUGGLING

SMUGGLING[1] is a real crime against sovereign and nation; but punishment for it should not involve disgrace, since the public do not think of an act of smuggling as disgraceful.

Yet why is it that this crime brings no dishonour upon the man who commits it, seeing that in fact he robs his prince, and therefore the nation as well? My answer would be that offences which men cannot conceive of as being directed against themselves, do not interest them enough to cause a public outcry against the offender. Smuggling is of this nature. The public, little impressed by consequences remote from themselves, do not see the damage which smuggling can do them; and they often enjoy its immediate advantages. Nor do they see the harm it does to the prince. So they are not so concerned to disapprove of a smuggler as they are of someone who has robbed an individual, or forged a document, or committed some other crime that might happen to themselves, the obvious principle being that every sentient creature is concerned only about the evils which fall within his experience. This is a crime which has its origin actually in the law. The higher the duties, the higher the profits of smuggling; the smaller the object to be smuggled and the longer the frontiers to be guarded, the more tempting and the easier smuggling becomes. Loss, both of the prohibited merchandise and all other belongings accompanying

[1] In Beccaria's time this was often punished with death. [Tr.]

it, is a very just punishment; but the lower the duty, the more effective this will be, since men only take risks in proportion to the advantages produced by the success of their undertaking.

It may be asked if such a crime should go unpunished when a man has no other belongings to forfeit. It should not: there are some forms of smuggling which have such an effect upon the revenue, so necessary and so difficult a part of a good system of law, that they deserve a considerable penalty, to the extent even of prison or penal servitude—though sentences of the kind should fit the offence. For example, a man who smuggles tobacco should not be imprisoned with a cut-throat or a thief; the most suitable penalty would be to confine such a smuggler's labour to the work and service of the very crown rights he had wished to defraud.

32. OF DEBTORS

THE bona fides of contracts, and the safeguarding of commerce, compel the legislator to secure, on behalf of his creditors, the person of an insolvent debtor. But I believe it important to distinguish in bankruptcy between the fraudulent and the innocent. The former should be punished as severely as those who counterfeit money, since to counterfeit a piece of minted metal, which is a pledge of the obligations of citizen to citizen, is no worse than to counterfeit the obligations themselves. But the innocent bankrupt, the man who has proved in rigorous examination before his judges that he was stripped of his goods by someone else's malice or misfortune, or by those vicissitudes which it is beyond man's prudence to escape—what barbarous reason can justify throwing a man of that kind into prison,[1] where, deprived of his one poor remaining possession, his bare liberty, he experiences the anguish of the criminal and, with the desperation of honesty trodden underfoot, is brought perhaps to regret that innocent life he once peacefully lived under the

[1] Imprisonment for debt in Italy ceased formally in 1865, but had not been applied for some time. [Tr.]

tutelage of laws, which he broke through no fault of his own? Laws dictated, let me add, by the greed of the powerful, laws which the weak are enabled to endure only by that hope which glimmers in the minds of most of us and makes us believe misfortune to be only for others, fortune only for ourselves! Left to their everyday feelings men prefer cruel laws, since the fear of being injured is always greater than the will to injure—though, since they are themselves subject to the laws, it is in each man's interest that they should be mild.

Returning to the innocent bankrupt; granting that his obligations should not be discharged until he has met them in full, granting that he should not be allowed to evade them without the consent of the interested parties, that he should not be allowed to remove to some other jurisdiction a business which he should be constrained, under penalty, to conduct so as to satisfy his creditors in proportion to its profits; I ask how any lawful pretext, such as the security of commerce or the sacred rights of property, can possibly justify depriving an innocent bankrupt of his freedom? This would be useless, except in a case—likely to be very rare if there has been a rigorous examination—in which the evils of servitude may be expected to compel a supposedly innocent bankrupt to reveal his secrets. I believe it to be a sound legislative maxim that the worth of penalties may be measured directly by the damage which has been inflicted on the public, and inversely by the difficulties of verifying that damage.[2]

It should be possible to distinguish fraud from grievous fault, grievous fault from slight fault, and the latter from entire

---

[2] Commerce and the ownership of goods are not an end of the social contract, but may be a means of achieving that end. To expose the members of society to the evils which are the reason why society has in so many ways combined, would be to subordinate ends to means, a fallacious proceeding common in all the sciences, and especially in politics, and one into which I fell in earlier editions of this work, when I said that the innocent bankrupt should be kept in prison in pledge of his debts or be made to work like a slave for his creditors. I am ashamed of having written in such a way. I have been accused of sedition, without deserving it: I offended against the rights of man, and nobody complained!

G

innocence; and, assigning to the first the punishment given for crimes of forgery, to the second penalties less severe (though still including the loss of liberty), to reserve to the last a free choice of the means of restitution, a freedom which should be denied to offenders of the third class and left to their creditors instead. But the distinctions between grievous and less grievous should be fixed by the blind impartiality of the law, not by the dangerous and arbitrary discretion of judges. It is as necessary to fix limits in government as it is in mathematics, in measurement of the public good as in measurement of size.

How simple it would be for the far-sighted legislator to do away with much culpable bankruptcy, while remedying the misfortunes of the man who is at once innocent and industrious! Public registration of all contracts, and freedom for all citizens to inspect these properly ordered documents; a public bank established by a wise distribution of tax upon prosperous trade, which would advance timely assistance to its unfortunate but innocent members—these would have no real drawbacks and might produce advantages beyond number. But the easiest, the simplest, and the best laws, which at a nod from the legislator would spread vigour and plenty throughout the nation, laws which would be followed by an outpouring of hymns of gratitude from generation to generation, are the ones least thought of, or least desired. A restless and niggling spirit, a timid caution which confines itself to the moment, a wary rigidity in the face of anything new, possess the minds of those by whom the bustling activities of humble mortality are controlled.

33. OF PUBLIC TRANQUILLITY

FINALLY, among the crimes of the third kind are those in particular which disturb the public tranquillity and quiet; uproar and merry-making, for instance, in public streets intended for business and traffic; or fanatical speeches which in an attentive crowd excite those easy passions the strength of which increases with the number of listeners, and which owe more to the obscure mystery of enthusiasm than to clear, quiet reasoning, which never has any effect upon a large gathering.

Lighting a city by night at the public expense, stationing guards in the different quarters, simple moral discourses on religion delivered only in the silent and sacred calm of churches under shield of public authority, speeches aimed at the sustention of private and public interests delivered at national assemblies, in parliament, or wherever the majesty of the sovereign power resides, are all effective ways of preventing a dangerous intensification of public hysteria. Such things are a chief part of that magisterial vigilance, which the French call *la police*; but if the magistrate should be guided in this vigilance by regulations which are arbitrary and not established by a code endorsed by every citizen, the door is open to that tyranny which is always to be found on the circumference of political freedom. I can find no exception to this general axiom, that every citizen should know when he is guilty and when he is innocent. If in any government there is need of censors, and in general of arbitrary magistrates, the cause, since they are foreign to the nature of well-organized government, lies in the weakness of its constitution. More victims have been sacrificed to hidden tyranny by uncertainty of their fate than by public and solemnized cruelty. Such cruelty revolts rather than demoralizes the spirit of man. The tyrant begins always by gaining control over opinion, which is the forerunner of courage, since courage can shine forth only in the clear light of truth, or in the fire of the passions, or in ignorance of danger.

34. OF POLITICAL IDLENESS

WISE governments do not put up with political idleness in the midst of labour and industry. I would call politically idle those who contribute neither work nor wealth to society; who accumulate but never spend; whom the vulgar regard with stupid

worship and admiration, and the wise with disdainful compassion for its victims; who, since they are deprived of that
stimulus to a life of activity which consists of safeguarding and
augmenting the means of existence, devote their whole energy
to cultivating those passions of opinion which are strong indeed.
Declamatory puritans have confused idleness of this kind with
the idleness which comes from wealth accumulated by hard
work; however, it is a matter for the law, not for censorious
virtue of a limited and puritanical nature, to determine the
kinds of idleness which should be punished. Political idleness
cannot be ascribed to the man who enjoys the fruits of the vices
or virtues of his forebears, and who provides the industrious
poor, in exchange for his pleasures, with their bread and existence; nor to the man who employs his wealth to conduct in
peace the silent campaigns of industry, instead of the hazardous
and bloody campaigns of war. The necessity and utility of such
idleness increases with the expansion of society and the restric-
tion of controls.

35. SUICIDE AND EXPATRIATES

SUICIDE[1] is a crime that does not properly appear to admit
of punishment, which in this case must fall either upon the
innocent or upon a body already lifeless and cold. In the latter
case it will make no more impression on the living than would
be made by flogging a statue, in the former it will be unjust
and tyrannical, inasmuch as man's political freedom necessarily
presupposes that punishment should not be other than personal.
Men love life too well, and are confirmed in this love by everything around them. Pleasure's seductive image, and Hope,
sweetest deceiver of mortal man, which makes us gulp down
draughts of evil mixed with but a few drops of content, are too
alluring for it to be feared that the inevitable impunity attaching to this crime could have a bad effect on mankind. Men who

[1] British law regarded suicide as a crime until 1961. [Tr.]

fear pain obey the laws; but death destroys every source of bodily pain. So what reason can there be for restraining the suicide's desperate hand?

The man who kills himself does less harm to society than the man who leaves his country for ever. The suicide leaves all his possessions behind him, the expatriate takes part of his property with him. Also if the strength of society depends upon the number of its citizens, the man who removes himself and adheres to a neighbouring country does twice as much damage as the man who simply removes himself from society by death. The question then reduces itself to whether a nation is served or harmed by allowing each of its citizens to be at all times free to take himself elsewhere.

A law should never be promulgated unless there is a force behind it, and unless circumstances are such as to make it effectual. Opinion obeys legislative influences if their impact is slow and roundabout, and resists them whenever their approach is direct and violent. Similarly the contempt which men have for ineffectual laws inclines to spread to laws of a more salutary nature, which are then looked upon more as obstacles to be surmounted than as strongholds of public welfare.

Moreover, if our sensibility, as we have said, is limited, the more respect we have for objects outside the law, the less we shall have left for the law itself. This is a principle from which the wise dispensator of public happiness can draw a number of useful conclusions, though to enlarge upon them would take me too far from my subject, which is to prove the uselessness of turning the state into a prison. There is no point in such a law; unless a country is divided from all neighbouring countries by unscalable crags or unnavigable seas, how can its surrounding frontiers be closed at every point, and who is to keep watch on the watchers? Once a man has carried his possessions away with him, how is he to be punished? From the moment of its commission, such a crime is beyond punishment; to punish it beforehand would be to punish the will and not the act, would be to take charge of a man's purpose, that freest part of him which is independent of the authority of human law. To punish the man who has absented himself by seizing the property he has left behind him—even supposing there was no collusion, which would be easy and inevitable and could be prevented only by tyrannical interfering in agreements—would bring all commerce between nation and nation to a standstill. To punish the guilty man if he should return would mean that no one would return, and thus prevent reparation for the harm done to society. The very refusal to allow men to leave their country would increase their desire to leave, and be an advertisement to foreigners against settling in that country.

What must we think of a government which can keep men in a country, to which they are naturally attached by their first childhood impressions, by no other means than fear? The best way of keeping citizens at home is to increase their individual and mutual prosperity. Just as every effort should be made to hold the balance of trade in our favour, it is in the very best interests of sovereign and nation that the sum of happiness should be raised above that of surrounding countries. Though the pleasures of luxury are not the principal elements in that happiness, they are needed to cure that inequality which increases with a nation's progress; and without them wealth would accumulate only in one pair of hands.[2]

[2] When the confines of a country increase at a greater rate than its population, luxury favours despotism, for where there is a scarcity of men there is less industry, and where there is less industry the poor have to depend more on the display of the wealthy, and the union of the oppressed against the oppressors is less to be feared. In such conditions, also, homage, office, distinctions, and deference, which make the gap between the strong and the weak even more noticeable, are more easily available to the few than the many, since men are the more independent the less they are observed, and the less observed the more there are of them. But when the population increases at a greater rate than the confines of the country, luxury is opposed to despotism, because then it stimulates the industry and activity of men, and the poor afford the rich too many pleasures and comforts to leave much room for those pleasures of ostentation which add to a conviction of dependence. Hence we may observe that in vast, weak, and thinly-populated states, if nothing else interferes, the luxury of ostentation prevails over the luxury of comfort; whereas in states which are populous rather than large, the luxury of comfort always diminishes this luxury of ostentation.

But trade in the pleasures of luxury, and their circulation, have this inconvenience, that though many people are engaged in their production, they are in fact from start to finish enjoyed only by a few; and it is the majority of the population which has the least share of them—a share insufficient to prevent that feeling of want which is less occasioned by the fact than by the comparison. But the bases of that happiness I mentioned are security and freedom, to which only laws ascribe a limit; given these two, the pleasures of luxury favour the people; without them, such pleasures become the instruments of tyranny. Just as the noblest of beasts and the freest of birds withdraw to solitudes and inaccessible thickets, leaving smiling fertile country to men with their snares, so men will flee even pleasure when it comes from the hand of tyranny.

The law then which imprisons subjects in their own country has been shown to be ineffective and unjust. It is the same with punishment for suicide; and on that account, though it be a fault which is punished by God, who alone is able to punish after death, it cannot be a crime before men, since the punishment falls, not upon the guilty person himself, but upon his family. If anyone tells me that such a punishment will nevertheless deter someone who has decided to kill himself, I answer that a man who calmly renounces the benefits of life, and hates existence so much that he prefers an eternity of unhappiness, is not at all likely to be swayed by the less powerful and more distant consideration of his children or his parents.

36. CRIMES DIFFICULT TO PROVE

THERE are some crimes which are at once of common occurrence in society and difficult to prove. Among these are adultery, pederasty, and abortion.

Adultery is a crime which, politically considered, derives its strength and direction from two causes, the variability of the laws in force among mankind, and that very powerful attraction which compels one sex towards the other.[1]

If I were speaking to nations still deprived of the light of religion, I should add that there is another considerable difference between adultery and other crimes. Adultery comes from the abuse of a need which is constant and universal with all mankind; a need which existed before society itself, and on which society is founded; whereas other crimes destructive of society have an origin determined less by natural need than by momentous passions. Those who have studied history and their fellow men agree that needs of this kind appear to be maintained quantitatively in the same region at a constant value. Supposing this to be true, laws and customs which have attempted to reduce rather the sum total of such needs would be useless and actually dangerous, since they would have the effect of loading every quarter of the world with the needs of every other quarter, as well as its own. On the contrary, sensible laws and customs would, so to say, follow the gentle declivity of the plain, dividing and distributing the sum total into as many small equal portions as would uniformly and generally prevent both flood and drought.

Conjugal fidelity is determined by freedom to marry and the rate of marriage. Where marriages are governed by hereditary prejudice, where they are made or marred by family power, the bonds are secretly broken by affairs of the heart, to the shame of that everyday morality whose business it is to decry the consequences but condone the causes. Such considerations, however, will not be required by men who live by the light of true religion, and have sublimer motives with which to remedy the forceful effects of nature.

The act of adultery is so quickly performed, in such a

[1] This attraction may be likened in many cases to that force of gravity which moves the universe. Like gravitation it diminishes with distance; and if gravitation controls most of the movements of bodies, this other force, while it lasts, controls all the movements of the mind. But they differ in this, that the force of gravity is counterbalanced by obstacles, while attraction of the sexes gathers force and vigour with the increase of obstacles opposed to it.

mysterious way, so entirely covered by that very veil which the laws have woven (a necessary veil, but a fragile one, which increases rather than diminishes the worth of the thing it conceals), the opportunities for it occur so easily and the consequences of it are so equivocal, that it is one of those crimes which the legislator will find it easier to prevent than to punish. It is a general rule that in every crime which, on account of its nature, frequently goes unpunished, penalties act as an incentive. Characteristically our imagination is stimulated in the liveliest way by difficulties, if they are not insurmountable or too much for the mental laziness of the individual; they increase the desirability of the object; they serve as so many barriers which prevent our wandering, fickle imagination from deserting that object. Thus compelled to examine its every aspect, our imagination fastens upon the pleasanter side, to which our minds naturally run, withdrawing speedily from the painful and the sad.

Pederasty, so severely punished by law and so freely subjected to tortures which triumph over innocence, is based less on man's needs when he lives in freedom and on his own, than on his passions when he lives with others in slavery. It draws its strength, not so much from a surfeit of every other pleasure, as from that education which begins by making men useless to themselves in order to make them useful to others. In those institutions packed with hot-blooded youth natural vigour, as it develops, is faced with insurmountable obstacles to every other kind of relationship and wears itself out in an activity useless to humanity, and which brings on premature old age.

Abortion, too, results from an inescapable dilemma involving the woman who has given way either to her own weakness or to violence. With a choice before her of disgrace or killing a being which cannot feel the pains of death, can a woman be expected not to prefer the latter to the misery which inevitably awaits both herself and her luckless offspring? The best way of preventing this crime would be by laws capable of protecting weakness from the tyranny which exaggerates all vices that cannot be hidden under the cloak of virtue.

I do not pretend to diminish the horror justly evoked by these crimes; but by pointing to their source I believe I may draw this general conclusion: that no punishment can be called exactly just (in other words, necessary) if the law, given the circumstances of the country, has not adopted the best possible means of preventing the crime.

37. OF ONE PARTICULAR KIND OF CRIME

THE reader of this essay must notice that I have written nothing of crimes of a particular kind which covered Europe in blood; crimes which raised those ghastly funeral pyres, the flames of which were fed by live human bodies, affording the blind mob the enjoyment and sweet harmony of hearing the confused groans of wretched victims emerging from violent swirls of black smoke—smoke from men's limbs, from their crackling and burning bones, their sizzling, still palpitating tripes. But the rational man will agree that neither the place nor the age nor the matter in hand allow me to examine the nature of such crimes. It would take too long, and stray too far from my subject, to show how essential to a state is a perfect uniformity in thinking, the example of many nations notwithstanding; or to show how opinions which differ on a few subtle and obscure points altogether beyond human grasp, can in fact upset the public welfare if one of them should not be given authority above the rest; or to show that the nature of opinion is such, that while some opinions are made clear by contrast, by a process of mutual fermentation and conflict which brings the true ones to the top and allows the false ones to sink into oblivion, other opinions, ill secured by the nakedness of their substance, require to be vested with force and authority. It would take me too long to prove that, although the triumph of force over the human mind may appear odious, its only trophies dissembling, and consequent degradation, though it may seem to contradict the spirit of gentleness and brotherly love enjoined by reason and by the authority we most revere, it may also be necessary and indispensable.

All this we may take as clearly proved, and when put into practice by recognized authority, as conformable to the true interests of mankind. I speak only of crimes which are the outcome of human nature and the social contract; and not of sins, the punishment of which, even in this world, requires to be governed by other principles than those of a narrow philosophy.

38. FALSE IDEAS OF UTILITY

THE false ideas of utility arrived at by some legislators are one source of error and injustice.

Such a false idea of utility sets particular inconveniences above the general inconvenience; it commands the feelings instead of exciting them; it tells reason that it must obey.

A false idea of utility sacrifices a thousand real advantages for one disadvantageous or imaginary or unimportant consequence; it would deprive man of fire because it might burn him and of water because it might drown him; it can mend evils only by destroying them.

Laws which prohibit the carrying of arms are of this kind, because they disarm only those who are neither inclined to crimes nor determined upon them. Can the man who has courage enough to violate the most sacred laws of humanity and the most important laws of the criminal code be expected not to disregard those lesser, purely arbitrary laws, so easy to break with impunity, the strict enforcement of which would deprive him of that personal liberty so dear to him, and so dear to the wise lawgiver, subjecting the innocent to all the vexations deserved by the guilty? Such laws weaken the assaulted and favour the assailant; instead of reducing the number of murders they increase them, since an unarmed man may be attacked with more confidence than an armed one. Laws of this kind must be called, not preventive, but fearful of crime, which has its origin not in a rational estimation of the drawbacks and advantages of a general decree, but in the tumultuous excitement set up by particular events.

A false idea of utility tries to impose upon a multitude of sentient beings that ordered symmetry which is the lot of unfeeling and inanimate matter; it ignores those immediate influences which alone act with force and firmness upon the multitude, in favour of remoter influences the effect of which is brief in the extreme and feeble, unless some altogether extraordinary imaginative power exaggerates them and makes up for their remoteness.

Finally it is a false idea of utility which, by sacrificing things to names, divorces the public from the private good. There is this difference between the state of society and the state of nature—that the savage does no more harm to another man than is necessary to do good to himself; whereas civilized man is sometimes moved by bad laws to injure others, without doing good to himself. The despot plants fear and dejection in the minds of his slaves; but these rebound on him and return to plague his own mind with redoubled force. The more solitary and domestic fear is in its effects, the less it endangers the man who makes it an instrument of his fortunes; but the more widely it ranges, and the more men it agitates, the easier it becomes for some rash, or desperate, or audacious and clever man to compel other men to his own purposes, arousing in them feelings which are the more welcome and the more seductive, the wider he is able to spread the risks of his enterprise; for the value which these unhappy creatures place on their own lives diminishes in proportion to the miseries they undergo. Hence crimes give birth to new crimes; for hatred is more durable than love, inasmuch as it derives its strength from the very acts by which love is weakened.

39. OF THE SPIRIT OF THE FAMILY

LEGALIZED injustices of a grievous kind have had the approval even of the most enlightened of men, and have been committed under the freest of commonwealths, because society has been regarded rather as a union of families than a union of men.

Let us imagine a hundred thousand men, or twenty thousand families, each one made up of five individuals including the representative head of the family; if union in society is reckoned by families, this will give us twenty thousand men, and eighty thousand slaves; if it be reckoned by men, we shall have a hundred thousand men, and not a single slave. In the former case, we shall have one commonwealth made up of twenty thousand little monarchies; in the latter the spirit of the commonwealth will breathe, not only in the market place and assemblies of the nation, but between the walls of the home, where most of all men find their happiness or misery. Since laws and customs result from the habitual sentiments of the members of a commonwealth, in the former case, its members being the heads of families, it follows that the spirit of monarchy will be introduced little by little into the commonwealth itself, and that its effects will be hindered only by the conflicting interests of individuals, not by a sentiment which breathes liberty and equality. The spirit of the family is one of detail, confining itself to the small facts of life. The spirit which regulates a commonwealth has a mastery of general principles: it sees the facts, and classifies them under their main heads for the general good. In a commonwealth made up of families the sons go on living under the sway of the head of the family until he dies, and it is only his death, which they have awaited so long, that allows them to lead an existence dependent entirely upon the law. If in their greener and more vigorous age, when their feelings were less influenced by that fear born of experience which we call moderation, they were accustomed to tremble and submit in this way, how are they going to overcome the obstacles which vice always opposes to virtue, in the languor of their declining age when their disposition to enjoy its fruits will allow no vigorous alteration in their ways?

When the commonwealth is one of men, the family is subordinated, not to command, but to contract; and the children, when they emerge from the natural state of dependence consequent upon their weakness and their need of education and protection, become free members of the community, who submit themselves to the head of the family only for their share of its advantages, as free citizens do *vis-à-vis* society at large.

In the commonwealth of families, the young people, who make up the larger and more useful part of the nation, are at the disposal of their fathers; in the commonwealth of men, they are bound by no other ties than the sacred and inviolable one of affording each other the help they require, and showing gratitude for the benefits they have received; such ties are less often destroyed by the wicked malice of the human heart than by ill-understood subjection imposed by law. These contradictions between the laws of the family and the fundamental laws of the commonwealth are a fecund source of other contradictions between domestic and public morality; and so give rise to a perpetual conflict in the individual mind. Domestic morality inspires subjection and fear, public morality inspires courage and liberty: domestic morality teaches that beneficence should be confined to a small number of persons without spontaneity of choice, public morality teaches its extension to every class of man. Domestic morality demands unending sacrifice to a vain idol which calls itself the 'good of the family' and often fails to do good to any of its members, public morality teaches men to help themselves within the law, and by endowing them with that zeal which is the prelude to action, excites them to self-sacrifice for their country. Such contrasts make men disdain to follow after virtue, which they find involved, confused, and separated from themselves by that remoteness which is occasioned by the obscurity of objects, whether physical or moral. How often is a man astonished to look back over his past actions and discover how dishonest they have been!

When a society increases, each of its members becomes a smaller part of the whole, and the sentiments of commonwealth are proportionately lessened if the law has taken no care to reinforce them. Societies, like the human body, have their circumscribed limits, which cannot be exceeded without upset to their economy. The size of a state, it seems, should be inversely proportioned to the sensibility of its members; otherwise, if both state and population increase together, good laws will find the prevention of crime to be an obstacle to the very benefits they have produced. Too large a commonwealth can only save itself from despotism by subdividing into a union of many small federal states. But this requires the absolute authority of a dictator with the courage of a Lucius Sulla, and as great a genius for building up as he had for knocking down. If such a man were ambitious, the glory of all the ages would await him; if he were a philosopher, the blessings of his fellow citizens would console him for the loss of his authority—if he had not clearly become indifferent to their ingratitude. As the sentiments which unite us to the nation weaken, so sentiments which unite us to surrounding objects grow stronger; which is why a more powerful despotism makes friendships more durable and the always middling virtues of the family more common, if not the only ones. Everyone can see from this how limited the outlook of most of our legislators has been.

40. OF THE EXCHEQUER

THERE was a time when almost all punishments were fines. The crimes of men were the patrimony of the prince. Attempts against the security of the public were an object of gain; those who were appointed to defend the public safety had an interest in seeing it violated. The business of punishment was accordingly a suit between the exchequer (which exacted the punishment) and the accused; a civil affair, contentious, private rather than public, which gave the exchequer other rights than those enjoined upon it by public defence, and inflicted upon the guilty man wrongs other than those required by the need of example. The judge became in this way an advocate of the exchequer rather than an impartial searcher after truth; an agent of the revenue rather than guardian and administrator of the law. But as, in this system, to confess to a crime was to confess to owing a debt to the exchequer, which in those days was the aim of criminal proceedings; so confessing to a crime, confessing to it in a way which favoured and did no harm to the revenue account, became and remains to this day (since effects always continue a very long time after causes) the central point around which all criminal proceedings revolve.

Without such a confession a guilty man convicted on unassailable evidence will have a lighter punishment than the one laid down for his offence; and without it, he will escape the torture which would have been inflicted for other crimes he may have committed of the same kind. But with a confession, the judge becomes master of the body of the accused, and tears it to bits with methodical formality, so as to extract from it, as if it were some capital he had acquired, all the profit it can produce. Once the existence of a crime has been proved, confession makes the proof convincing; and to make this proof still less open to doubt it is forcibly wrung out by spasms of agony and despair; while at the same time an extra-judicial confession obtained in a calm and detached way, without the overwhelming terrors of judicial torture, is considered insufficient for a verdict. Inquiries and evidence which elucidate the crime but weaken the revenue are excluded; it is not compassion for misery and weakness which sometimes saves the accused from torture, but concern for the revenue which this imaginary and inconceivable entity might perhaps lose. The judge becomes the enemy of the accused, of a man in chains, abandoned to squalor, to torment, and the most terrible of futures; he does not look for the true facts, but looks for the crime in the prisoner; he tries to trap him, and believes it will be his loss if he fails to do so, that it will do harm to that infallibility which man arrogates to himself in everything. The grounds of arrest are in the power of the judge; for a man to prove himself innocent, he must first be declared guilty. This is called an *offensive prosecution*. Such are criminal proceedings in the eighteenth century, in almost every corner of our enlightened Europe. The true form of prosecution, the *informative,* in other words, impartial inquiry into fact, the kind of prosecution demanded by reason, adopted under military laws, and used even under Asiatic tyrannies in trivial and unimportant cases, is used least of all by the courts of Europe. How incredible this complicated labyrinth of strange absurdities will appear, beyond any doubt, to a more fortunate posterity! Only the philosophers of that future time will be able to read in human nature proof that such a system could ever have existed.

41. HOW CRIMES MAY BE PREVENTED

IT is better to prevent crimes than to punish them. That is the chief purpose of all good legislation, which is the art of leading men—if one may apply the language of mathematics to the blessings and evils of life—towards the maximum of possible happiness and the minimum of possible misery.

But the means hitherto employed are for the most part mistaken, and contrary to the end proposed. It is impossible to reduce the turbulent activities of mankind to a geometrical order devoid of irregularity and confusion. Just as nature's immutable and very simple laws do not prevent disturbance in the movement of the planets, so human laws cannot prevent disturbances and disorders in the infinite and utterly opposed attractions of pleasure and pain. Yet such is the chimera entertained by men of narrow mind, who have authority in their hands. To prohibit a multitude of trivial acts is not to prevent the crimes which they may occasion, but to create new ones, and to define at pleasure virtues and vices, which we are exhorted to regard as eternal and immutable. What a situation it would reduce us to, if everything which might tempt us to crime were

H

forbidden! Man would have to be deprived of the use of his sense. For every single thing that drives men to commit a single real crime, there are a thousand things which drive them to some trivial act that a bad law insists on calling a crime; and if the likelihood of crimes is proportionate to the number of motives, then to extend the sphere of crime is to increase the likelihood that they will be committed. The majority of laws are nothing but privileges, a tribute, that is to say, by all to the comfort of the few.

We want crime to be prevented? Then we must see to it that laws are clear and simple, and that the whole strength of the nation is concentrated upon their defence, and that no part of its strength is used to destroy them. We must see that the law favours individual men more than classes of men, that men fear the law and nothing but the law. Fear of the laws is salutary, but fear between man and man is dangerous and productive of crime. Men in a state of slavery are more sensual, more debauched, more cruel, than men who are free. Those who are free study the sciences, study the interests of the nation, look upon great things and imitate them; slaves, content with the day, seek in the clamour of debauchery a distraction from the emptiness of their lives; never sure of how anything will end, the dubious issue of the crimes they commit favours the passion by which crimes are determined.

If climate makes a nation indolent, uncertainty in its laws will maintain and aggravate that indolence and that stupor. If a nation likes its pleasures but is lively, uncertainty in its laws will dissipate that liveliness in numberless little cabals and intrigues, which sow distrust in every heart and establish treachery and dissimulation as the foundation of prudence. If a nation is courageous and strong, all uncertainty in its laws will in the end disappear, but only after much wavering between freedom and slavery, slavery and freedom.

We want crime to be prevented? Then see to it we must that light and freedom go hand in hand. The evils born of knowledge are in inverse ratio to its diffusion; the benefits in direct ratio. A daring impostor, always a man above the ordinary, wins the adulation of an ignorant people and the hisses of an enlightened one. By making comparisons easier and by multiplying points of view, knowledge opposes sentiment to sentiment and makes them modify each other, a process which becomes all the easier when different people may be expected to hold the same views or advance the same objections. When light falls profusely over a nation, slanderous ignorance is reduced to silence, authority is disarmed of its reasons and starts to tremble, and nothing can shift the forceful vigour of the law; because there exists no enlightened man who does not approve the compacts, public, open, and effective, which uphold the security of the people, who does not compare the small share of useless liberty he has sacrificed with the sum of all the liberty sacrificed by others who, had there been no laws, might have joined in conspiracy against him. Every man of sensitive outlook who glances at a well-made code of laws and sees that all he has lost is a fatal liberty to do injury to others, must be constrained to bless both the throne and its occupant.

It is not true that the sciences have always been prejudicial to mankind; and when they were, it was an evil men could not avoid. The multiplication of mankind upon the face of the earth introduced war, the cruder arts, and the first laws, which were temporary agreements born of a necessity and perishing with it. This was the first philosophy of man, the few elements of which were just, because men's apathy and want of learning preserved them from error. But the needs of men always multiplied with their numbers. Hence it was necessary to impress men in stronger and more durable ways so as to dissuade them from returning repeatedly to their original state of disunity, which proved more and more disastrous. Of great benefit to mankind therefore were those first errors which peopled the earth with false gods (I mean great social benefit), and created an invisible universe to control our universe. They were benefactors of man, who dared deceive him and dragged him in docile ignorance to the altar. By presenting man with things beyond his senses, which fled before him just as they seemed to be within his grasp, and which were never despised because never properly understood, they reconciled man's divided passions and focused them upon a single thing that powerfully absorbed them.

These were the events which first lifted every nation from savagery; this was the epoch which saw the formation of great societies; and such was the nature of the bond—the only bond perhaps—which they required. I do not speak of God's Chosen People; among whom the place of human politics was taken by the most extraordinary of miracles and the most signal of favours. But just as it is the property of error to divide and divide again *ad infinitum*, so the sciences, which were born of error, transformed mankind into a fanatic multitude of blind men, pushing and shoving one another in a closed labyrinth, in such utter confusion that some minds of philosophic sensibility have even looked back with envy to man's first savage state.[1] Here then was the first epoch in which knowledge, or rather opinions, were harmful.

The second epoch was that terrible and difficult one of transition from error to truth, from the darkness of the unknown to light. The mighty clash between error, which serves the few men of power, and truth, which serves the multitude of the weak, the fermenting brew of passions aroused at such a time, brought upon suffering mankind an infinity of evils. If we reflect upon history, the chief epochs of which, after certain intervening periods, are so little different from each other, we must observe that again and again a whole generation has been sacrificed to the happiness of succeeding generations, in the painful yet necessary transition from the shadows of ignorance to the light of philosophy, and from tyranny to liberty. But when the minds of men have calmed and the fires which purged the nations of the evils oppressing them have been extinguished, and truth, whose pace quickens after the first slow steps, sits side by side with kings upon the throne and is worshipped at her altar in the parliaments of every commonwealth, who then will dare ever to assert that the light which lightens the multitude can be more harmful than the darkness, or that a clear

[1] An allusion to J. J. Rousseau. [Tr.]

understanding among them of the true and simple relationships of things can ever be fatal to men?

If blind ignorance is less fatal than a confused modicum of knowledge, which adds the evils of ignorance to the evils of error arising inevitably from a narrow view of the confines of truth, then the most precious gift a sovereign can make to the nation and to himself is an enlightened man as depositary and guardian of the sacred laws. Accustomed to see the truth, and not to fear it, freed for the most part of the demands of reputation, which are so rarely satisfied and which put the virtue of most men to the proof, used to contemplating mankind from the loftiest viewpoint, the enlightened man will regard his country as a family of brothers, and the more of mankind he has before his eyes the less of a gulf he will find between the great and lowly. Philosophers are distinguished by needs and interest unknown to the common man; above all they do not deny in the light of day the principles they advocate in private; and they acquire the habit of loving truth for its own sake. A good choice of such men makes the happiness of a nation; but that happiness only lasts if good laws so increase their number as to reduce the always considerable likelihood of a bad choice.

Another way of preventing crime is to make the tribunal of those who execute the laws more interested in observing than in corrupting them. The greater their number, the less danger there will be of encroachments upon the law. Corruption is more difficult among members of a tribunal who keep watch on one another, and so are the less tempted to increase their authority, the smaller the share of it that would fall to each of them— compared to the dangers of such an undertaking. If by pomp and display, by the severity of edicts and by allowing complaints both just and unjust to be laid by anyone who believes himself oppressed, the sovereign accustoms his subjects to dread magistrates more than they dread laws, it is the magistrates who will gain by this, and not private or public security.

Another way of preventing crime is that of rewarding virtue. On this proposition I observe a total silence in the laws of every nation at the present time. If prizes awarded by academies for the discovery of useful truths have multiplied both knowledge and good books, why should prizes distributed by the sovereign's beneficent hand not increase virtuous actions? The coin of honour is always inexhaustible and fruitful in the hands of one who distributes it wisely.

Finally, the surest but most difficult way of preventing crime is to improve education; this is too vast a subject, and one which exceeds the limits I have set myself; a field of public happiness, I would even dare to say, too intimately connected with the nature of government not to remain, till the remotest of centuries, barren, and cultivated only here and there by a handful of the wise. One great man,[2] who gives light to the humanity which persecutes him, has explained in detail the principles of an education truly useful to mankind; which should comprise, not a sterile multitude of subjects, but subjects chosen with precision and care; which should substitute, both in the moral and the physical phenomena which chance or diligence present to the fresh minds of the young, originals for copies; which should lead to virtue along the easy path of feeling, and divert from evil along the never-failing path of necessity and trouble, instead of using the uncertain method of command which produces no more than a momentary and counterfeit obedience.

42. CONCLUSION

FROM all I have written a very useful theorem may be deduced, little though it conforms to custom, that common lawgiver of the nations. It is this: *In order that punishment should never be an act of violence committed by one or many against a private citizen, it is essential that it be public, speedy, and necessary, as little as the circumstances will allow, proportionate to the crime, and established by law.*

[2] J. J. Rousseau again. [Tr.]

Alessandro Manzoni

THE COLUMN OF INFAMY

translated by Fr. Kenelm Foster O.P.

PREFACE

THE *Storia della colonna infame* (last translated into English in 1845) was finished in 1829, shortly after the first edition of *I promessi sposi* (1825–27) and published in 1842, as a sort of appendix to the revised definitive edition. It was the fulfilment of Manzoni's promise, in Chapters XXXI and XXXII of his great novel, to return in another work to the subject of the plague in Milan in 1630, and to examine in more detail one of its effects: the panic aroused in the city by rumours that poison had been spread on walls and houses, and the consequent arrest, trial, torture, and execution of the persons suspected of having done this (the presumed *untori*).

The public had expected something in the style of the novel and the work fell flat. 'Quand ma petite histoire a paru,' Manzoni wrote to a French admirer, 'le silence s'est fait.' And for all his modesty and freedom from illusions, he seems himself to have felt disappointment, to judge from a comment in the same letter, which is worth citing for the light it throws on his motives in writing the book:

Événement isolé, et sans relation avec les grands faits de l'histoire; acteurs obscurs, les puissants autant que les faibles; erreur sur laquelle il n'y a plus personne à détromper, *parmi ceux qui lisent*; institutions contre lesquelles on n'a plus à se défendre; il m'avait semblé que sous tout cela *il y avait pourtant encore un point, qui touchait aux dangers toujours vivants de l'humanité . . . à sa lutte perpétuelle sur la terre* (my italics).

Clearly, the 'point' Manzoni alludes to here is that the growth of knowledge and the reform of institutions are not of themselves a guarantee against further lapses into injustice and cruelty as evil, if not outwardly as barbarous, as those committed by the Milanese authorities in the summer of 1630. And they are no such guarantee because they do not and cannot go to the moral root of the matter, which is the perpetually recurring conflict in the human heart between justice and expediency—a conflict, moreover, which is particularly liable to be decided in the wrong way whenever expediency can claim the sanction of patriotism or public interest, of 'that public utility which has ever served as a pretext for violating justice';[1] as was in fact the case in that trial of the *untori*. For Manzoni the *lutte perpétuelle* of mankind on earth was the conflict between right and wrong; the fight for justice, or, better, man's struggle to *be* just; and he chose to write about that particular episode because he thought it an especially instructive instance of how justice can in fact be defeated.

Written in 1829, *The Column of Infamy* already belongs to the second of the two periods into which—allowing for minor changes and developments—his long life as a writer can be divided: the first, from 1800 to about 1827; the second, from this date to his death in 1873. The first period closes with the final decline of his poetic powers; the second is marked by a predominance of the rational and reflective faculty. With the publication in 1827 of the last volume of *I promessi sposi*, Manzoni's imagination had given all it could to literature: the revision that led to the edition of 1840–42 is important only in respect of style and diction. The poet's work was done; that of the moralist, the historian—if one whose historical writing is so penetrated by moral concern may be so called—the philosopher, and the linguistic reformer continued.

A few details to fill in the above outline. Alessandro Manzoni was born in Milan on 7 March 1785. He may have been illegitimate, but officially his father was Don Pietro Manzoni, a minor Lombard nobleman, and certainly his mother was Giulia, eldest daughter of Cesare Beccaria (see page vii). Educated by a religious teaching Order, he was unhappy at school and became fervently anti-clerical, writing a long poem inspired by the French Revolution, *Il trionfo della libertà*, before he was sixteen. Between 1805 and 1810 he lived mostly in Paris with

---

[1] *Opere di A.M.*, ed. M. Barbi and F. Ghisalberti, Vol. II, p. 208.

his mother (who had long been separated from Don Pietro), forming friendships and connexions particularly among the 'Idéologues', which greatly influenced his intellectual development; he was always to feel perfectly at home with the French mind and culture. Residence in France ended with the turning-point of his life, his return to the Catholic Church. This was linked with his marriage in 1808 to Henriette Blondel, daughter of a Swiss Calvinist. Her conversion to Catholicism in 1809–10 was followed by Manzoni's reconversion, after a long spiritual journey which seems to have come to a crisis during an incident in Paris on 2 April 1810. Two months later the young couple returned (with Donna Giulia) to Milan. There—or in its neigh-bourhood—Manzoni was to spend the rest of his life, apart from a few journeys and some years on Lake Maggiore after the reconquest of Lombardy by Austria in 1849. Between 1812 and 1814 he wrote his religious poetry, the *Inni sacri,* completed in 1822 by the magnificent *La Pentecoste*; and in 1816–19 his work in Catholic apologetics, *Osservazioni sulla morale cat-tolica.* He became the chief poet and theorist of Italian Roman-ticism, and between 1820 and 1827 gave expression to this movement and clarified its principles in a series of major creative and critical works: *Il Conte di Carmagnola* (1820), the *Lettre à M. Chauvet,* the *Adelchi,* with its long prose pendant on Lombard history (1822), the *Lettera sul romanticismo* (1823), *I promessi sposi* (1825–27). After his brief creative period Manzoni wrote relatively little; but four later works, besides the *Colonna infame,* are important: an essay on the historical novel, *Del romanzo storico*; a philosophical dialogue on art, *Dell'in-venzione*; a critique of Utilitarianism, published in 1855 as an Appendix to a new edition of the *Osservazioni*; and a compara-tive study of the French and Italian Revolutions. This last work was left incomplete, as was one on the Italian language, the subject that most engaged Manzoni's energies in his last years. He died at Milan on 22 May 1873.

KENELM FOSTER

INTRODUCTION

THE judges who, at Milan in 1630, condemned to a horrible death certain persons accused of spreading the plague by methods no less stupid than disgusting, thought they were doing something so worthy of record that, in the very sentence of condemnation, along with a clause ordering the destruction of their victims' houses, they decreed that in the space where these houses had stood a pillar be erected, to be called the 'Column of Infamy', and on this pillar an inscription written where all posterity might read of the crime which they had prevented and the punishment they had imposed. And they were right; that judgement of theirs was indeed memorable.

In the course of the preceding work[1] the author stated his intention of one day publishing some account of this affair. And this promise he now fulfils: but in offering his account to the public he is uncomfortably aware that some of his readers were expecting something much longer and more learned. Yet, while he is ready to be mocked by those whom he has disappointed, he feels free to disclaim responsibility for their expectations: if he has only a mouse to offer, he never said that mountains were giving birth. All he said was that while a concern for brevity prevented him from including the affair as an episode in his novel, and though he was aware that it had already been discussed by a deservedly famous writer,[2] he considered nevertheless that the subject might very well be studied afresh and from

[1] *I promessi sposi*, Ch. XXXII, *in fine*.

[2] Count Pietro Verri, 1728–97; Milanese writer and social reformer. In 1764, with his brother Alessandro and Cesare Beccaria, he founded the short-lived but important journal *Il Caffè*, for the propagation of liberal and progressive ideas in literature, politics, and economics. Broadly speaking, Verri and his circle were the Milanese counterpart of the French Encyclopaedists. Though loyal to the Austrian Empire (to which Milan then belonged) Verri welcomed the French Revolution. His *Osservazioni sulla tortura* was written in 1777 but not published until 1804 (see p. xvii). [Tr.]

a different point of view. Let this difference suffice to explain why the present work was undertaken. Whether it has been usefully undertaken is another question; which, alas, has more to do with effects than with causes.

Pietro Verri was concerned, as the title of his book suggests, to draw from the affair in question an argument against torture; inasmuch as the only effect of torture, in this case, had been to extort confessions to a crime that was physically and morally impossible. And his argument was as cogent as his intentions were noble and humane.

But from the history of a matter so complex as this (however briefly it may be described) and of so much evil inflicted without reason by men on their fellow men it should, I think, be possible to draw conclusions of a more general character and of an equal, if less immediate, utility. Indeed there is a danger in restricting one's comments only to such points as are most relevant to the particular argument referred to above; the danger, I mean, that the reader might come to take a view of the episode that would be not only incomplete but also false; for he might ascribe its evils merely to the ignorance prevalent in those times and to a barbarous legal system, and so come to think of them as necessitated and inevitable; which would be to deduce a mischievous falsehood from data which could be most instructive. Ignorance of natural science may have undesirable effects, but it cannot cause wickedness. Nor do bad institutions function automatically. It was certainly no necessary result of believing in the infectiousness of certain unguents to believe that Guglielmo Piazza and Giangiacomo Mora had used them; and the fact that the law in those days had recourse to torture did not compel the judges in this case to apply torture to all the accused, nor to find guilty all whom they tortured. This is a truth that may seem too obvious to be interesting; but it not infrequently happens that the most obvious truths, which ought to be taken for granted, are in fact forgotten; and it is only by not forgetting the truth I have stated that one can form a right judgement on that appalling sentence. What I have attempted, then, is to bring this truth into the light of day; to show clearly that those judges were guilty of condemning men who were innocent and men whose innocence they were perfectly capable of recognizing, notwithstanding their conviction of the infectiousness of the unguents and notwithstanding the laws permitting the use of torture. I will go further and say that in order to find those persons guilty, in order to suppress the truth which appeared and reappeared all the time and on every side, and with features as visible then as they are now and always will be, the judges had continually to exercise the utmost ingenuity and have recourse again and again to expedients of the injustice of which they could not have been ignorant. It would of course be absurd, and also dishonourable, to attempt to deny that ignorance and torture had their share in the vile business. A deplorable ignorance gave the evil its chance in the first place, and torture was the cruel weapon it found ready to hand (though not, certainly, the only nor the chief one). But what matters, I think, is that we grasp the real and effective cause of what was done. And what could this have been if not a passionate perversion of the human heart?

Only God could see clearly into the hearts of those judges and measure the exact degree of control that emotion had gained over their wills. Anger, no doubt, played its part, stirred up by a vague sense of undefined dangers; an anger that desired an object on which to vent itself and so clutched at the first that came to hand; anger impatient for evidence and that would not listen to the thought that the evidence in fact presented might be false; which had cried 'At last!' and now absolutely refused to say 'We must start again': an anger made pitiless by prolonged fear and now become a self-righteous hatred of its poor struggling victims. Again, there was a fear of seeming not to respond to what the public was expecting, with an expectation as confident as it was hasty and rash; a fear of seeming less intelligent if the accused were found innocent; a fear that if the clamour of the crowd were not heeded it would turn against themselves; a fear too, perhaps, that resistance to that clamour might provoke a serious disturbance of the peace—which may seem a more respectable sort of fear but which is really no less evil and ignoble, if it usurp the place of that other, that genuinely wise and noble fear of committing an injustice. Only God could tell whether those magistrates who found people guilty of a crime they had never committed, but which others desired them to have committed,[3] were more the accomplices or the tools of a public blinded not by ignorance but by rancour and rage, and whose clamour for revenge was directly opposed to the divine law which it professed to revere. So much only God could judge; but lying, and abuse of power, and violation of the ordinary and obvious rules of behaviour, and playing tricks with the scales of justice—such things we men can recognize for ourselves, when they occur; and, having recognized them, we can relate them with absolute certainty to the passions which corrupt the human will. Nor need any other passions be looked for, as we seek to understand the objective iniquities of that court of law, than the anger and the fear I have mentioned: both natural enough, and both vile.

Such causes of crime are not, unfortunately, confined to a particular age; nor can the fact that emotion—these particular passions and others—have driven men who were anything but professional criminals to public or private wickedness be attributed solely to such ignorance of natural science as may have occasioned their crimes, or to their having had the power to inflict torture. 'If,' wrote Verri, 'only one torture the less be inflicted in future, as an effect of my having described these horrors, I shall consider that the grief that impels me to write will not have been in vain; and in this hope I find my consolation.'[4] And for my part I shall consider it well worth while to have reminded my readers of horrors they already know if, by so doing, I can stir their indignation also, and chiefly, against the influence of evil passions—which cannot indeed be discarded like false ideas, nor abolished like harsh institutions, but which can at least be rendered less potent and poisonous by recognizing and detesting their effects.

Moreover this way of looking at the matter has its consoling

[3] *Ut mos vulgo, quamvis falsis, reum subdere.* Tacitus, *Annales,* I, 39.
[4] *Osservazioni sulla tortura,* c. vi.

side. If we regard a complex series of cruelties inflicted by man on man merely as the effect of times and circumstances, the horror and pity we feel is accompanied by a sense of discouragement, by a sort of despair. We seem to see human nature driven irresistibly to evil by forces beyond its control, caught in the toils of some evil and exhausting dream which it can neither throw off nor even become clearly conscious of. And so the indignation that spontaneously springs up in us against the men who did such things begins itself to appear unreasonable, even while, at the same time, we feel it to be noble and religious. Our horror remains, but the deed itself seems to have lost its guilt; and our mind, seeking the true culprit, the right object for its revulsion, is dismayed to find itself hesitating between two alternatives, equally blasphemous and insane: a denial, or an indictment, of Providence. But if, on a closer examination of the facts, we are able to discern an injustice which those who committed it could themselves have recognized; a violation of rules which they themselves accepted; an acting in clean contradiction to principles not only admitted in that age but also evidently respected, in similar circumstances, by the very men who acted in this way—then we can with relief conclude that if these men did not know what they were doing it was because they did not choose to know, and that theirs was the kind of ignorance which men adopt and discard as they please; not an excuse for crime, but itself a crime; and that such things as they did may indeed be suffered, but not done, under compulsion.

With all this I do not want to suggest that Pietro Verri was entirely unaware of the personal and voluntary injustice of the judges in this case; but only that he did not make it his business to study this aspect of the matter, still less to prove that such injustice was the chief—or, more precisely, the sole—cause of the sentence which they passed. Indeed, he could not have carried out this demonstration without, in effect, spoiling his case against torture; the upholders of which (for the most irrational institutions never lack supporters so long as there is life in them at all, and even when dead they often still find upholders for the same reasons which once kept them alive)

I

would have turned the proof of the judges' wickedness into a defence of torture. 'Don't you see,' they would have replied, 'the fault is not in the system but in those who abuse it.' A strange defence indeed—to point out that something in any case absurd has also served, in certain cases, as passion's tool for deeds both absurd and atrocious. Such, however, is the usual reasoning of prejudiced minds. But in any case those who aimed, like Verri, at the abolition of torture had no wish to complicate their case with distinctions, nor to make torture itself seem less horrible by denouncing anything else. Experience would have taught them that whoever strives to inculcate a truth which is in dispute is apt to find his own supporters, as well as his adversaries, a hindrance to its perfect elucidation. True, he can always count on that very numerous third party of the neutral, the indifferent, the unconcerned; those for whom that truth has no interest whatsoever.

As regards the materials for the story I am about to relate, I must say at the outset that all my efforts to discover the original minutes of the trial—efforts which have met with the most courteous and diligent co-operation on the part of those who seemed best able to help me—have only led me to the conclusion that this document is irretrievably lost. A considerable portion of the minutes, however, survives in a copy. It happened that one of the accused, Don Juan Padilla (who, by the way, owed this unhappy position to one of his fellow victims), was a man of some importance, being the son of the Governor of the Castle of Milan, a Knight of St. James, and a captain in the cavalry. This gentleman was able to have a copy of his defence printed, to which he added an abstract of the trial communicated to him in his capacity as one formally charged with the crime in question. And certainly the judges had no suspicion, when they permitted the printing of this record, that they were erecting a monument more solid and enduring than that which they had built by an architect.

There is also extant another copy, in some places less complete, in others more so, of this abstract. It belonged to Conte Pietro Verri and was placed at my disposal, with a courtesy both generous and patient, by his son Conte Gabriele. It is in fact the document used by Verri in writing his book and it has marginal jottings in his hand reflecting the thoughts that passed through his mind, and the feelings of pity, distress, and indignation that moved him as he read it. It is entitled *Summarium offensivi contra Don Johannem Cajetanum de Padilla*. Many points are more fully reported in this copy than in the printed abstract. Numbers in the margins refer to the pages of the original minutes of the trial, and there are brief notes in Latin due to the same hand as wrote the text: *detentio Morae*; *descriptio domini Johannis*; *adversatur commissario*; *inverisimile*; *subgestio*, etc.—obviously, notes made by the barrister who was defending Padilla. From all this it appears that we have here a literal copy of the official abstract communicated to the defending counsel; and that when the latter had the text printed he caused the printers to strike out certain matters as unimportant and give a mere *résumé* of others. But why does the printed version include things omitted in the manuscript? A likely explanation is that the defending counsel had been able to re-read the original minutes and so make a fresh selection of material which he thought might be useful to his client.

From these two abstracts then, the printed one and the manuscript, I have naturally drawn most of my materials; and since the former has recently been reprinted (it had hitherto been extremely rare) the reader may, if he likes, use it to check the facts which I have culled from the manuscript copy.

The speeches for the defence, referred to above, have also provided certain facts and the material for some observations. As these have never been reprinted and very few copies are extant, I shall be careful to quote *verbatim* such passages from them as I have occasion to use.

Finally, a few details have been picked up from sundry scattered documents surviving from that confused and rather careless epoch, and now preserved in the archives to which reference was made, more than once, in the foregoing work.[5]

To my account of the trial I thought it worth while to subjoin

[5] *I promessi sposi.*

a brief history of the opinions held with regard to it down to the time of Verri, that is for a century and a half; I mean, the opinions which found expression in books; these being for the most part the only ones of which we can know anything with certainty, and being, in any case, those which have a special importance. It will, I think, be found curious to watch a succession of writers following one after the other, like the sheep in Dante, without taking the slightest trouble to inform themselves about the matter on which they were writing. I say 'curious', not 'amusing'; for the spectator of that bitter conflict, which ended so horribly with a victory of error over truth and brute force over unarmed innocence, can feel nothing but distaste, I had almost said exasperation, as he reads these writings (and the particular author makes no difference, they are all the same), with their pompous assertions of falsehood, their smug dogmatizing on a basis of irresponsible credulity; so much denunciation of the victims, all that topsyturvy indignation. Yet the distaste will not be futile if it serve to increase any reader's aversion from and distrust of the old and never sufficiently discredited habit of repeating things without examining them; of—if I may so express myself—serving the public with wine of its own making, and which has sometimes gone to its head already.

With this in mind I thought at first of putting before the reader all the judgements on the matter in hand of all the writers I had read who had anything to say about it. But on second thoughts I decided to spare the reader's patience. Better, I thought, to limit myself to a few authors, of whom none are completely forgotten, while most have still fame enough to make their errors particularly instructive, now that they have lost their power to do harm.

CHAPTER ONE

AT about half past four in the morning of 21 June 1630 it unfortunately happened that a woman was looking from the window of a sort of bridge which at that time crossed the Via della Vetra de' Cittadini at the end where it meets the Corso di Porta Ticinese, almost opposite the columns of San Lorenzo. The woman's name was Caterina Rosa. As she stood there she noticed a man in a black cloak with his hat pulled down over his eyes and in his hand a piece of paper on which, so she was to say in her deposition, 'he seemed to be writing'. She watched the man enter the street 'and draw near the wall immediately after turning the corner', and then 'from time to time draw his hands along the wall'. It was then, she said, 'that it occurred to me he might perhaps be one of the people who had recently been going about smearing on the walls'. Her suspicions aroused, she went into another room, to a window that looked down the length of the street, in order to keep the stranger in view; 'and I saw', she said, 'that he kept on touching the wall with his hands'.

There was another watcher, at the window of a house in the same street, a woman called Ottavia Bono. Whether she formed the same crazy suspicion on her own account, or only after Caterina Rosa had started the rumour, we cannot say; in any case, on being interrogated, she too declared that she had seen the man from the moment of his entering the street, though she did not mention his touching the wall as he went along it. 'I saw him stop,' she said, 'at the end of the garden wall of the Crivelli's house, and I saw a paper in his hand on which he seemed to be writing with his right hand, and then I saw him raise this hand from the paper and rub it on the garden wall where there is a white patch.' The man was probably rubbing ink off his fingers, for he seems in fact to have been writing: at his interrogation the next day, when asked whether 'his actions that morning had anything to do with writing', he answered, 'Yes, my lord.' And as for his keeping close to the wall, a good enough reason for this was that it was raining, as Caterina herself mentioned, though she drew her own conclusion from the fact, saying: 'And mind you, this is important; it was raining yesterday when he was doing the smearing, and he must have chosen the time on purpose as then more people would get the stuff on their clothes, because they would go close to the wall for shelter.'

After stopping (as Ottavia said) the man turned back down the road again; he reached the corner and was about to pass out of sight when, again unfortunately, he was met by another man who entered the street and greeted him. Caterina Rosa, who by this time, to keep the 'smearer' in sight, had returned to her first window, asked the second man who it was he had greeted. The second man, as he was to declare later at the trial, replied that the other was someone he knew only by sight but that he knew he was a Commissioner of the Sanità. 'And I then said to him,' reports Caterina in her deposition, 'that I had seen the other man doing things I didn't like the look of at all. And then the news got around' (chiefly through her, of course), 'and people came out and saw the walls smeared with a sort of thick yellowish paste; and especially the people who live at Tradate said they had found the walls of the approach to their gate all smeared.' The other woman said the same. Asked if she knew why the man rubbed his hand on the wall, she answered, 'the walls were found smeared afterwards, especially round the Tradate gate.'

There are things here that would be reckoned implausible in a novel, though alas the blinding of reason by passion accounts for them only too well. It never occurred to either of these witnesses that in thus describing (especially the first witness) step by step the man's walk up the road and back, neither was able to say that he had entered that particular street; nor did it seem to them 'important' that he appeared to have taken no precautions not to be observed—despite the fact that he had waited until the sun was risen before starting his peculiar business; that he never even glanced up at the windows; that having passed up the street he calmly turned round and came down it again, as though criminals were in the habit of loitering in the place where they have just committed a crime; that he was handling with apparent impunity stuff that was supposed to kill those who 'got it on their clothes'; and many other equally strange improbabilities. But the strangest and most dreadful feature of all was that such things did not seem improbable to the official who interrogated the accused; that he asked for no explanations. Or, if he did, it is still worse that no mention of this was made in the trial.

The people of the neighbourhood hurriedly began to apply burning straw to the walls to burn off heaven knows how much dirt that had probably been there, under their eyes, for heaven knows how long before panic brought it to their notice. Giangiacomo Mora, the barber at the corner of the street, agreed with the rest that the walls of his house had been smeared; unaware, poor wretch, of the very different danger that threatened him from the aforesaid and, as it turned out, equally unlucky Commissioner of the Sanità.

The story told by the two women was quickly enriched with fresh details—unless perhaps what they were afterwards to say to the Chief of Police did not exactly tally with what they had said to their neighbours. The son of the unfortunate Mora, on being asked later 'whether he knew for himself, or had heard, how the said Commissioner smeared the walls and houses', answered, 'I heard that one of the women who live in the arch that crosses Via Vedra[1] (I don't know her name) said that he smeared with a pen, having a small jar in his hand.' And very likely Caterina Rosa did mention having seen a pen in the man's hand; and as for her 'small jar', its nature may easily be guessed; to a mind obsessed with smearing a pen must have seemed much more directly related to jars than inkpots.

Unfortunately, however, all the babble and chatter conveyed this much truth, that the man was a Commissioner of the Sanità, a clue which pointed at once to a certain Guglielmo Piazza,

[1] Via Vetra was the correct name. Via *Vedra* was the dialect form, and so used only when citing the words of witnesses. [Tr.]

son-in-law of a well-known midwife of the neighbourhood called Paola. The news spread to other quarters of the city, carried in part by someone who had happened to find himself where the hubbub began. It came to the ears of the Senate, which at once ordered the Chief of Police to collect information and take such action as was required. 'A report has come to the Senate,' said the Chief of Police to the notary whom he took with him on his investigations, 'that yesterday morning the walls and houses of Via Vedra de' Cittadini were smeared with a deadly paste.' With these words—so full already of a lamentable assurance, passing as they did, without the slightest correction, from the populace to the authorities—the case was opened.

So firm a conviction, such insane terror of a crime that was never committed may well remind my readers of events which took place a few years ago, in various parts of Europe, at the time of the cholera epidemic; but there is this difference, that in the latter case no one with any education (with a few exceptions) showed a like disastrous credulity; indeed most people did what they could to make sanity prevail. And no one was arrested by the authorities on suspicion of similar 'crimes', unless it was to save the person suspected from the fury of the mob. A great improvement, certainly; but even were it greater, even if one could be sure that similar pretexts would never again give rise to the same sort of persecution, yet one cannot be certain that the danger of such follies—which would differ indeed as to their subject matter, but not necessarily as to their mode of expression—is altogether a thing of the past. Men can, alas, deceive themselves, and terribly deceive themselves, on much less absurd presuppositions. A similar fear and fury can equally well be provoked by evils that may really be, and sometimes are, an effect of human depravity; but fear and fury, when not controlled by reason and charity, are unhappily liable, on the flimsiest pretexts and following the wildest assertions, to presume the guilt of men who are simply unfortunate. For example, not so long ago—a little before the cholera epidemic—when there was an outbreak of arson in Normandy, what was it led the mob to fix the guilt, immediately, on one particular man? Simply that he was the first to be found on the spot or near it; that he was a stranger and could give no satisfactory account of himself (a thing doubly difficult when a man is terrified and his interrogators angry); that he was accused by a woman of the type of Caterina Rosa and by a boy who, himself suspected of being an accomplice and being ordered to say who had told him to start the fires, gave the first name that came into his head. Happy the juries appointed to try the accused (when there *was* a trial, for more than once in fact the mob gave effect to its own judgement) if they entered the court fully persuaded that so far they knew nothing at all; if their minds were deaf to the clamour outside; if their thought was not: 'We are the People' (one of those abstractions which only too often blind men to the particular and proper nature of the facts before them, and are especially odious and cruel when the People have already made up their ignorant minds on the matter)—but rather: 'We are a group of men entrusted with the sacred, necessary, and fearful authority—and with this authority only—of deciding whether other men are guilty or innocent.'

The man whom the Chief of Police had been advised to interrogate had nothing to say, except that on the previous day he had seen people scorching the walls of Via della Vetra, and that he had heard that these had been smeared that morning by 'the son-in-law of midwife Paola'. The Chief, with his notary, went to the place indicated, saw the fire-blackened walls, and noticed that those of one house, the barber Mora's, had just been whitewashed. And they too were told, by people there, the reason for the scorching: the walls had been smeared. 'The Chief of Police and I,' wrote the notary, 'saw, in fact, on the burnt patches traces of a yellowish pasty stuff, as if someone had been smearing with his fingers.' What a way to check evidence of crime!

A woman of the Tradate household was questioned: she had found the walls of the street 'dirtied with some yellow stuff, a lot of it'. Caterina Rosa and Ottavia Bono were questioned, and we know how they replied. Some other persons were questioned who had nothing to say that threw any light on the facts; among these, the wayfarer who had met and greeted the Commissioner of the Sanità; asked whether he had then seen dirt on the walls of Via Vedra he said, 'I didn't look, because nothing had yet been said about it.'

An order was already out for the arrest of Piazza, and this was easily effected. On the same day, the 22nd, 'one of the Baricello di Campagna guard reported to the aforesaid Chief of Police, the latter being still in his carriage on the way home . . . how he had found the aforesaid Guglielmo standing at the doorway of the Lord Senator Monti, President of the Sanità, and had taken him off to prison as ordered'. That this evident unconsciousness of peril on the part of the Commissioner did nothing to diminish the judges' suspicion of him is a fact that can certainly not be explained away by the ignorance of those times. Those judges knew that the flight of a suspected person was technically an indication of guilt; odd then that this man's *not* fleeing, and so obviously not fleeing, was not taken as indicating the contrary! But it is ridiculous to insist that what could *not* have been seen *could* have been seen; one can always choose not to consider what one sees.

Piazza's house was then thoroughly searched, *in omnibus arcis, capsis, scriniis, cancellis, sublectis,* for jars of paste and for money. Nothing was found; *nihil penitus compertum fuit.* But not even this was of the least use to him, as became only too clear at his first examination, that very day, by the Chief of Police, assisted by an auditor supplied, probably, by the Tribunal of the Sanità.

He was questioned about his profession, his usual occupations, the walk he had taken the previous day, the clothes he had been wearing. Finally he was asked: 'Whether he knew anything about any fouling of the walls of the houses of the city, especially in the neighbourhood of Porta Ticinese.' He answered: 'I know nothing about it; I never spend any time by Porta Ticinese.' They replied, 'Not plausible'; they wanted to prove he knew something. Four times they asked, four times he gave the same answer in different words. They then passed to other matters, but keeping the same end in view. And we shall see why presently; we shall see what cruel cunning was concealed in their insistence on that 'implausibility', and then in their change of ground.

Among the events of the previous day mentioned by Piazza in his replies was his having met with some 'parochial deputies' —gentlemen chosen from each parish by the Tribunal of the Sanità to see that its orders were carried out. Asked for the names of these deputies, Piazza answered that he knew them only by sight, not by name. Again the reply came, 'implausible'. But to make the full—and fearful—meaning of this word clear I must ask the reader now to bear with some rather general considerations on the criminal law procedure of those times. I shall be as brief as the matter allows.

CHAPTER TWO

As everyone knows, that procedure was regulated principally, both in this country and nearly everywhere else in Europe, by the authority of the writers on the law; and for the simple reason that in most cases it was the only authority available. For the absence of any accepted legal system framed for society as a whole had two consequences: that those who interpreted the law became in effect its makers; and that their authority to do so was pretty generally admitted. When what needs doing is left undone by those whose business it is to do it—or, if done at all is incompetently done—then there will always be found people who think they can supply the lack, and others who are prepared to accept whatever is provided, regardless of who provides it. Nothing is harder and more wearisome than to live without rules of some kind.

For example, the Statutes of Milan laid down no other rules or conditions with regard to the power to torture a man accused of crime (a power itself admitted implicitly by everybody, as a natural consequence of the right to put such a man on trial) than that the accusation be supported by public opinion; that the crime in question be punishable by death; and that there be some evidence of guilt—the degree of evidence being, however, left vague. On this last point the Roman law itself, which operated in cases not foreseen by the Statutes, was no more precise, though it had more to say. 'The judges,' it declared, 'must not begin with torture; they must first have recourse to arguments both plausible and probative. But if, having weighed the matter, they consider that they have sufficient grounds to warrant the use of torture in order to find out the truth, then let them use it, having regard to the condition of the accused.'[1] In fact the Roman law explicitly left it to the judges' discretion to decide as to the quality and force of the evidence in each case; and this power of the judiciary was presupposed by the old Statutes of Milan.

The so-called New Constitutions, promulgated by order of Charles V, do not even mention torture; and thenceforward, down to the period of our trial and for a long while after, though many decrees were passed inflicting torture as a punishment, there was not one, so far as I know, that regulated its use as a means of obtaining proof.

And here again the reason is not far to seek. What was at first an effect had become a cause; a substitute had been found, here as elsewhere, for the legislative authority, and especially in the sphere of judicial procedure; a substitute that operated in such a way as to make the need for any intervention of that authority to be felt less and less, to the point of being almost forgotten. The writers on the law, particularly from the time that mere commentaries on Roman law began to go out of fashion and works of a more independent character, whether on criminal procedure as a whole or on this or that special point, began to increase, these writers took to elaborating their material systematically and at the same time with a minute attention to detail; creating new laws by reinterpretations of the old; extending their application by comparing case with case, and so drawing general rules out of particular decisions. And where all this still seemed insufficient they provided rules of their own in line

[1] *Codex*, IX, tit. 41, 'De quaestionibus', l. 8.

with what they thought reason or equity or natural law required; and doing this sometimes concordantly—one writer copying and quoting the others—and sometimes not. And the result was that the judges—men trained in the subject and sometimes themselves writers of this kind—came to have to hand, in almost every case and for every detail of each case, a set of ready-made conclusions to follow or to choose from. Law, in fact, had become a body of knowledge, a science. And it was to this science, that is, to the Roman law so interpreted, and to such ancient customs of various regions as had not been obliterated by the authority of Roman law, and were interpreted in the same way, as well as to such customs as were approved by the jurists, along with the latters' precepts now become customary, it was to all this that the name 'Law' came to be almost exclusively applied; whereas the acts of the ruling authority in the State were merely entitled 'orders', 'decrees', 'proclamations', and so forth, and had about them an air of things vaguely contingent and temporary. To give one example, the proclamations of the government of Milan (which was certainly a legislative authority) were valid only so long as a particular government held office; so that the first act of its successor was always provisionally to confirm them. Each *gridario*, as it was called, was a sort of Praetor's Edict made for the time being, as the occasion required. But legal science, on the other hand, was continually operative and over the whole field. It developed indeed and changed, but only by degrees too small to be noticed. Those who were masters in it had always started their careers as pupils. One might almost call it a continual revision, in part a continual recompilation, of the original Twelve Tables, entrusted, or rather relinquished, to a perpetual Decemvirate.

Now this age-long and extensive authority of private persons over public law came in time to be regarded—and, if I am not mistaken, is still regarded—as a thing anomalous in itself and pernicious in its effects; especially in the sphere of the criminal law, and more particularly in that of the procedure of the courts. Opposition to it began when men became aware of the desirability and the possibility of abolishing it and of replacing it by a new legal system more complete and precise and logical than the old. Yet we have seen that the old system was in its way a natural product; nor had it arisen as a novelty, but rather as a sort of extraordinary extension of a phenomenon as old as the hills and destined perhaps, in one form or another, to go on forever: for let laws be as precise as you please, they will always, perhaps, require interpretation; and perhaps judges will always be inclined—at one time more, at another less—to have recourse, for the law's interpretation, to writers who have established themselves as the acknowledged experts on the subject as a whole. And for my part I am not at all sure that, on a calmer and more thorough examination of the facts, we should not have to conclude that the authority of those old jurists was, relatively and comparatively speaking, beneficial; for the state of affairs that preceded it had been far worse.

For after all it is improbable that men accustomed to take into consideration a great number of possible cases, and to endeavour to regulate these either by existing positive law or by more general and higher principles, should recommend procedures more unjust and more unreasonable, more violent and more capricious than such as are only too likely to commend themselves to an authority which deals *ad hoc* with one case after another, in a field so wide open to emotional influences. The very number of volumes and authors, the multiplicity and ever-increasing particularization of the rules they prescribed are themselves some indication of a desire at work to set limits to the play of arbitrary power and to guide it, so far as was possible in those times, towards reason and justice. Men do not need such minute instructions on how to abuse power. If you want a horse to run wild, you don't lecture him on the art of running; just off with his bridle, if he has one!

But so it is as a rule with reforms that are brought in by degrees (I mean real reforms, not everything so named). To those who first embark on a course of reform some slight alteration of the *status quo* seems already much—a correcting this or that particular abuse, an adding here, a removing there. But for those who come on the scene later, and sometimes much later, and who find, rightly, much still to blame in the system as it stands, it is only too easy to stop short at a superficial judgement as to the causes of the system; to denounce as its creators those whose name it bears, and which it bears only because they were the men who gave it the form in which it continues to exist and be powerful. And a mistake such as this was made, I think, by the author of *Osservazioni sulla tortura,* along with other distinguished men of his time. It was almost an enviable mistake, the kind of error that sometimes accompanies great and beneficent innovations. But the force and cogency with which Pietro Verri demonstrated the irrationality, injustice, and cruelty of the hideous practice of torture was only equalled by the rashness, as I would call it, with which he attributed all that was worst in it to the authority of those writers of the law. And certainly it is not as claiming any superiority to so justly celebrated a man, nor as ignoring the nobility of his work, that I venture to criticize Verri on this point. It is merely that I have had the luck to be born later and that I have the advantage (taking as my principal theme a point which for him was quite secondary) of being able to study dispassionately, and with an eye to its effects as a whole and in its historical setting, a system which he had to challenge at a time when it still held the field and stood as a powerful obstacle to novel and urgently-needed reforms. And in any case the matter I speak of here is so much part and parcel of our common theme that neither he nor I could avoid discussing it—not Verri, because, the authority of the writers on the law being acknowledged by the men responsible for that iniquitous sentence of the court of Milan, he regarded it as an accomplice and part cause of the iniquity itself; not I, because, having closely studied what this authority prescribed and taught, I am in a position to use it as a subsidiary but very important standard of comparison to bring out the *peculiar* iniquity, as I would call it, of that sentence.

'It is certain,' wrote Verri (his judgement a little disturbed by strong feeling), 'that our laws give no ruling as to who may be tortured, nor as to the circumstances which may justify torture, nor as to the manner of its application (whether by burning, dislocation, or wounding), nor as to the duration of the agony, nor as to the number of times it may be repeated. All this tormenting of human beings depends purely on a decision of the judge, guided by nothing but the teaching of the aforesaid criminal jurists.'[2]

But those laws of ours explicitly prescribed torture; and not our laws only but those of a great part of Europe, not to mention the Roman law which for so long had the name and authority of a universal code; all explicitly prescribed torture.[3] Hence the real question is whether the writings of the interpreters (as I shall call the old jurists, to distinguish them from those who were to have the merit, and the good fortune, of finally discrediting them), whether these writings were such as to tend to make torture more or less cruel than it actually was in the hands of the judges to whom the law almost entirely, in fact, committed its execution. And the strongest argument in those writers' favour is hinted at, to say the least, by Verri himself when he says: 'the same Farinaccio, speaking of things that occurred in his own time, says that the judges used to devise new tortures in order to gratify the pleasure they took in inflicting pain on those accused of crime, *judices qui propter delectationem quam habent torquendi reos inveniunt novas tormentorum species*'.[4]

I say in those writers' favour because such appeals to the judiciary to cease inventing new methods of torture—along with

[2] Verri, op. cit., c. xiii.

[3] England was an exception. In the English criminal courts the guilt or innocence of an accused person did not depend on his answers to interrogation; and this indirectly ruled out the cruel and deceptive method of extracting confession of guilt by torture. In the kingdom of Aragon, too, F. Casoni and A. Gomez bear witness to the fact that, at least in their day, torture was not employed; and the same can be said of Sweden, on the evidence of J. Loccenio as quoted by O. Tabor. I do not know whether any other European country was immune from this evil, or had succeeded in getting rid of it, before the eighteenth century.

[4] Verri, op. cit., c. viii. Farinacci, *Praxis et theoria criminalis*, I, tit. 5, Q. xxxviii, 56.

other more general reproaches and complaints which bear witness both to the ingenious and unbridled cruelty of those who had the power to pass sentence and to a desire, at least, to expose this cruelty and stop it—are to be found not in Farinacci only but pretty generally in nearly all the writings of the criminal jurists. The very words quoted above were borrowed by Farinacci from an earlier writer, Francesco da Bruno, who in turn took them from another still earlier, Angelo d'Arezzo, together with other and yet stronger expressions which I give here in translation: 'corrupt and savage judges whom God will punish; men of crass stupidity too, whose doings are abhorrent to every enlightened and virtuous mind'.[5] Again, as early as the thirteenth century, earlier than any of the writers already cited, we find Guido da Suzara declaring his desire 'to put some check on the excessive cruelty of the judges' (this in a discussion of torture where the writer refers to a rescript of Constans on the detention of criminals).[6] Again, in the century following, Baldo turned the famous rescript of Constantine about masters who killed their slaves against 'judges who mangle the bodies of prisoners in order to extort confession of guilt'; if the prisoner, he says, dies under torture the judge should be beheaded for murder.[7] Later, Paride dal Pozzo inveighed against those 'blood-thirsty judges who love to inflict torture, not as a just retribution for crime, nor to deter others from crime, but only to exalt themselves (*propter gloriam eorum*). They are no better than murderers.'[8] Again, Giulio Claro writes: 'let the judge beware of applying strange tortures not approved by custom; otherwise he were better called a butcher than a judge'.[9] 'We must vehemently denounce,' says Antonio Gomez, 'those pitiless judges who devise new tortures for prisoners brought before them; their motive is mere vainglory and self-interest.'[10] What

[5] Fr. da Bruno, *De indiciis et tortura*, Part 2, Q. ii, 7.
[6] G. de Suzaria, *De indiciis et tortura*, 1.
[7] B. de Ubaldis, commenting on *Codex*, IX, tit. 14, 3.
[8] P. de Puteo, *De Syndicatu*, 'Crudelitas officialis', 5.
[9] J. Clarus, *Sententiarum receptarum*, V, Q. lxiv, 36.
[10] A. Gomez, *Commentariorum variarumque resolut.*, III, c. 13, 5.

K

a motive for glory! What charmingly appropriate feelings! To enjoy inflicting pain on a fellow man and take pride in humiliating one who lies at your mercy! But at least the writers who drew attention to such motives cannot be supposed to have favoured them.

Let me remark in passing, *à propos* of these texts and of others that I shall adduce, that in all the relevant literature known to me I have not found a single complaint against a judge for using torture too leniently. Should a text of this kind be brought to my notice I would regard it as a genuine curiosity.

Some of the authors I have cited or shall cite are included in a list drawn up by Verri of 'writers who, if they had expressed their inhuman principles in plain language, and their careful descriptions of nicely calculated torments in a style less insufferably barbarous to any sensitive and civilized reader, could hardly have escaped that abhorrence and contempt with which we regard tortures themselves'.[11] Well, certainly the things these authors describe are quite horrible; and the things they acquiesced in we rightly abhor; but whether what they themselves contributed, or wished to contribute, to the system be matter for abhorrence and contempt is a question concerning which there may, even on the evidence so far adduced, be two opinions.

In their books—or rather in some of them—you will find, it is true, the various methods of torture set out in greater detail than they appear in the legal codes; but as accepted and customary practices, not as inventions of our authors. And Ippolito Marsigli, a jurist and judge of the fifteenth century who gives, in part from his own experience, a ghastly and grotesque and disgusting list of such methods, nevertheless calls those judges 'bestial' who seek to devise new ones.[12]

Again, it was, to be sure, these writers who brought up the question how often a torture might be repeated; but, as we shall see, they did so precisely to set some limits and conditions on arbitrary power; taking advantage of the vagueness and am-

[11] Op. cit., c. xiii.
[12] H. de Marsiliis, *Ad tit. Digest. de quaestionibus*; § 'In criminibus', 29.

biguity of Roman law on this point. Again, it was they who discussed the length of time appropriate to each application of a given torture; but once more, this was to impose limits, to put some control (the law itself putting none) on the tireless cruelty of 'certain judges, as ignorant as they are wicked, who will go on torturing a man for a space of three or four hours'. So wrote Farinacci,[13] and a century earlier Marsigli had inveighed against 'unjust judges, infamous wretches from the dregs of society, ignorant, worthless, brutal: when they get a man in their power (through no fault perhaps of his own, *forte indebite*) they refuse to speak to him until he is actually under torture, and if he does not reply as they wish they leave him hanging at the rope's end all day and night'.[14]

The reader will have noticed, in these passages and in others I have quoted, that the idea of cruelty is linked with that of ignorance. Knowledge, no less than conscience, is invoked on the side of moderation, humanity, kindness—all infuriating words I admit, in a context such as this, but they do at least show that those who used them aimed at taming the monster, not goading it on.

As for the statement that 'our laws' gave no rulings as to who could be subjected to torture, I cannot see that this matters in view of the relative abundance of directives on this unsavoury point provided by the Roman law, which was in effect ours also.

Verri continues his indictment:

Ignorant and brutal men, indifferent to those questions of principle without a firm grasp of which it is impossible to frame a system of laws in harmony with nature and reason and conducive to the good of society; men who never thought of asking themselves whence comes the right to punish crime, or what is the purpose of punishment, or how to gauge the gravity of crimes and their relation to punishment, or whether a man may ever be constrained to surrender his right to self-defence. Men of no standing in society, mere private individuals, they took it on themselves to elaborate with ignoble subtlety a system for inflicting the maximum pain on their fellow men, and then

[13] Op. cit., Q. xxxviii, 54.
[14] *Practica causarum criminalium*; § 'Expedita', 86.

solemnly to publish their conclusions with all the impassivity of physicians recommending remedies for disease. And such men were set up as authorities, nay as legislators; and the books in which they give careful instructions as to how to dislocate living bodies and how precisely to prolong its agonies and add pain to pain, these inhuman writings found a welcome in all legal libraries and were seriously and calmly studied.

But really, is it credible that men of no social standing or culture—I mean, social standing in their own day and culture by the standards of their time—should have been allowed so much authority? For the question is necessarily a relative one; it is not whether those writers were as enlightened as one would wish legislators to be, but whether they were more or less so than the men who had formerly applied, indeed to a large extent invented, the law on their own bare authority. And as between a man who works out theories in the abstract and then debates them in public, and a man who executes his arbitrary decisions in private, which after all is the more 'brutal'?

As for Verri's series of questions, it would be extremely awkward if the first one, 'Whence comes the right to punish crime?', had to be answered before anyone could draft a reasonably satisfactory penal code. No doubt Verri's contemporaries thought they had found the right answer, but today the question is more than ever disputed—and a good thing too, for it is better to be perplexed and uncertain than peacefully in error. And the other questions, those of more immediate and practical importance, were they answered and answered correctly, had they even been examined and discussed, when our writers came on the scene? Are we to believe that the emergence of these writers upset some juster and more humane system? That their follies replaced a long heritage of wisdom? Put out of court a better reasoned and more reasonable jurisprudence? The answer, obviously, is No; and this suffices for my immediate argument. But I could wish that some competent scholar would take the matter further; would examine, that is, whether it was not on the contrary our jurists who, just because they were private persons and not legislators, and so were perforce obliged to back their conclusions with reasons, whether they were not in fact the first to seek to relate the whole matter to general principles, by collecting and co-ordinating such principles as lay scattered through the body of Roman law and seeking to complete them by others drawn from the abstract idea of justice; whether it was not these writers who, in their endeavour to form a complete and coherent system of criminal practice out of old and new materials, did in fact adumbrate the concept and indicate the possibility—and in part the pattern—of a complete and coherent criminal law; whether, in short, their conception of an ideal order in this matter did not open the way to other writers—by whom they have been too summarily condemned—to conceive the idea of a general reform.

As for the accusation, so sweeping and unqualified, that our authors 'took it on themselves to elaborate with ignoble subtlety a system for inflicting the maximum pain', we have seen, on the contrary, that this is what most of them expressly detested and did their utmost to prevent. Many too of the texts cited could serve to acquit them of a cold impassivity in their treatment of the matter; let me quote once more from Farinacci: 'I cannot contain my fury against the judges who keep a man bound in chains day after day before putting him to torture; this is adding cruelty to cruelty.'[15] Words that seem to protest in advance against Verri's charge.

In fact, from the evidence adduced and from all we know of the practice of torture in its latest period, we can in all sincerity conclude that the interpreters of the criminal law left that practice a great deal less barbarous than they found it. It would of course be absurd to attribute this improvement to one cause alone, but it also seems to me unreasonable not to reckon among its many causes the censures and warnings repeated publicly, time and again down the centuries, by writers who, as their critics themselves point out, did have a certain authority over the practice of the courts.

Verri goes on to cite some of their statements, though not

[15] Op. cit., Q. xxxviii, 38.

enough to support a general historical judgement, even were
these all cited accurately. Here, for example, is an important
one cited inaccurately: 'Claro asserts that, to put a man to
torture, it suffices that there is some evidence against him.'[16] If
Claro had really said that, it would be an oddity rather than an
argument, so much opposed is it to what a host of other interpreters said. But in fact Claro says just the contrary. Verri was
probably misled by a misprint: he read *nam sufficit adesse
aliqua indicia contra reum ad hoc ut torqueri possit*,[17] instead
of the *non sufficit,* etc., which I find in two earlier editions of
the text. But in order to become aware of his error Verri did
not need to compare texts; he had only to continue reading the
one before his eyes, which goes on: 'if such evidence be not
legally proved', a phrase which would clash with the antecedent
clause if this were in the affirmative. And note how Claro
continues:

I have said that it does not suffice that there is evidence *(dixi
quoque non sufficere)*; but even legal proof does not make such
evidence sufficient, if this be not of a kind sufficient to justify torture;
which is a point that God-fearing judges ought always to bear in
mind lest they inflict torture unjustly. And if they do such injustice
then they themselves must answer to the court of appeal; and de
Afflictis tells of a reply that he made to King Frederick, that not even
the king had authority to order a judge to put a man to the torture,
against whom there was no sufficient evidence.

So speaks Claro, and his words make it pretty clear that Verri
has misunderstood another sentence which he renders as
follows: 'As to what torture has to do with evidence of guilt,
there being no definite rule, everything is left to the decision of
the judge.'[18] Verri understands this as allowing an absolute
authority to the judiciary. But the contradiction would be too

[16] Op. cit., c. viii.
[17] Clarus, op. cit., V, Q. lxiv, 12. The corrected reading 'non sufficit',
which Manzoni found in Venice editions of 1580 and 1595, appears also
in the Lyons edition of 1590. [Tr.]
[18] Op. cit., c. viii.

glaring if this were the true meaning of Claro's words; and it becomes, if anything, still more so in the light of another passage: 'although it belongs to the judge to give judgement, he must respect the common norms of justice . . . and let the agents of justice take care not to proceed too boldly, on the pretext that the decision lies with them'.[19]

What then is the sense of that *remittitur arbitrio judicis* which Verri renders as 'everything is left to the decision of the judge'?

It means . . . but good heavens, why look for Claro's personal opinion in these words? In writing them he was merely repeating a commonplace, a conventional tag that turns up in all these writers. Bartolo refers to it as a commonplace: *Doctores communiter dicunt quod in hoc* (the question of what evidence suffices to justify torture) *non potest dari certa doctrina, sed relinquitur arbitrio judicis.*[20] And for the jurists this was simply a matter of fact, not of theory or principle: since in fact the law did not specify the evidence required, it left this to the judge to decide in each case. So Guido da Suzara, writing about a century before Bartolo, after stating or repeating the same *dictum,* that the decision as to the evidence was left to the judge, adds, 'as, in general, every matter that the law leaves undetermined'.[21] Again, to cite a later authority, Paride dal Pozzo, having repeated the same formula, comments: 'where neither law nor custom has fixed the procedure, the wisdom of the judge must supply the defect; which is why this matter of evidences lays a grave responsibility on his conscience'.[22] And finally Bossi, a fifteenth-century writer on criminal law and a Senator of Milan, writes: 'judgement here only means (*in hoc consistit*) that the judge can look for no definite ruling from the law, which merely states that he must begin with probable and plausible arguments. His business, then, is to discover whether a given piece of evidence is plausible and probable'.[23]

---

[19] Clarus, op. cit., V, Q. lxiv, 13.
[20] Bartolus de Saxoferrato, *Ad lib. Digest.* XLVIII, tit. 18, l. 22.
[21] *De tormentis,* 30.
[22] *De Syndicatu,* 'Mandavit', 5, 18.
[23] Aegidius Bossi, *Tractatus varii,* 'De indiciis ante torturam', 32.

In short, what they called 'decision' or 'judgement' was the same as what later, to avoid ambiguities, came to be called discretionary power; a thing which, though dangerous, is inevitable in the application of laws whether good or bad, and which a wise legislator will always endeavour, not to abolish, for that would be impossible, but to limit to certain well-defined circumstances of minor importance; restricting its application, as far as possible, even in these. And such, I venture to say, was the aim from first to last of our laborious interpreters, and particularly in the matter of torture where the law left a terrifying range of power to the judges. Thus Bartolo, after the words I quoted above, adds, 'but I will give such rules as I can'. Others before him had given rules, and his successors in their turn added more, some proposing rules of their own, others recalling and approving those of their predecessors; but none omitting to repeat the formula which expressed the law as it stood in fact; for they were, after all, only the law's interpreters.

But with the passing of time and as their work progressed, they began to express a desire that the formula itself be modified. We can see this in Farinacci, who wrote after the authors I have been citing in the last few paragraphs, but before the period of the trial that we are studying, when he was reckoned a major authority. After repeating and confirming with a great parade of authorities, the principle that a judge's power of decision 'must not be regarded as free and absolute but as bound by justice and equity'; after deducing and confirming, with more authorities, the consequence that 'the judge ought to lean towards mercy, conform his judgement to the general tenor of the law and the teaching of approved authors, and refrain from manipulating evidence as he pleases'; after discussing, at greater length I think, and more systematically than anyone had hitherto done, the kinds of relevant evidence, Farinacci concludes in these terms: 'Thus it appears that the traditionally accepted ruling of learned authorities—that whether the evidence justifies torture is to be left to the free decision of the judges—has been so much and so concordantly limited by the same authorities that not without reason many jurists maintain that the contrary ruling should hold, namely that this assessment of the evidence should never be subject to the judge's decision.'[24] And he cites Francesco Casoni: 'It is a common error of judges to think that whether torture is to be used or not depends entirely on their own good pleasure; as though Nature had formed the bodies of prisoners only that judges might torment them at will.'[25]

With these words we come in sight of an important moment in the history of legal science. This science is now taking stock of its achievements and is claiming that the time has come to give effect to its findings. Not that it declares openly for reform; it did not presume so far, nor would such presumption have been tolerated. But, declaring itself a real co-operator with the positive law, and appealing in support of its own authority to that of a higher, eternal law, it admonishes the judges to conform their practice to its findings; and this both for the sake of those who would otherwise suffer without cause and for the sake of the judges themselves, who would otherwise be guilty of shameful injustice. We may think these efforts rather pathetic, applied as they were to a practice which of its nature could never be made acceptable; but they do at least make nonsense of Verri's contention that 'what is horrible is not merely the suffering caused by torture . . . but also the teaching of the jurists on the circumstances attending its application'.[26]

I have not space to examine all the texts quoted by Verri, though a thorough treatment of the question would require this and more: but I may be allowed one last observation. It concerns his reference to Claro in the following passage:

Let one horror stand for all, one that we learn of from Claro, the celebrated Milanese jurist and a main authority on this matter. 'When a woman,' he writes, 'is in prison as under suspicion of some crime, the judge concerned with her case has the right to have her brought secretly to his room and there caress her and make pretended love

---

[24] Op. cit., Q. xxxvii, 193–200.
[25] Fr. Casoni, *Tractatus de tormentis*, c. i, 10.
[26] Op. cit., c. viii.

to her, promising her freedom on condition she confess her guilt. It was thus that a certain judge induced a young woman to confess the crime of murder and so was able to have her beheaded.' And lest anyone imagine that I exaggerate in recounting this horrible violation of religion and virtue and the most sacred principles of human life, here are Claro's very words: *Paris dicit quod judex potest*, etc.[27]

Horrible indeed: but what are the facts? In the first place, this Paris (Paride dal Pozzo) was not stating a private opinion; he was recounting, and alas with approval, something actually done by a judge, one of a thousand misdeeds caused by the arbitrary power of the judiciary and without the slightest encouragement from the jurists. In the second place, observe that Baiardi, who mentions this opinion in his supplement to Claro (Claro himself does not refer to it), does so only in order to express his abhorrence and to denounce the judge in question as a 'diabolical deceiver'.[28] In the third place, Baiardi cites not a single other author in support of Paride's opinion during the hundred years that elapsed between Paride and himself. And it would be stranger still to find it upheld in any later period. And as for Paride, heaven preserve us from calling him, as Giannone does, an 'excellent jurist', but other words of his which I have already quoted suffice to show that even he is not quite fairly represented by the deplorable passage to which Verri refers.

In all this I do not of course claim to have proved that the teaching of the interpreters of the law, taken as a whole, was not a factor making for evil, as having been turned to evil uses. A most interesting question this—involving as it does an assessment of the aims and general effects of intellectual labours that extended over several centuries and had to do with matters of vital importance for mankind. It is a question, really, for our own generation to answer, for, as I have already remarked and as indeed everyone knows, the generation that is actually engaged in overturning a system is not in the best position to write its history. But that answer cannot be given, that history cannot

[27] Op. cit., c. viii.
[28] *Ad Clari Sentent. recept.*, V, Q. lxiv, 24; additions 80, 81.

be written in a few disconnected observations such as I have offered in this chapter. Let these serve, however, as I think they will, to show that the view of the matter I criticized was one too hastily adopted. In a way, too, they introduce the narrative that follows, for in the course of this we shall often have occasion to regret that the authority of the writers on the law was not more effective. Indeed I feel sure that my readers will finally join with me in saying, 'If only they had been obeyed !'

CHAPTER THREE

To return now to the trial. It was the usual, almost universal teaching of the law-writers that if an accused man lied to the judge who was interrogating him this amounted to 'legitimate evidence', as they called it, sufficient to justify torture. Hence the reply made to the unfortunate Piazza, under interrogation, that it was 'not plausible' that he should not have heard of the fouling of the walls around Porta Ticinese, nor have known the names of those deputies whom he had met.

But did any lie suffice?

'To constitute evidence sufficient to justify torture the lie must be connected with the nature of the crime and its essential circumstances (namely such as pertain to the crime in such a way that it could be inferred from them). Otherwise it does not suffice: *alias secus*.' Again: 'A lie is not relevant to the question of torture if it concern matters which would not be to the disadvantage of the accused had he confessed them.'[1]

Moreover, was it enough, in the view of the same authorities, to justify torture, if it merely seemed to the judge that the accused had lied?

'To be evidence justifying torture the lie must be conclusively proved, either by the accused's own confession or by two witnesses . . . , it being commonly accepted that two witnesses are required to establish a piece of "remote evidence" such as a lie.'[2]

[1] Farinacci, op. cit., Q. lii, 11, 14.　　　　[2] Ibid., 13.

I am citing, and shall often cite, Farinacci, who was reckoned a major authority at that time and was a diligent collector of the more commonly held opinions. Some jurists, it is true, were content with only one witness, provided he or she were thoroughly trustworthy. But that a lie had to be proved by the forms of law, and could not rest merely on the judge's conjecture, was common doctrine contradicted by no one.

These conditions were deduced from the clause in the Roman law which forbade the judge to begin a trial with torture (the things men have to forbid, once other things are allowed !).

If the judges [wrote Farinacci] were authorized to use torture on prisoners in the absence of legitimate and sufficient evidence, this would amount to allowing them to begin with torture. . . . And by legitimate evidence is meant such as is plausible and probable; not trivial indications nor mere formalities, but weighty, serious, certain, and clear evidence—clear as daylight, as people say. . . . It is a question of handing a man over to torture, and to torture that might prove fatal *(agitur de hominis salute)*. Do not wonder then, you severe judges, that the law and the men learned in it require evidence so precise and so definite, and have expressed this requirement so emphatically and so often.[3]

I would not say, to be sure, that such pronouncements as these were rational. How could they be? They involved self-contradiction. They represented a hopeless attempt to combine certainty and uncertainty; an endeavour to avoid the risk of torturing the innocent and of extorting false confessions of guilt, while at the same time admitting torture as precisely the means for discovering whether a man was innocent or guilty by compelling him to confess his guilt. The logical consequence of the underlying intention would have been to say outright that torture was absurd and unjust: but against this stood the barrier of a blind reverence for antiquity and the Roman law. That little book *Dei delitti e delle pene,* which played a notable part not only in the abolition of torture but in the reform of all our criminal legislation, opened with these words: 'Certain

[3] Op. cit., Q. xxxvii, 2, 3, 4.

residues of the laws of a race of conquerors'; a phrase which at the time seemed (as indeed it was) audacious, the bold stroke of a brilliant mind; but a century earlier it would have seemed paradoxical to the point of extravagance. And no wonder: have we not seen a similar reverence survive still longer? First, and with even renewed power, in politics, then in literature, and finally in some branches of the fine arts. There comes a moment, in great matters as in small, when something which men have striven, despite its contingency and artificiality, to perpetuate as natural and necessary, must at last succumb to experience, or to rational argument, or to mere satiety and change of fashion—or to some other factor, if any there be, more trivial even than fashion—according to the nature and relative importance of the matter in question. But that moment must be prepared for; and it stands a good deal to the credit of the old jurists if they did in fact, as I think they did, prepare for such a moment in the history of jurisprudence, however slowly and unwittingly they did so.

But in the case of our trial, even the rules by that time established were enough to convict the judges of definite illegality. For they chose in fact to begin with torture. Completely ignoring the circumstances, whether 'essential' or not, of the presumed crime, they bombarded their victim with questions from which nothing relevant could result, except only a pretext for them to say 'not plausible'; and, on this pretext—giving to asserted implausibilities the character of proved lies—to warn him that they would use torture. They were not in fact seeking the truth at all; their only object was to extort a confession. Uncertain of their advantage if they were to stop to examine the facts, they wanted as quickly as possible to inflict the pain which would give them a certain and swift advantage. They were in a hurry: all Milan knew (that is the word used in such cases) that Guglielmo Piazza had smeared the walls, doorways, and approaches of Via della Vetra—and those who had him in their power, couldn't *they* make him own up?

Someone may say perhaps that all this was justified, in law, at least, if not in conscience, by the principle—a revolting one but accepted in those days—that when threatened by a crime of more than usual enormity the public authorities need not scruple to use illegal methods to suppress it. But in point of fact it was—and heaven knows, this was only right—the common, nay almost the universal opinion of the jurists that this principle did not apply to the actual process in court, but only to the punishment eventually imposed. As one of them expressed it, 'the enormity of the crime one may be concerned with is no proof that the accused committed it; and until such proof be shown, let all legal formalities be observed'.[4] And here I should like to put on record another text, if only because it seems to me to represent one of those moments that occur from time to time in history when a gleam of eternal justice itself shows through human speech. I refer to a phrase used early in the fifteenth century by Nicolò Tedeschi, Archbishop of Palermo, but more famous, so long as he had any fame, as the Abate Palermitano, and whom our ancestors called the 'Bartolo of Canon Law'. 'The graver the crime,' wrote this author, 'the stronger should be the proofs of guilt, for where the danger is greater there is the greater need of prudence.'[5] However, these texts do not— from the strictly legal point of view—apply to our case, for we have it on Claro's authority that in the practice of the courts of Milan a contrary custom prevailed—namely that in such cases (of especially grave crimes) the judge was permitted to set the law aside, even in examining the accused; 'A rule,' remarks Rimaldi, another erstwhile celebrated jurist, 'which other nations would do well not to adopt'—on which Farinacci comments, 'well said'.[6] But observe how Claro himself interprets this rule: 'Recourse is had to torture although the evidence be not altogether sufficient (*in totum sufficientia*), nor proved by altogether unimpeachable witnesses, and often also without having given the accused a copy of the minutes of the investigation.' But where he treats particularly of evidence that would justify torture, he expressly states the necessity of some such

[4] P. Folerius, *Pract. crim.*, § 'Quod suffocavit', 52.
[5] *Commentaria in libros decretalium*, 'De praesumptionibus', c. xiv, 3.
[6] Op. cit., Q. xxxvii, 79.

evidence—'not only in the case of petty crimes but for the greatest crimes too, not excluding high treason'.[7] Claro, then, allowed that certain cases called for a less thorough scrutiny of evidence, but not that it could ever be right to dispense with such scrutiny altogether. He allowed that in certain cases one might go ahead without witnesses of the highest character; not that there need be none at all; that the evidence could be slighter, but not that none need be adduced—and such as was adduced must, he insisted, be real and relevant. Claro, in short, aimed at making things easier for the judges in their task of discovering crime, but not at giving them power to torture, on whatever pretext they chose, whomsoever might fall into their hands. No abstract theory could ever allow, ever conceive, ever dream of conceiving such a power. The passions, however, are far more practical.

And so Piazza was warned by that unspeakable interrogator: 'Tell us the truth—the real reason why you say that you do not know that the walls have been smeared, and that you do not know the names of the deputies. Otherwise, these statements being implausible, we shall put you on the rope to discover the truth behind the implausibilities.' 'Hang me up if you want to, but I know nothing of the things you have asked me about.' So the poor wretch replied, with that sort of desperate courage with which reason will sometimes challenge violence as though to make it understand that, do what it will, violence can never change its nature and become reasonable.

And notice the paltry cunning of these gentlemen in finding an extra excuse for their proceedings by ferreting out a second 'lie', as though to have the term in the plural gave them more assurance—another zero to swell a sum which so far contained nothing else.

He was put to the torture. They said: 'Tell us the truth at last.' Howling and sobbing, praying and supplicating, he answered, 'My Lord, I have told the truth.' They persisted with their questions. 'Ah for the love of God,' he cried, 'let me down my Lord and I will tell all I know. . . . Give me a drop of water,

[7] *Sentent. recept.*, V, Q. lxiv, 9.

please.' He was let down, put in a chair, and questioned again. He again replied, 'I know nothing . . . give me some water, please.'

The blindness of panic! It never crossed their minds that from the very thing which they were determined to force Piazza to say he could have made a very strong argument in his defence—if it had been true, as they so cruelly insisted it was. 'Yes, sir,' he could have replied, 'I had heard that the walls of Via della Vetra had been smeared; and then I went and lounged about at the door of your house, my Lord President of the Sanità!' And the argument would have been all the stronger for the fact that the two rumours, of the smearing and of Piazza's responsibility for it, were going around together; so that Piazza must have been aware of his danger, along with the rumour of the smearing. But this obvious consideration, to which the minds of his judges were blinded by passion, could not occur to him either, poor fellow; because they had never told him what he was accused of. Before anything else they wanted to break his spirit with torture. It was this that represented for them the 'plausible and probable arguments' which the law required. They wanted to make him feel the terrible and immediate consequences of answering them in the negative; to make him admit himself a liar once, in order to gain the right not to believe him as soon as he should declare himself innocent. But this particular villainy did not succeed. Put to the torture again, lifted up on the rope, warned that the torture would be repeated, subjected to it again time after time, and continually pressed to 'tell the truth', Piazza's answer, screamed out at first and then spoken in a low voice, was always the same: 'I have told you the truth.' Until at last the judges, seeing that he was past giving any answer at all for the present, ordered him to be let down and taken back to prison.

On 23 June a report of this interrogation was made to the Senate by the President of the Sanità, himself a Senator, and by the Chief of Police (who could also sit in that assembly when invited). The Senate thereupon decreed, in its capacity as Supreme Court, that 'Piazza be shaved, given a purgative, dressed in clothes provided by the court, and then tortured again', this time 'tied by the rope'—a very cruel addition, since it meant that now his hands, as well as arms, would be dislocated. This torture 'was to be repeated as often as the two aforesaid magistrates thought fit, because of certain lies and implausibilities which the trial has brought to light'.

The Senate alone had, I will not say the authority but the power, to take things so far with impunity. With regard to the repetition of tortures the Roman law was interpreted in two ways; and the legally weaker of the two was the more humane. Many authorities—perhaps following Odofredus, who is the only one quoted by Cino da Pistoia and the earliest quoted by the other writers who maintained this view—held that torture could not be repeated unless in the meantime new and weightier evidence had come to light; with, later, the added qualification that this evidence should be different in kind from that adduced in the first instance. On the other hand many writers followed Bartolo in holding that torture might be repeated if the original evidence were very plain, clear, and pressing; and if—again a condition added later—the first application of torture had been mild. Now clearly, neither of these interpretations had the slightest relevance to the Senate's decree. No new evidence had been shown. And what was the original evidence? That two women had observed Piazza touching a wall, and that (here 'evidence' and 'crime' became the same thing) the magistrates had seen 'some traces of oily material' on the scorched and blackened walls of a part of the street where in fact Piazza had not been! Moreover, these so evidently 'plain, clear, and pressing' signs of guilt had not been tried out or tested in any discussion with the accused. Discussion indeed! The Senate's decree makes no mention of evidence in regard to the crime: the decree was not even a misapplication of the law; it proceeded as though there were no law. In the teeth of all law and all accepted authorities, not to speak of all reason, it ordered that Piazza be tortured anew 'because of some lies and implausibilities'; that is to say, the Senate ordered its ministers to do again, and still more cruelly, what it ought to have punished them for doing in the

L

first place. For it was a universally admitted principle of jurisprudence (and how could it not have been?) that a subordinate judge who had put a man to torture without due evidence of guilt should be punished by his superiors.

But the Senate of Milan was the supreme court of justice (in this world, to be sure), and it would not do for the Senate of Milan—to which the public was looking, if not for protection, at least for revenge—it would never do for this body to be less adroit, persistent, successful in discovery than Caterina Rosa. For in fact the whole business was going forward under this woman's authority. They were her words which had started the trial on its course—'then it occurred to me that he might perhaps be one of the people', etc.—and the same words were still controlling and ruling it; except that, while she began with surmises, the judges began with assurance. And let us not be surprised to see a court of justice playing the eager disciple to a couple of illiterate women; for where passion calls the tune, it is only natural that the blind should be leaders. Nor need we be surprised to see men whom we cannot suppose to have been, indeed who certainly were not, of the kind that choose evil for its own sake, to see such men so cruelly and blatantly violate every rule of justice; for once a man allows himself to think unjustly he will proceed to act unjustly and continue down this path as far as the unjust thought can take him; and if conscience hesitates, and grows uneasy, and starts to send out warnings— well, it is all too easy for popular clamour to overwhelm all scruples, or even prevent any ever arising, in the mind of one who forgets that he has to answer to another judge.

As for the humiliating (to say the least) directions with regard to shaving, clothing, and purging the accused, they are sufficiently explained by Verri. 'It was the belief of those times,' he writes, 'that a criminal might have some diabolical charm or some pact with the devil concealed on his person, in the hair of his head or body, or in his clothes, or even in his stomach; so that shaving, stripping, and purging were employed to render him defenceless.'[8] And it is true, such was the belief of those

[8] Op. cit., c. iii.

times; and violation of human rights was a fact of those times, and is of all times, under one form or another; but was never at any time accepted in principle.

Piazza's second interrogation was only a repetition of the first one—just as absurd, still more cruel, and equally ineffective. The poor wretch was first questioned, his answers being contradicted with captious objections which one would call childish if such a term could apply to anything done in this affair; and the questions still bore on circumstances irrelevant to his presumed crime, about which he was still kept entirely in the dark. This done, they began to torture him again, and more cruelly, in obedience to the Senate's decree. All they obtained were cries of anguish, cries for mercy—not a word of what they desired to hear, and to extort which they had the nerve to cause such cries and to listen to them. 'Oh my God! Oh, my Lord, what are you doing to me . . . get it over quickly, at least . . . cut my hand off . . . let me die . . . give me at least a moment to breathe. . . . Ah, Lord President! For the love of God give me something to drink. . . .' Yet still, with all this: 'I don't know anything; I have told you the truth.' Having answered thus again and again, to their coldly and yet furiously repeated demand, 'Tell us the truth', Piazza's voice failed him, he went dumb; during four repetitions of the torture he was silent. Then, at last, he found strength to say once more in a low voice: 'I know nothing, I've already told you the truth.' And with this they had to make an end, and return him, unconfessed, to prison.

And now they no longer had any reason, any sort of pretext, for beginning again; they had taken a short cut and it had led them astray. Had the torture produced its effect of extorting the confession of a lie, they would have had Piazza at their mercy; and, horrible to say, the less important the subject of the lie, the more indifferent and trivial, the more effectively would it have served them as an argument of his guilt; as showing his need to keep clear of the whole business, to appear completely ignorant of it—in short, to lie. But, having tortured him once, illegally, and then again still more illegally and still more savagely (or, to use their term, 'severely'), it would have been just a little too extravagant to begin a third time to torture a man for denying that he had heard certain rumours or known the names of some parish functionaries. So they were back at their starting point, as though nothing had yet been done; obliged after all, with nothing gained so far, to begin the investigation of the supposed crime, and therefore to tell Piazza what he was charged with and commence his cross-examination. And what if he denied the charge? What if, as he had shown himself able to do, he persisted in denying even under torture? And this torture would have had to be absolutely the last, unless the judges chose to bring on themselves the fearful judgement pronounced by a fellow judge, one who had died almost a century earlier but whose authority was stronger now than ever before—I mean that Bossi who has been quoted already: 'I have never,' said Bossi, 'known torture to be ordered more than three times, except by judges who were murderous brutes, *nisi a carneficibus*.'[9] And he meant torture ordered with due regard for the law !

But unfortunately the passions are ingenious and intrepid in finding new ways to take when the right way seems long and unsure. The judges had begun with the 'dislocation torture'; they now continued with torture of another kind. By order of the Senate (as we know from a letter of the Chief of Police to the Governor of Milan, Spinola, who at the time was besieging Casale) the Auditor of the Sanità, in the presence of a notary, promised Piazza his liberty on condition—as was to appear in the course of the trial—that he confessed the whole truth. In this way they managed to convey to him that of which they accused him without being compelled to discuss it; to inform him of it, not in order that his replies might help them to discover the truth, not in order to hear his opinion; but to bring to bear on him a powerful stimulus to say what they themselves wanted to hear.

The letter to which I refer was written on 28 June, that is to say when the trial, as we have seen, was already well on its way.

[9] *Tractatus varii*, 'De tortura', 44.

It begins thus: 'I think that Your Excellency should be informed of things that have come to light concerning certain criminals who have recently gone about smearing the walls and gates of this city.' And it will not be without interest, or profit, to see how those in charge of the proceedings represented the facts. 'I was commissioned,' the writer continues, 'by the Senate to set up an inquiry, as a result of which, on the evidence of certain women and of a man whose words could be trusted, a certain Guglielmo Piazza (a man of the lower class, but who holds the office of Commissioner of the Sanità) came under suspicion of having, in the early morning of Friday, 21 June, smeared the walls of a district by the Porta Ticinese, called the Vetra de' Cittadini.'

And the man whose words could be trusted, thus brought in at once to corroborate the testimony of the woman, had said that he had met with Piazza, adding 'and I greeted him and he returned my greeting'. And so Piazza 'came under suspicion'! As though the crime imputed to him was of having entered the Via della Vetra! Incidentally, the Chief of Police does not mention his own visit to the scene of the crime to verify the facts; nor was it mentioned during the rest of the trial.

'Piazza,' the letter goes on, 'was therefore immediately arrested.' But the writer says nothing of his own visit to Piazza's house, where 'nothing suspicious' had been found. 'And since his interrogation by the judges made him still more suspect' (as we have seen!) 'he was very severely tortured, but did not confess his guilt.'

If someone had informed Spinola that in fact Piazza had not been interrogated at all about the crime, Spinola would have replied: 'But I have positive information to the contrary. The Chief of Police has written to tell me, not indeed of this precisely, for that was not necessary; but he has informed me of something else which implies that and necessarily presupposes it; for he has written to say that the man, though severely tortured, did not confess the crime.' And if the objector had stuck to his point, that eminent and powerful personage might very well have retorted: 'What! Do you suppose the Chief of Police would make fun of me, to the extent of telling me, as an important item of news, that something did not happen which could not have happened?' And yet this precisely was the case: not, of course, that the Chief of Police had tried to make fun of the Governor; but the authorities had, in fact, done a thing of such a kind that they were unable to present a truthful report of it. For the fact was, and is, that bad conscience more easily finds pretexts for acting than formulae in which to render account of what it has done.

But on the matter of impunity that letter contained another deception which Spinola could—and indeed should—have observed for himself, if he had had a mind for anything except the taking of Casale (which he never took). For the letter continues: '. . . Until by order of the Senate (indeed in execution of the last decree which Your Excellency caused to be published on this matter) Piazza, being promised impunity by the President of the Sanità, finally confessed,' etc.

In the thirty-first chapter of the foregoing work[10] mention was made of a decree in which the Tribunal of the Sanità promised a reward and impunity to whomsoever should reveal the agents responsible for the smearings found on the doors or walls of houses on the morning of 18 May; and reference was also made to a letter of the same Tribunal to the Governor on this point. This letter, after declaring that the Tribunal's decree had been published 'with the approval of the Grand Chancellor', who was deputizing for the Governor, begged the latter 'to confirm it with a fresh decree which should promise a greater reward'. And in fact the Governor did cause another one to be promulgated on 13 June, in which (so it ran) 'he promises to any person who, within thirty days, should identify the person or persons who have committed, favoured, or aided the said crime a reward of, etc. . . . and in the event of such a person being himself involved in the crime, he is also promised impunity from punishment'. Now it was as in execution of *this* decree, which so explicitly referred to something done on 18 May, that the Chief of Police said that impunity had been promised to a man accused of something done on 21 June; and

[10] *I promessi sposi*, Ch. XXXI.

he said it to the very man who had, to say the least, signed this decree. Such confidence they had, it seems, in the siege of Casale! For it would be too much to suppose that their own minds were confused to such a degree.

But why did they need to use such a subterfuge with Spinola?

It was because they needed the support of his authority to disguise an action which was irregular and unjust both by common jurisprudence and by the laws of the country. For it was a commonly accepted principle that a judge could not, on his own authority, grant impunity to an accused person; and the Constitutions of Charles V, while conceding very wide powers to the Senate, nevertheless did not concede the power 'of granting pardons for crime, remission of punishment or safe-conducts; these things being reserved to the Sovereign'. And Bossi, from whom I have already quoted, and who was among those who compiled the Constitutions, being a Senator at the time, says expressly, 'the promise of impunity pertains exclusively to the Sovereign'.[11]

But why should they have involved themselves in subterfuge when they could have had recourse to the Governor in the first place for the power to grant the impunity? For the Governor certainly had this power, as the Sovereign's representative, together with authority to delegate it; and the proof that the judges could have obtained this power from him is the fact that they did so later on with regard to another unfortunate man who was to be involved in this same inhuman trial. The Governor's reply is registered in the Acts of the trial:

Ambrosio Spinola, etc. In conformity with the views expressed by the Senate in a letter of the 5th instant, we herewith authorize you to concede impunity to Stefano Baruello, condemned for distributing and manufacturing certain pestilent unguents which have been disseminated in this city for the destruction of the populace; if, within a period of time to be fixed by the said Senate, he shall reveal the agents of the said crime and their accomplices.

The promise to Piazza of impunity was not made in writing and officially; but informally, by the Auditor of the Sanità,

[11] Op. cit., 'De confessis per torturam,' 32. 11.

outside the trial. Naturally enough; for a formal assurance would have been obviously false, if based on the Governor's decree; and clearly a usurpation of authority if based on nothing. But why, I repeat, did the judges renounce, as it were, the possibility of giving a proper official form to so important an action?

These questions cannot be answered with certainty, but we shall see presently the advantage the judges gained from acting in this way.

In any case the irregularity of their procedure was so evident that Padilla's counsel frankly drew attention to it. Although— as he very rightly protested—he did not need, in order to disprove the charges against his client, to refer to matters in which the latter was not directly concerned; and although—wrongly and rather inconsistently—he conceded that a real crime and real criminals were involved in all this muddle of fantasy and invention; nevertheless for good measure, as people say, and with the general object of weakening the case against his client, he made various objections to the conduct of the trial as this had affected others of the accused. And in connexion with the impunity, without impugning the Senate's authority in the matter (for men are sometimes more touchy on the subject of their power than of their honesty), the advocate objected that Piazza 'was brought only before the said Lord Auditor who had no jurisdiction . . . and whose actions were therefore null and void and contrary to law'. And referring to the mention that was made in passing, later on, of that impunity, he said: 'And yet there had been nothing said or written hitherto, in the course of the trial, about any impunity, though according to law there ought to have been some such record of it before it was claimed.'

In this part of the defence a very pregnant remark was made in passing. Reviewing the actions which had preceded the promise of impunity, the advocate, without directly expressing any disapproval of the tortures inflicted on Piazza, nevertheless referred to them in these terms: 'He was tortured on implausible pretexts.' This seems to me a fact worth noting—that the thing should have been called by its true name even at that time, even in the presence of those responsible for it, and by one who was not in the least concerned to defend the innocence of the man who suffered by it.

This promise of impunity must have been little known to the general public: Ripamonti does not mention it in his history of the plague, which gives the main facts of this trial; indeed he indirectly denies its existence. It was not in Ripamonti's nature to misrepresent things deliberately; but he is inexcusable for not having read either Padilla's defence or the digest of the trial which was printed with it; and, touching the impunity, he says that Piazza, immediately after he had been tortured and while they were unbinding him to take him back to prison, came out with a 'spontaneous and quite unexpected revelation'. This false revelation was certainly made, but not until the following day, after Piazza had spoken privately with the Auditor; and it was made to men who very much expected it. Thus if the few documents above-mentioned had not survived, if the Senate had only had to do with the public and with historians, it would have succeeded in its attempt to conceal a fact which was of fundamental importance in the trial and was the starting point of all that took place subsequently.

No one knows what took place in that meeting between Piazza and the Auditor. We are left to conjectures and probabilities. Verri writes:

It was probably while he was actually in prison that the unhappy man was assured that if he persisted in his denials, the torture would be repeated every day; that his guilt was held to be certain, and that there was nothing that he could do now except to accuse himself and give the names of his accomplices. In this way he would save his life and escape from the daily torture prepared for him. Piazza therefore begged for impunity, and it was granted him, on condition that he made a clean breast of the facts.[12]

And yet it does not seem at all likely that Piazza himself asked for impunity; as we shall see as we follow the rest of the trial, he never took a step on his own initiative; he had to be dragged

[12] Op. cit., c. iv.

forward all the time; and in order to make him take that first step, and such a strange and horrible one, of calumniating himself and others, it is much more likely that he was offered the impunity by the Auditor. Moreover, the judges would surely not have omitted, when they spoke to him of it later, to mention so important a circumstance and one which gave so much more weight to his confession; nor would the Chief of Police have overlooked it in his letter to Spinola.

But who can imagine the struggle that went on in Piazza, with the memory of the torture so fresh in his mind, making him feel at the same time a terror of suffering again and a horror of causing others to suffer; having been offered the chance of escaping a ghastly death only at the cost of bringing it upon some other innocent person! For he could not have believed that they were going to let go one prey without trying to catch another, that they were resigned to doing without any condemnation at all. He yielded; he seized on the chance they offered, however horrible, in its conditions, and however doubtful it must have seemed; he accepted, deliberately, the loathsome and difficult task of finding another victim to take his place. But how find such a victim? Where should he begin? How choose with no one to choose from? In his own case, there had been a real fact to serve as the occasion and pretext for an accusation. He had, after all, gone into the Via della Vetra, he had walked along it touching the wall; and though the woman who saw him was warped in mind, she had at any rate seen something. We shall see that it was another equally innocent and equally trivial fact which suggested both the person he would accuse and the story he would invent.

There was a barber called Giangiacomo Mora who compounded and put out for sale an ointment as medicine against the plague—one of a thousand such things which had gained credit with the populace, as was only to be expected when an evil of which no one knew the remedy was working such havoc and in an age when medicine had as yet so little learned how not to dogmatize and had as yet taught people so little what not to believe. Now a few days before his arrest, Piazza had asked this barber for some of his ointment and the latter had promised to get some ready for him; and then, meeting Piazza on the Carrobio on the very morning of the day after the arrest, he had told him that the jar was ready and asked him to come and take it. But a story about ointment, about agreements between people, about the Via della Vetra, was just what the judges wanted from Piazza; hence these circumstances, all so fresh in his mind, supplied him with the materials to compose such a story—if you can call it composing to take a number of real circumstances and tack on an invention inconsistent with them.

On the day following, 26 June, Piazza was brought before the court of inquiry and ordered by the Auditor 'to declare in the presence of the notary Balbiano, and in conformity with the confession he has made extra-judicially to me, whether he knows who is responsible for compounding the unguents with which the gates and walls of the houses of this city have so many times been smeared'. But the poor wretch, who was lying against the grain, tried to move as little as possible away from the truth; he answered: 'It was the barber who gave me the ointment.' This is a literal translation of his words as recorded, which Ripamonti, as we have seen, places in the wrong context: *dedit unguenta mihi tonsor*. They told him 'to name the said barber'; and the latter's self-styled accomplice and instrument in crime replied: 'I think the name is Giovanni Giacomo, but his family [surname] I don't know.' He only knew for certain where the man's house, or rather shop, was; as was to appear in a later interrogation.

Piazza was then asked whether 'from the barber, thus identified, he has received little or much of the ointment'. He replied: 'He gave me as much of it as could be contained in the inkstand on that table.' If he had received from Mora the little jar of the stuff he had ordered, he would have described it; but, finding his memory empty, he grasped at an object he could actually see, as being at least something real. Their next question was 'whether this barber was a friend of his', and he, without noticing that what he really did remember was quite inconsistent with the story he was making up, answered: 'He is a friend, my Lord, yes indeed, an old friend, my Lord'; which simply meant that they knew one another enough to say 'good morning', if so much.

Without comment, the cross-examiners went on to ask him in what circumstances 'the barber had given him the unguent'. Piazza replied: 'As I was going along, he called me and said, "I've something for you." So I said, "What?" And he said, "a sort of ointment". And I said, "All right, I will come and get it from you later." And so, two or three days later, he gave it me.' In this account what had actually occurred was altered enough in its details to fit in with Piazza's story; but a good deal survived the process; and some of the words quoted probably had been spoken when the two men met. Phrases spoken in consequence of a previous agreement about a safeguard against disease were now reported as having been used in order there and then to concoct a plan—as crazy, to say the least, as it would have been wicked—to spread poison in the city.

The judges, nevertheless, proceeded with questions on the place, the date, and the time of day of the proposal, and the acceptance. Then, as though satisfied with Piazza's replies on these points, they asked, 'And what did he say to you when he actually gave you the ointment?' 'He said,' answered Piazza, ' "Take this jar and smear the walls of the streets here behind us; and then come to me and I'll give you a lot of money." ' At this point Verri comments with some impatience: 'But what prevented the barber from safely doing the smearing himself during the night?' And the next reply brings out still more plainly the implausibility noted by this comment. Asked, 'Did the barber tell the witness precisely where he was to smear the stuff?' Piazza answered, 'He told me to do it in the Vedra de' Cittadini, and that I was to start at the street corner, which I did.'

'So the barber didn't even smear his own street-corner!' notes Verri; and to be sure *his* intelligence was hardly required for that observation; whereas either a blindness caused by passion was needed for it not to be made, or downright malice, due to the same cause if, as seems more likely, the same idea occurred to the judges.

It cost the unhappy Piazza such an effort to invent his story, it had to be forced out of him by so many questions, that one is left wondering whether that promised bribe was a mere product of his imagination as it cast about for some likely reason for having agreed to do as he was doing, or whether it had really been suggested to him in that secret interview with the Auditor. The same doubt arises when we find his story stumbling, indirectly, against another difficulty—namely how on earth he could have handled so deadly an ointment without taking any harm from it himself. On the judges asking him, 'Whether the barber told him why he was having the said doors and walls smeared', Piazza replied, 'He didn't say anything, but I think the ointment was a poison harmful to the body, because the next morning he gave me a glass of water to drink, saying that it would be a safeguard.'

To all these replies, and to others which it would be tedious to repeat, the judges found nothing to object, or rather they expressed no objection. Regarding one point only they thought fit to require an explanation: why had the witness not confessed all this before? Answer: 'I don't know—I can't think of any reason except perhaps the water which he gave me to drink; for Your Excellencies know that, in spite of all the tortures, I couldn't say a thing.' But this time they were not so easily satisfied; they repeated the question: 'Why had he not confessed the truth sooner, especially in view of the tortures he had undergone both on Saturday and yesterday?'

The truth!

He replied: 'I didn't admit it because I couldn't, and if I had stayed hanging on that rope a hundred years I still couldn't have said anything; I just couldn't speak: whenever I was asked about anything to do with this business it all went out of my head and I couldn't answer.' This said, the judges concluded the interrogation and sent the unfortunate Piazza back to prison.

Yet is it enough merely to call him unfortunate? This is a question one's conscience shies away from and would rather declare itself incompetent to answer: how cruel, how arrogant, how pharisaically presumptuous it seems, at first, to pass judgement on a man trapped and tortured as Piazza was! But the question cannot be avoided, and there is only one possible answer: he was also guilty. The sufferings and fears of an innocent man are great things, powerful things, but they do not alter the moral law; they cannot make calumny to be no longer wrong. And the very pity that makes us wish we could find excuses for the sufferer turns us against the calumniator. Another innocent man has been named; we foresee another's sufferings and fears, and perhaps another's similar sins.

And the men who did the trapping and the torturing—shall we excuse them on the plea that they sincerely believed the tale about the poison, and that to torture was normal procedure at that time? But we too believe that men may be killed with poison; but what should we say of a judge who based the justice of a death-sentence for poisoning on this persuasion? The death-penalty is still inflicted; but what should we say to a man who thereby justified every death-sentence? No, the fact is that as far precisely as Guglielmo Piazza was concerned there might as well have not been any practice of torture; it was his judges who deliberately brought it into this particular case, who in a sense invented it for this occasion. Had he deceived them, the fault would still have been theirs, for he was acting under pressure from them; but we have seen that he did not deceive them. And even supposing they were deceived by his statements in the final interrogation—that they believed the story he told, with all the details that we have heard—what was it that started Piazza speaking in this way? How did they obtain his statement? With a device, the illegality of which they had no business to be deceived about, and in fact were not deceived about, since they did their best to conceal it and disguise it.

And if *per impossibile* all that took place subsequently had been nothing but an accidental convergence of factors tending to confirm them in their deception, they would still have been to blame for having prepared the ground for such a deception in the first place. But we shall see, on the contrary, that the whole affair went forward as the effect of, and controlled by, their intention to maintain that 'deception' to the bitter end; to do which they were prepared not only to dodge the law but also to shut their eyes to evidence, and not only to harden their hearts against pity but also play fast and loose with justice.

CHAPTER FOUR

THE Auditor hastened to Mora's house with a squad of police. They found him in his shop—this second criminal, untroubled by any thought of flight or concealment, though his accomplice had now been four days in prison. With Mora was his son. They were both arrested by order of the Auditor.

When Verri examined the parish registers of San Lorenzo, he found that the unlucky barber may also have had three daughters, one aged fourteen, one twelve, and one just six. I find it moving that a man like Verri, rich, celebrated, well-born, invested with public authority, should have gone to such trouble to unearth the records of people who were poor, lowly, forgotten, and what is more, technically criminals; that he should have thus gone seeking fresh objects for a wise and generous compassion at a time when his contemporaries still blindly and obstinately repeated the foolish denunciations of an earlier generation. It is, to be sure, unreasonable to pit compassion against justice. Justice must sometimes punish in spite of pity; it cannot condone crime out of compassion for the innocent who may suffer when guilty men are punished. Yet compassion too is a kind of justice, when stirred by violence and bad faith. That first sudden dismay of a wife and a mother, the terror that must have gripped the hearts of those children, so utterly unprepared for what occurred—their grief and horror at seeing a father and a brother suddenly seized and bound and insulted—if the men who caused this had had nothing worse on their consciences it alone had been a grievous thing to answer for. For it exceeded anything that justice required or even that the law allowed.

Because, of course, to arrest a man, you had to have some evidence against him, and against Mora there was none— neither ill-repute, nor attempted flight, nor complaint of an offended party, nor accusation lodged by anyone worthy of belief, nor testimony of any witness; nothing but the statement of a presumed accomplice; and before a judge could act on such a statement many conditions had to be fulfilled. We shall see that more than one essential condition was in fact lacking, and it would be easy to show the same of many others; but there is no need for this, because, even had every condition been scrupulously observed, there was one circumstance in this case which rendered the accusation absolutely invalid from the start —namely, that it was made in virtue of a promise of impunity. 'Whatever is testified,' says Farinacci, 'as a result of a hope of exemption from punishment (whether such exemption be con- ceded by the law or promised by the judge) ought not to be received as evidence against the persons named in the testi- mony.'[1] And Bossi writes:

> That testimony is defective which a witness makes in consequence of a promise of impunity . . . considering that a witness ought to speak disinterestedly and not with a view to gaining some advantage. . . . And this holds even in cases when, for other reasons, the rule which disallows the evidence of an accomplice is dispensed. . . . The witness who testifies because of a promise of impunity is called 'corrupt' and deserves no credence.[2]

This was a principle universally admitted.

As the police were about to search his house and shop Mora said to the Auditor: 'Oh, Your Excellency, I know you have come for that ointment of mine. Your Excellency can see it there—a little jar of it that I got ready to give to the Commis- sioner of Police, but he hasn't come for it. I've done nothing wrong. You don't need to keep me bound.' The poor fellow

---

[1] Op. cit., Q. xliii, 192.
[2] *Tract. varii*, 'De oppositionibus contra testes', 21.

thought that it was for making and distributing the specific without a licence that they were arresting him.

They turned everything upside down, examining big jars, little jars, flasks, casks, every sort of container (at that time barbers went in for rudimentary surgery, whence it was only a step to dabbling in medicine and pharmacy). They found two things that roused their suspicion; and, with apologies to the reader, I must speak of them, because it was just this suspicion shown by the police in the course of their examination of his house which led to poor Mora's finding something to accuse himself of when he later came to be tortured. Besides, the whole affair offers greater objects for our disgust.

In time of plague it was natural that a man who had to have dealings with many people, and particularly with the sick, should live apart from his own family as much as possible (an observation which Padilla's advocate was to make, as we shall see, when pointing out to the prosecution the lack of material evidence of crime in this case). Besides, the plague itself had lowered the standard of cleanliness—not in any case a high one then—in that afflicted population. So it is hardly surprising that in a small room behind the shop the police should have found, as the records say, 'two pots full of human excrement'. But one policeman was surprised by this find and remarked (since anyone was free to speak against 'the smearers') that 'the privy was upstairs'; to which Mora answered, 'I sleep down here and don't go upstairs.'

The second thing was that in a little yard they found 'an oven and in it, behind a low wall, a brass cooking-pot containing dirty water and at the bottom some sticky yellowish-white stuff which, on being thrown against a wall, stuck to it'. Mora said: 'It is *smoglio*' (i.e., lye), and the records note that he said this very emphatically, an observation which shows the sinister importance the police attached to this discovery. But how did they come to take such risks in handling so mysteriously potent a poison? Their, fear, no doubt, was overcome by the fury which was yet one of its causes.

They found also, among Mora's papers, a recipe which the

M

Auditor handed to him, asking him to explain it. Mora tore it
up because in the confusion he took it for the recipe of his
specific against the plague. The scraps were picked up at once,
and we shall see later how this paltry incident was used against
him.

The report of the trial does not say how many people were
arrested along with Mora. Ripamonti says that the whole
household was taken away, including those who worked in the
shop—wife and children and whatever other relatives happened
to be there, and the youths and boys in Mora's employment.

On leaving his house (to which he never returned and which
was destined to be razed to the ground to make room for the
Column of Infamy) Mora said: 'I haven't done anything wrong.
If anything has been wrong, I am ready to be punished for it;
but since I made that ointment I've done nothing else. If that
was a crime, I ask for mercy.'

He was interrogated that same day, chiefly concerning the lye
found in his house and concerning his relations with the Commissioner of Police. His answer on the first point was: 'My Lord,
I know nothing about it. The women must have been responsible for it; ask them, they will tell you. As for me, I had no
more idea that it was there than that I should be taken to prison
today.' With regard to the Commissioner, Mora told of the jar
of unguent which he had promised to let this man have, specify-
ing its ingredients. He denied having had anything else to do
with the Commissioner, except that about a year before the latter had come to his house for some professional service or other.

Immediately after Mora they had his son up for questioning,
and it was then that this poor lad repeated the stupid story
about the little pot and the pen which I mentioned at the
beginning. For the rest, they got nothing conclusive out of him.
Verri, in a note, observes that they ought to have asked the
barber's son about the lye, so as to find out how long it had been
in the cooking-pot, and how it had been made, and why. 'But,'
he adds, 'they feared to find Mora not guilty.' This goes to the
root of the whole affair.

However, they did question Mora's wife on this point. The

gist of her replies was that she had done the household washing
ten or twelve days previously; that after every such washing she
put aside some lye for certain surgical purposes, which was how
the police came to find it; but that this time she had not in fact
found any use for the stuff. The lye itself they then had
examined by two washerwomen and three doctors. The women
said it was lye but that it had been altered in some way; the
doctors said it was not lye at all. The reason for both replies was
the same: the stuff stuck to the pot and only came off in strings.
'In a barber's shop,' comments Verri, 'where linen soiled by
wounds and plasterings has been washed, what more natural
than to find a sticky, oily, yellowish sediment, especially in the
summer?'[3]

But to conclude, all this searching of Mora's house brought
no discovery to light; its only results were negative. And
Padilla's counsel was to draw the conclusion quite correctly:
'From my reading of the case for the prosecution,' he was to
say, 'I cannot see that it has established circumstantial evidence
of crime such as a sentence of guilt of necessity requires.' And
he went on to observe that such evidence was the more necessary, in this case, in that the effect which was being ascribed to
criminal activity, i.e., the death of so many people, had its
proper natural causes. 'How necessary,' he exclaimed, 'to turn
back from such vague ungrounded opinions to the certainties
of experience. Men have studied the unfavourable influences
of the constellations; the mathematicians have made their
prognostications; from which it had become perfectly clear
already that the year 1630 would bring plague—the plague
which in any case has desolated and destroyed so many fine
cities of Lombardy, not to speak of other parts of Italy, without
any thought or fear of unguents ever crossing anyone's mind.'
Here even error, we see, comes to the aid of truth, although
truth needed no such assistance. But one is sorry to hear this
advocate, after this and other equally cogent observations in dis-
proof of the 'crime', and after ascribing to the force of torture
the deposition which had accused his client, it is sad to hear him

[3] Op. cit., c. iv.

come out on another occasion with the following strange remark: 'It must be admitted that sheer wickedness caused the
said persons and their accomplices to attempt so heinous a crime
against the fatherland; for, as the barber himself confessed, their
motive was to enrich themselves by robbery.'

In the letter in which the Chief of Police informed the
Governor of these events, we read: 'The barber has been
arrested, his house having been found to contain certain com-
pounds which competent judges consider very suspect.' Suspect!
A word that a judge may begin with, but never willingly ends
with, without first trying every means in his power to change
suspicion into certainty. And if there really was anyone who did
not know or could not guess what means were available even in
those days for establishing the truth, means which certainly
could have been adopted had anyone genuinely desired to know
exactly how poisonous the dirt found in Mora's house was—
well, the President of the Court was there to give such information. In fact, in the letter already referred to, in which the
Tribunal of the Sanità told the Governor about the great fouling of walls on 18 May, mention had been made of an experiment with dogs, in order to 'ascertain whether the smearings
were poisonous or not'. But when that letter was written the
Tribunal had not yet got a man in their clutches on whom to try
the experiment of torture, and against whom the mob was
yelling *Tolle!*

However, before putting Mora to this test, they desired
clearer and more precise information (and the reader will agree
they needed it) from the Commissioner of the Sanità. So they
had him brought before them and asked him whether what he
had deposed on oath was true and whether he had since remembered anything else. But Piazza only confirmed his previous
statement and found nothing to add to it now. Then they said:
'It seems highly implausible that nothing passed between you
and the barber other than what you stated in your deposition.
For you were concerned with a matter of the gravest consequence such as one does not normally entrust to another's
execution in the off-hand way described in your statement.'

A remark much to the point; but made too late. Why had they not made it *à propos* of Piazza's first deposition which did not differ from this one? Why did they call that first deposition 'the truth'? Was their sense of what was plausible so dull and slow that it took them a whole day to wake up to an implausibility? *They* dull and slow? On the contrary! Their sense of the implausible was wonderfully, even excessively, delicate. Had they not immediately found it implausible when Piazza denied having heard of the fouling of the walls in Via della Vetra? When he said he did not know the names of those parish deputies? What made them so hard to please in one case, so quick to decide in the other?

They well knew the reason; and He who sees all things knew it too. And there is something that even we can discern—that they found an implausibility when this served them as a pretext for torturing Piazza, and did not find one when it would have proved too obvious an impediment to the arrest of Mora.

We have, to be sure, already seen that since Piazza's deposition was basically invalid, the judges had no right to make any use of it against Mora. But because they were in any case resolved to use it, they had no choice but to uphold it. If, when Piazza first made his statement they had declared it 'highly implausible'; and if Piazza had not succeeded in getting round this difficulty by putting out a more plausible story, and this without contradicting the first one (an unlikely event); then the judges would have found themselves faced with the alternatives of either leaving Mora alone or of imprisoning him after having themselves protested, as it were, in advance against such an action.

The remark about implausibility was followed by a terrible admonition: 'If the witness is determined not to speak the whole truth, as he promised to do, then let him take warning that the promised impunity will not avail him—in so far, that is, as his declaration as to what took place between him and the barber be found to come short of the entire truth; whereas on the contrary, if he speaks the truth, the said impunity will avail him.'

Here, by the way—to recall a point already alluded to—it

becomes clear what an advantage it was to the judges not to have had recourse to the Governor for the concession of this impunity. Had he conceded it, on his sovereign authority and with all the due formalities, there could have been no question of withdrawing it so casually now. But what a mere Auditor said, an Auditor could unsay.

We may also note here that it was not until 5 September that an impunity was requested, from the Governor, for Baruello; that is to say, after the punishment inflicted on Piazza, Mora, and a few others. By that time one could take the risk of letting someone escape; the animals having been fed, their bellowings became naturally less impatient, less imperious.

On receiving that warning, Piazza—who was resolved to stick to the wretched course he had chosen—had fairly to cudgel his brains for all they were worth; but the only result was a repetition of his original story. 'I will tell Your Excellency. Two days before the barber gave me the ointment, he was standing in the street leading to Porta Ticinese with three other men, and seeing me pass by, he said to me: "Commissioner, I have some ointment for you." I said: "Do you want to give it to me now?" He answered, "No." And just then he did not tell me about the effects of the ointment. But when he gave it to me later he said that it was for smearing on the walls so as to make people die. And I didn't ask him whether he had already tried it out.' To be sure, in the original story Piazza did not say: 'He said it was ... to make people die', but rather: 'he didn't say anything, but I think the ointment was a poison'. However, the judges let this contradiction pass and asked him, 'Who were the men with the barber and how were they dressed?' Piazza did not know who they were; he only suspected that they were friends of Mora. As for their dress, he could not remember. He only insisted that what he had deposed against Mora was the truth, and on being asked whether he was prepared to maintain this to Mora's face, he answered 'yes'. They then put him to the torture again in order to 'cleanse him from disrepute' and 'make it possible for him to bear witness' against the unlucky barber.

The use of torture is, thank God, so much a thing of the past that these phrases need to be explained. Roman law had laid it down that 'the testimony of gladiators and suchlike was invalid, unless corroborated by torture',[4] and later jurisprudence had specified the persons to whom this rule applied, naming them 'disreputable'. And to this class belonged everyone convicted of crime, whether by his own confession or by a process of proof. But how did torture 'cleanse' from such disrepute? The jurists reasoned as follows. An accomplice to a crime is not as such an acceptable witness. But if he persist in an assertion that is very much against his own actual and tangible self-interest, then one may admit that he does so as constrained by the force of truth. So then if, after a man convicted of some crime has become the accuser of someone else, the former is told that he must either withdraw his accusation or submit to torture; and if he persist in the accusation, and persist even when the threat is carried out and he actually *is* tortured; then in that case, they said, his testimony becomes credible. Torture has 'cleansed his disrepute'—giving his testimony the authority which it could not get from his personal character.

But then why had they not made Piazza confirm under torture his first deposition? Was it so as not to imperil this deposition—so flimsy in itself but so necessary for the arrest of Mora? The omission, in any case, lent an added illegality to that arrest; for while it was admitted that the accusation of a 'disreputable' person, not corroborated by torture, might, like any other weak evidence, be of some use in the process of collecting information, it was not admitted as a ground for taking action against the one who was accused. Claro states this as, without exception, the practice of the courts in Milan: 'For an accomplice to be accepted as a witness, it is necessary that he first be tortured; for as such he is in disrepute on account of his crime. This is our practice: *et ita apud nos servatur.*'[5]

Was it then legally correct to torture Piazza, at least this last time? By no means; even in law it was unjust, for their purpose in torturing him was to confer validity on an accusation which, being the effect of a promise of impunity, could never in fact

---

[4] *Digest*, XXII, tit. 5, 'De testibus'.   [5] Op. cit., Q. xxi, 13.

become valid. Why did they not heed their own Bossi's warning on this point? 'Since the harm,' he writes, 'done by torture cannot be remedied, care must be taken not to inflict it to no purpose, i.e. when no further presumption or evidence of crime has been brought against a man.'[6]

Then whatever they did, they broke the law—torturing or not torturing. Certainly: and why should we be surprised? If one takes a wrong turning one may well come to a choice between two roads that are both wrong.

For the rest, I need hardly tell the reader that the torture used on Piazza to make him withdraw an accusation did not have to be so efficient as that used on him to force him to accuse himself. And in fact they had no howls or groans to record this time; he confirmed his testimony quite calmly.

Then they asked him, and twice over, why he had not made it when they first interrogated him: clearly, they could not get the suspicion out of their minds (and a sting of remorse from their hearts) that perhaps his absurd story had been prompted by their promise of impunity. He answered: 'It was because of the water that I told you I drank.' They would no doubt have preferred a better reason, but they had to put up with this one. They had neglected—indeed shunned and shut out—every means that might have helped them to discover the truth; they had made their choice between the two opposite conclusions to which the inquiry might have led, and had then used one means after another to obtain, at any cost, the conclusion they had chosen: had they now any right to find in this the joy which the sight of a truth that has been sincerely sought for can give? To put out the light is an excellent way to avoid seeing what one does not want to see, but not to see what one does want to see.

When the rope was let down and while they were untying him, the Commissioner said: 'My Lord, please wait until to-morrow, when I will tell you whatever else I can remember about the barber and about other people too.' And then, as they were taking him back to prison, he stopped and said: 'Wait, I have something to say now'; and proceeded to name, as friends

[6] Op. cit., 'De indiciis . . . ante torturam', 152.

to Mora and as shady characters, the aforenamed Baruello and two *foresari*,[7] Girolamo Migliavacca and his son Gaspare.

In this way the wretched man tried to make names a substitute for the evidence that he knew was lacking. But could his interrogators have possibly failed to see that with this Piazza only gave further proof of not being able to answer their questions? It was they who had asked him to state circumstances that might corroborate his account of what had happened; and presumably he who calls for corroboration sees the need of it. But with these vague new accusations Piazza was as good as saying: 'You tell me to show you quite clearly the existence of a fact. This I can't do because there was no fact. But after all, what you really want is to get hold of people you can condemn. Very well then, here are some—and now it is up to you to get what you require from them. You are sure to succeed with at least one of them; after all you did so with me.'

I shall not mention again the three men named by Piazza— nor others named subsequently, on no better grounds, and condemned with equal assurance—except so far as this may be required for telling the story of Piazza and Mora (who, being the first to fall into the hands of the police, were always regarded as the principal criminals) or so far as they offer an occasion for some particular comment on the affair. I omit also, here as heretofore, various minor happenings, and pass straight to the second examination of Mora; which took place on the same day.

In the course of various question about his unguent-specific, about the lye, and about some lizards he had had caught by the shop-boys in order to concoct a medicine used at that time (questions which he answered like a man who has nothing to hide and no need to invent) they produced the pieces of the paper that was torn up by Mora when the police visited his home. He said: 'I see it is the paper I tore up without thinking what I was doing, and if you will put the pieces together so that the writing can be read, I will also be able to remember who gave it to me.'

---

[7] Grinders of scissors for cutting gold thread. The fact that there was a distinct profession of this kind shows that the industry which it subserved was still flourishing in Milan.

They then asked him: 'How is it that if (as you said in the preceding interrogation) you are not a particular friend of Commissioner Piazza, he so readily had recourse to you for the jar of preservative against the plague, and you so freely and readily agreed to let him have it, and asked him to come and fetch it?'

Notice the appeal, once again, to the *stricter* standard of plausibility. When, the first time, Piazza asserted that his 'good old friend' the barber had offered him, no less 'freely and readily', stuff intended to spread death through the city, the judges accepted the story at once; but not now, on hearing that the stuff was intended as a safeguard. And yet surely one should be less hesitant in looking for the accomplice without whom some minor illegality, and one involving actions in themselves innocent, could not have been committed, than in seeking a superfluous 'accomplice' to a crime both abominable in itself and extremely dangerous to its perpetrators. Nor is this a discovery made in these last two hundred years. The judges' topsyturvy reasoning was not the reasoning of 'seventeenth-century man', but simply of frightened and furious men. As for Mora's answer, it was: 'I did it for the money.'

They asked him next whether he knew the other men named by Piazza; to which he replied that he did, but they were no friends of his, being 'persons better left alone'. Then they asked: Did he know who had fouled the whole city with those smearings? Answer: No, he did not. Did he know, then, who had provided the Commissioner with the unguent to be smeared? No, again he did not. And then their final question: does he know whether anyone offered money to the said Commissioner to induce him to smear the walls of Via Vedra de' Cittadini, and then gave him a glass jar of unguent to be used for the purpose? To which Mora replied, in a low voice and with his head bowed *(flectens caput et submissa voce)*: 'I know nothing about it.'

It was perhaps only now that he began to see to what a strange and horrible conclusion all the twists and turns of these questions might be leading him. If so, he must have guessed the truth from the way they questioned him; but who can tell what exactly it was that opened his eyes? But certainly, his judges, in the degree that they were still, willy-nilly, unsure of having discovered what they were seeking, must have been led to hint that now at last they *were* sure—that now they were forearmed against foreseen denials. But they could not see, of course, nor record the faces and gestures that he saw.

They put the direct question to him: 'Did you seek out Guglielmo Piazza, Commissioner of the Sanità, in order to induce him to smear the walls at the corner of the Via Vedra de' Cittadini, and to this end give him a small glass jar containing unguent for that purpose; promising him a sum of money in payment?'

His reply was more of a cry than an answer. 'My Lord, no! *Maidè*,[8] no! No, no, forever, for eternity! Would *I* do such things?' Words which could be spoken either by a guilty man or an innocent man, but not in the same way by both. But they answered: 'What then will you say when this truth is maintained to your face by Guglielmo Piazza?'

This truth once again! Their entire knowledge of the matter was based on the statement of a presumed accomplice; to whom they themselves, that very day, had replied that the story, as he told it, was 'most implausible'; and who had since then failed to add to it a single grain of plausibility, unless self-contradiction be such. And now to Mora they coolly say, 'this truth'! Was this due to the grossness of the times? Or to a barbarous legal system? Or to ignorance? Or superstition? Or was it one of those occasions when iniquity gives the lie to itself?

Mora answered: 'If he maintains this to my face, I will tell him he is a scoundrel, and that he cannot say this, because we have never spoken of any such thing, so help me God!'

They summoned Piazza and, in Mora's presence, asked him if this and that and the other were true; one thing after the other, his entire deposition. He answered, 'Yes, my Lord, it is true.' Poor Mora cried, 'God in heaven, this can never be shown to be true!' The Commissioner: 'I have come to this by helping you.' Mora: 'It can never be shown; you cannot prove that you

[8] An old Milanese expression meaning originally 'my God'.

have ever been in my house.' Piazza: 'I wish I never had, but I have been there; and now I've come to this because of you.' Mora: 'You will never prove that you've been to my house.' Then they were taken away, each to his own prison.

In the letter—mentioned more than once above—of the Chief of Police to the Governor, this encounter was described as follows: 'Piazza vigorously maintained to his [Mora's] face that he really had received from Mora an unguent of this kind, giving the circumstances of time and place.' Spinola then must have been led to believe that Piazza had specified these circumstances, and, so doing, had been contradicted by Mora on each of them. As for that 'vigorously maintained', all it boiled down to in fact was, 'Yes, my Lord, it is true.'

The letter ended with these words: 'Further inquiries are on foot to discover other accomplices and ringleaders. Meanwhile, I thought it well to inform Your Excellency of what is being done in the matter. Humbly kissing Your Excellency's hands, I wish Your Excellency every success in your present undertakings.' There were probably other letters which have not survived. As to the Governor's undertakings, the well-wishing went for nothing: not receiving reinforcements, Spinola lost all hope of taking Casale, fell sick (partly out of chagrin) and died on the 25th of the same month; having failed in the end to live up to his illustrious title, acquired in Flanders, of 'the taker of cities'; and exclaiming (in Spanish), 'They have dishonoured me.' What 'they' had done was, in fact, worse—placed him in a position involving many grave responsibilities, only one of which he appears to have taken seriously; this being probably also the only one they had in mind when appointing him.

The day after his confrontation with Mora, the Commissioner asked to be heard again. Brought before the court, he said: 'The barber has denied that I was ever in his house; so I beg your Lordships to interrogate Baldassar Litta, who lives in Antonio's house in the district of San Bernadino, and Stefano Buzzio, a dyer who lives opposite Sant' Agostino, near Sant' Ambrogio. These men know that I have been in the barber's house and shop.'

Was Piazza acting on his own in saying this? Or on a suggestion from the judges? If the former, it was an odd thing to do, as the event will show; on the other hand the judges would have had a very strong motive for urging him to this step. They wanted a pretext for having Mora tortured; and among the factors which, in the opinion of many learned men, could give to an accusation made by an accomplice the force which it otherwise lacked, and so render it sufficient grounds for torturing the person accused, was a relation of friendship between the latter and his accuser. But not any kind of friendship or acquaintance; for in that case, as Farinacci observes, 'any accusation by an accomplice could count as sufficient evidence, it being hardly likely that an accuser be wholly unacquainted with the man he accuses. What must be shown is that the two men have been in close and frequent contact, such as to make it plausible that the crime in question was planned by them together'.[9] And this in fact was why the judges had begun by asking Piazza whether the barber were a friend of his. And the reader will remember the answer they received: 'He is a friend . . . indeed, an old friend.' But more than this bare assertion they could not wring from him, even with threats; so that what they had sought for as a means to the end they were pursuing had become an obstacle in their path. True, it was never, and could never become, a legally valid means; for no friendship, however intimate and however well certified as a fact, could have given validity to an accusation already nullified by the promise of impunity. But this difficulty, like many others not actually raised in the course of the trial, they simply ignored; whereas, having explicitly made an issue of the friendship, or lack of it, between Piazza and Mora, they found themselves now compelled to settle this question once and for all. Thus it is that the records of the trial contain statements by jailers, policemen, and persons who were already in prison for other crimes, statements made in consequence of their being dragged into the affair for the sole purpose of 'getting them to say something' on this point. It is then very probable indeed that the judges had used some

[9] Op. cit., Q. xliii, 172-4.

such person to tell the Commissioner that his safety might depend on his supplying proofs of his friendship with Mora; and that the poor wretch, to avoid admitting that he had none, had had recourse to a stratagem which would otherwise never have occurred to him. For the actual testimony of the two witnesses cited by him showed how little he could have counted on them: Baldassare Litta, being asked whether 'he had ever seen Piazza in Mora's house or shop', answered, 'No, my Lord'; and Stefano Buzzi, on being asked 'whether Piazza and the barber were friends', answered, 'Perhaps they were; perhaps they exchanged greetings when they met; but I really wouldn't know, my Lord.' And when asked again, 'if he knew whether Piazza had ever been in Mora's house or shop', he said, 'I couldn't say, my Lord.'

After this they called another witness to verify a statement in Piazza's deposition, that a certain Matteo Volpi had been present when the barber had said to him, 'I have something for you.' Questioned on this, Volpi not only replied that he knew nothing about it, but, when his questioners persisted, answered with spirit, 'I am ready to swear that I have never seen them speaking together.'

The next day, 7 June, Mora was examined again; and you would never guess how this interrogation began.

'Please tell us why, at your last interrogation when you were brought face to face with Guglielmo Piazza, Commissioner of the Sanità, you said that you scarcely knew him and that he had never been in your house, although to your face he maintained the contrary; and again, despite the fact that in your first interrogation you showed that you knew him very well, as is also clear from the formal testimony of other witnesses, besides the fact that it clearly appears from your eagerness in offering him and preparing for him (as you have already admitted) a jar of your preservative.' Mora replied: 'It is true that the Commissioner often passes by my shop; but he is not well known to my household nor to me.' They answered: 'That is contradicted, not only by what you said in the first interrogation, but by the testimony of other witnesses. . . .'

Any comment would be superfluous.

However, they dared not torture Mora simply because of Piazza's deposition. So what then? Why, they went back to the pretext of 'implausibilities'; and, believe it or not, one of these was his having denied that Piazza was his friend and a frequent visitor at his house, while at the same time stating that he had promised Piazza some of the preservative! The other was that he had not sufficiently explained why he had torn up that paper. For Mora persisted in saying that he had done this inadvertently and under the impression that the paper could be of no interest to the police. Perhaps, poor fellow, he feared to make things worse for himself if he admitted to having torn it so as to destroy evidence of an illegality on his part; or perhaps he really could not explain to himself, here and now, what he had done in those first moments of confusion and panic. In any case, those bits of paper were now in the hands of his judges; and if they suspected that the writing on them contained evidence of crime, they had only to put the pieces together and read it, as Mora himself had suggested in the first place. And is it credible that they had not, in fact, already done so?

They ordered Mora, then, with threats of torture, to tell them the truth on the above two points. He replied: 'I have already told you about the paper. As for the Commissioner, he can say what he likes but what he told you is a damned lie, because I gave him nothing.'

He thought—and how could he not have thought?—that this was the truth they finally wanted from him. But of course not! They replied: 'Do not bother us with that point; it is not about that that we are asking you. All that we want to know here and now is why you tore up the piece of paper and why you have denied and still deny that the Commissioner has been to your shop, and so would almost have us believe that you do not know him.'

It would, I think, be hard to find another example of so shamelessly untruthful a respect for legal formalities. Since it was too obvious that they had no right to have Mora tortured on account of the main—indeed the only—charge that had been brought against him, they wanted to make it appear that the torture would be inflicted on other grounds.

But wickedness is like a cloak that doesn't fit: pull it down to cover one side of you, it will leave the other bare. For they were now left with only two pretexts for proceeding to physical violence, both entirely unjust: one which they themselves in effect declared to be such, in preferring not to make out what was written on the paper; the other shown to be so, and even more flagrantly, by the testimonies with which they had tried to give it the force of legal proof. And, as though this were not enough, there is the further point that, even if Piazza's second statement had been fully confirmed by those testimonies, and even had there not been the obstacle of the impunity, Piazza's deposition had no validity at all as legal evidence: 'If,' writes Farinacci, 'the depositions of an accomplice prove inconsistent and self-contradictory, then, as the statements of a perjuror, they cannot render the person whom he accuses liable to torture . . . or even to interrogation . . . and this is a principle commonly accepted, one can say, by all writers on the law.'

But Mora *was* put to the torture.

He was not so robust, poor man, as his calumniator. For a time, however, the agony only wrung pitiful cries from him and protestations that he had said the truth: 'Oh my God, I don't know the man, we have never been friends, and that's why I can't say . . . and that's why it's a lie he tells that he has often visited my house or been in my shop. Oh God! Mercy, my Lord, mercy! That paper I tore up thinking it was the recipe for my preservative . . . because all I wanted was the money.'

'That is not enough,' they said. He begged to be let down, saying that he would tell the truth. Let down, he said: 'The truth is that I do not know the Commissioner well.' The torture was resumed, with greater severity. To their pitiless questioning he then replied, 'My Lords, tell me what you want me to say, and I will say it'; the same reply that Philotas gave to the man who was torturing him at the command of Alexander the Great ('who himself was behind a curtain listening' [10]): *dic quid me velis dicere;* the same reply of who knows how many other poor wretches.

At last the pain overcame all aversion to self-calumny and all fear of the death-sentence; he said: 'I gave the Commissioner a jar of filth, of excrement, so that he should smear the walls with it. Your Lordships, let me down; I will tell the truth.'

So they had succeeded in making Mora confirm the policeman's suspicions just as they had succeeded before in making Piazza confirm the woman's tittle-tattle; the means being this time illegal torture, the other time an illegal promise of impunity. The weapons, in both cases, were taken from the armoury of jurisprudence; but were wielded by despots and deceivers.

Seeing that pain had produced its desired effect, they did not heed their victim's plea that at least he be spared further suffering. 'Speak,' they commanded.

He said: 'There was human excrement and *smojazzo*' (i.e. lye; so here is the result of their discovery of the cooking-pot on visiting Mora's house; that visit begun with such parade of authority and then cut short so cunningly) 'because that Commissioner asked me for it so as to smear on the houses; and also some of the stuff that comes from the mouths of the dead people on the carts.' And not even this last detail was Mora's own invention; for when, on a later occasion, they asked him, 'Where did you learn how to compose your unguent?' his reply was: 'People say that the Turks[11] use the stuff that comes from dead men's mouths, and then I thought I would add lye and excrement.' He might have answered: 'I have learned a good deal from my murderers—from you and the public.'

But there is something very strange about this confession; for it was not required by the terms of their questions; indeed they had expressly excluded it from the scope of this interrogation by the words quoted above: 'Do not bother us with that point; it is

[10] From Plutarch's 'Life' of Alexander.

[11] A free translation; the text runs, 'dicevano così in barbaria, che si adoperava di quella materia . . .'. [Tr.]

N

not about that that we are asking you.' If the pain compelled
Mora to lie, one might at least have expected that his lie would
correspond to their questions. He could have told them that he
was a close friend of Piazza; he could have invented some evil
motive, one that aggravated his guilt, for having torn up the
paper. But why go beyond the limit to which they were pressing
him? Was it, perhaps, that during his agony they had suggested
other ways by which he might make the agony cease? Did they
ask him other questions of which we have no record? If so, then
perhaps I myself was deceived when I said, with regard to
Piazza, that the judges had deceived the Governor when they
induced him to believe that Piazza had been interrogated about
the crime. But this suspicion—that perhaps the lie, after all, *was*
told in the actual trial, and not in that letter to the Governor—
I left unexpressed, as being insufficiently supported by the facts;
whereas here, in this matter of Mora's interrogation, it is precisely the strangeness of the fact itself which almost compels one
to suspect a further villainy to add to the many already so
evident. We find ourselves, I mean, placed between two alternatives: either to believe that Mora, without being asked, accused
himself of a horrible crime, which he had not committed, and
which would certainly bring him to a terrible death; or to hazard
the suggestion that the judges, while admitting *de facto* that
they lacked sufficient grounds for compelling Mora by torture to
confess the crime, took advantage of the torture which, on a
different pretext, they were inflicting to extort just that confession. I leave the reader to choose the alternative that seems
more probable.

The interrogation that followed the torture, like Piazza's
after the promise of impunity, was a blend, or, better, an inconsistent muddle of stupidity and guile—a barrage of uncalled for
questions together with an avoidance of matters the examination of which both common sense and jurisprudence plainly
and imperatively required.

Consider the requirements of jurisprudence. Presupposing
that 'no one commits a crime without some motive', and taking
note of the fact that 'many persons of weak character have

confessed to having committed crimes which later, after sentence has been passed on them and they are about to be executed, they have protested that they did not commit; and of which, afterwards, and too late, they have been found in fact innocent', the jurists had formulated this rule: that 'no confession is valid unless it contain a statement of the motive that led to the crime, and unless this motive be weighty and plausible in proportion to the crime in question'.[12] Now what had the miserable Mora said? Reduced to the necessity, in that interrogation, of inventing fresh stories to give support to the one which would certainly bring him to a frightful death, he said that the Commissioner had supplied him with saliva from those who had died of the plague and had suggested a criminal use of it; and that Piazza's motive in suggesting this, and his own for accepting the suggestion, was that the two of them would make a large profit as a result of the widespread illness that would ensue; Piazza in his capacity as Commissioner, Mora through the sale of his preservative. I need hardly put it to the reader whether the importance to the two men of such earnings (for which in any case Nature was already providing plentiful occasions) was proportionate to the enormity and the dangers of such a crime. But lest the reader suppose that it might have seemed so to those seventeenth-century judges, and that the motive might have seemed to them quite sufficient, let me assure him that he will soon hear the contrary from their own lips.

And there is yet another difficulty in the way of believing the motive stated by Mora; a difficulty perhaps no stronger, but more concrete and material. The reader may remember that when the Commissioner accused himself, he too stated the motive which had led him into crime, namely that the barber had said to him: 'Smear the walls ... and then come to me and you'll get a handful', or, as he said at the next examination, 'a great deal of money'. So there were two motives for the same crime; and two, not only different, but opposed and incompatible motives. The same man, according to one confession, bribes his accomplice with a large sum of money; and, according

[12] Farinacci, op. cit., Q. l, 31; lxxxi, 40; lii, 150, 152.

to the other, agrees to join in the latter's crime in the hope of a paltry profit. Let us put from our minds all we have seen hitherto—how these two motives came to be stated, how the two confessions were obtained—and consider the matter simply as it stands in the situation to which our narrative has brought the persons concerned. How then, in such a situation, would we expect judges to behave whose consciences were not perverted, darkened, and stupefied by passion? Such judges would be horrified at having (even through no fault of their own) gone so far; they would have drawn comfort from the thought that at least they had not yet taken the final, irrevocable step; would have halted at the obstacle that fortunately barred their path to the precipice; have given it all their attention, fully resolved to unravel its mystery; have exercised all possible diligence, perseverance, and subtlety in interrogating further; have looked up precedents; have not allowed the case to advance an inch until they had discovered (and would this have been so difficult?) which of the two men was lying or whether both were lying. But our judges, on receiving from Mora this reply, 'Because he would have made a good profit from the illness of so many people, and I would have made a good profit with my preservative', turned to other matters.

After this it will be enough, to say the least, to touch only in passing and partly on the rest of that interrogation. Asked 'whether there were any other accomplices in this affair', Mora replied, 'There may have been Piazza's companions, but I don't know who these are.' They objected: 'This ignorance is not plausible.' At the sound of this word, this fearful herald of torture, the unhappy man at once affirmed in the most positive way, 'They are the *foresari* and Baruello'; whose names he had heard at the previous interrogation. As for the poison, he said that he kept it in the oven, that is just where they imagined it might be. He told them how he concocted it, and ended by saying: 'I threw away what was left of it in the Vedra.' Here I cannot refrain from transcribing Verri's marginal note: 'He wouldn't, of course, have thrown this away after the imprisonment of Piazza!'

He answered various other questions they put to him on times and places and so forth, as though now the substance of the matter were quite clear and proved and only certain details were still lacking. Finally, he was tortured again in order to make his testimony valid against those named therein, in particular against the Commissioner—the man they had already tortured to give validity to a testimony which, on essential points, contradicted Mora's! No use citing legal texts or opinions here; for truly no such case was envisaged in jurisprudence.

A confession made under torture remained invalid unless it was ratified without the use of torture and in some other place, where the hideous instruments could not be seen, and on another day. This was an expedient devised by legal science to render an enforced confession, if possible, spontaneous; and to satisfy at once the promptings of common sense, which said only too clearly that words extorted by pain do not merit credence, and the Roman law which upheld torture. Indeed the jurists argued the desirability of such precautions from the Roman law itself, referring to the following strange words: 'Torture is a delicate, dangerous, and deceptive thing: for many persons have such strength of soul or body that they heed pain very little, so that it is not a means of getting the truth from them; while others are so susceptible to pain that they will tell any lie rather than suffer it.' [13] I call these strange words in a law that upheld torture; and to understand how it was that the only conclusion drawn from them in fact was that 'one cannot always believe what is said under torture', one needs to remember that originally the Roman law was a law made for slaves, and that slaves, in the degraded and corrupt pre-Christian world, could be regarded not as persons but as things; as objects therefore upon which one might carry out any experiment in order to discover the crimes of others. Later legislators, with other ends in view, made this part of the law apply also to free men; which is one example and a notable one, if by no means unique, of how laws may acquire a wider application than they had at first and, so extended, outlast their origins.

[13] *Digest*, XLVIII, tit. 18, ll. 1, 23.

The next day then, in observance of this formality, the judges summoned Mora again. But being now incapable of proceeding without guile, without seeking some advantage, without insinuations, instead of simply asking him whether he meant to ratify his confession, they asked: 'Have you anything to add to what you confessed yesterday after the torture?' Thus they precluded all doubt: jurisprudence required that the confession made under torture should now be open to further question; but they took its truth for granted, only asking that it be added to.

But in the meantime, whether prompted by the sense of his own innocence, or by horror of the death penalty, or by the thought of his wife and children, Mora seems to have regained some hope of bearing fresh tortures more bravely; for his reply was: 'No, my Lord, I have nothing to add; rather, something to subtract.' So they had to ask him what this was. Then he spoke out more frankly, as it were plucking up courage: 'That unguent I talked about, I didn't make it at all; I only said I did because of the torture.' Immediately they threatened him with a repetition of the torture; and this (apart from other flagrant irregularities) without taking account of Mora's contradiction of Piazza, that is without being themselves prepared to say whether the new torture would be on account of Mora's confession or of the Commissioner's deposition; whether inflicted as on an accomplice or as on the chief criminal; for a crime committed at another's instigation or for one which the sufferer himself had instigated; for a crime for which Mora had been willing to pay lavishly, or for one which he had hoped would yield him a pittance.

To this threat he replied as before: 'I repeat; what I said yesterday is completely untrue; I said it because of the torture'; and then: 'Your Lordships, let me say a *Hail Mary,* and then I will do what God shows me I ought to do'; and he knelt down before an image of the Crucified who would one day judge his judges. After a little he got up and, on their urging him to ratify his confession, said, 'In conscience, it isn't true.' They had the unhappy man taken at once to the torture-chamber and bound,

ordering the extra cruelty of the rope.[14] He then said: 'Your
Lordships need not torture me again. My confession was true
and I confirm it.' Unbound and taken back to the other room,
he once more said, 'It is utterly untrue.' So back to the torture-
room where again he said what they wanted; and now, the
pain having burnt away what little courage was left in him, he
upheld what he had said under torture, declaring himself ready
to ratify his confession; he did not even want them to read it to
him. But to this they would not consent—scrupulously respect-
ing a formality which now meant nothing, while violating
greater laws. So they read out the report of the interrogation,
and he said, 'It is all true.'

After this, persisting in their method of taking no step in the
inquiry, of facing no difficulty, except after using torture (a
procedure expressly forbidden in the law itself and one that
even Diocletian and Maximian had tried to suppress) they at
last thought of asking him whether he had had any purpose
other than profit in selling his preservative. 'As far as I know,'
he replied, 'I have no other purpose.'

'As far as I know'! Who else, if not he, could know his own
private thoughts? And yet these strange words were fitting in
the circumstances; no others that the wretched man might
have used could have better expressed his self-abdication, so
to call it, at that moment; his being ready to say yes and then
no, and have only such knowledge, and all such knowledge,
as suited the pleasure of those who had power to make him
suffer.

They continued to press him, saying: 'It is not very plausible
that you and the Commissioner should have planned, by smearing the gates, to spread death and destruction in the city, simply
in order that he should find work and you should sell your
preservative; therefore, tell us why and wherefore you two
started on this course of action for so trivial a motive.'

Ah, so now it seems implausible! So they had threatened and
repeatedly tortured him to make him ratify an implausibility!
What I said above can be repeated here: 'a remark much to the

[14] See p. 139.

point, but made too late'; the circumstances are so similar, they call for the same comment. Just as it had not occurred to these men that there was anything implausible in Piazza's deposition until, as a result of it, they had Mora in prison; so now they see nothing implausible in the latter's confession until after forcing him to ratify it and so obtaining the instrument they needed for his condemnation. Are we really to believe that this was the first time they noticed the implausibility? If so, how are we to explain, how shall we find words to describe, their subsequent upholding of the validity of the confession? Did Mora perhaps give them a more satisfying answer than Piazza had given? Here is Mora's answer: 'If the Commissioner doesn't know, I don't know; but he must know, and your Lordships will get the truth from him, because he started it all.' And clearly, the motive of all this passing on the principal guilt from each to the other and back again was not so much that each wanted to appear less guilty, as that they both wanted to be rid of the task of explaining things which could not be explained.

After that answer of Mora's they gave him to understand that 'having concocted the aforesaid unguent, in agreement with the said Commissioner, and having then given it to the latter to be smeared on the walls of houses (in the mode and manner stated by both in their depositions) in order to make people die (this purpose having been confessed by the said Commissioner), he had incurred the guilt of actively intending the death of people and thus had become liable to the penalties imposed by the law on whomsoever so intends and endeavours'.

To recapitulate. The judges ask Mora: How is it that you—the two of you together—decided to commit this particular crime for this particular motive? Mora answers: The Commissioner certainly knows why we decided; why he did and why I did: ask him. He refers them to another man for an explanation of an interior event in his own mind; that they might understand how a motive was sufficient to bring him, inwardly, to a decision. And to what other man? To a man who did not admit this particular motive, since he attributed the crime to a wholly different cause. And the judges conclude that the difficulty is solved; that the crime confessed by Mora has become plausible; so much so that they find him guilty of it.

Whatever brought them to see implausibility in such a motive, it was not ignorance; and whatever led them to treat in this way the rules and prescriptions of jurisprudence, it was not jurisprudence.

CHAPTER FIVE

IMPUNITY and torture had brought to light two stories; and while, for such judges as those, this sufficed to justify two sentences of guilt, nevertheless, as we shall now see, they did all they could to blend the two stories into one; and, all things considered, not without success. Finally, and in conclusion, we shall see them by their actions professing themselves convinced of the truth of this eventual single story.

The Senate confirmed and amplified the decision of its delegates. 'Having taken note of what has come to light from the confession of Giangiacomo Mora; having considered and compared the antecedent facts and all the circumstances [except that for one and the same crime there were two principal agents; two different causes; two different arrangements of the facts], the Senate ordered that the said Mora . . . be once more diligently examined, but without torture, to make him explain more clearly the things he has confessed, and to obtain from him the names of the other agents, instruments, and accomplices of the crime; and, this examination terminated, that he be pronounced guilty (after all the facts of the case are recounted) of having concocted the poisonous unguent and given it to Guglielmo Piazza; and that he be allowed three days to prepare his defence. And with regard to Piazza, let him be asked whether he has anything to add to his confession, this having been found incomplete; and in the event of his having nothing to add, let him be pronounced guilty of having spread abroad the said unguent; and be granted the same time for his defence.' That is to say: Do your best to get all you can out of both men, and in any case let them both be declared guilty, each on his own confession, in spite of the confessions being contradictory.

They began with Piazza, and on the same day. He had nothing to add and did not know that *they* had something; he had not, perhaps, foreseen that in accusing an innocent he was creating an accuser. They asked him why in his deposition he had not said that he had given the barber saliva from persons dead of the plague with which to make the unguent. 'I didn't give him anything,' was his answer; as though those who had believed his lies had to believe him when telling the truth. After more twists and turns of question and answer they declared that 'since you have not told the whole truth, as you promised to do, you cannot and should not any longer enjoy the impunity we promised you'. At once he said: 'My Lord, it is true that the barber came and asked me to get him some of that stuff, and I did bring him some, for making the unguent.' He hoped to save his impunity by admitting everything. Then, either to curry yet more favour or simply to gain time, he added that the money promised him by the barber was to have come from 'a great person', and that he learned this from the barber himself, but had never been able to make the latter say who the person was. He had not had time to think of a name.

So they asked Mora the next day; and probably the poor fellow would have thought up some name or other, as best he could, if they had tortured him. But, as we have seen, the Senate had ruled out torture this time—evidently to make the new ratification they desired of his previous confession seem less blatantly enforced. Hence, when asked 'whether you took the first step in approaching the Commissioner . . . and promised him a lot of money', Mora answered, 'No, my Lord; and where does your Lordship think I could have found this lot of money?' They might in fact have remembered that when Mora's house was thoroughly searched on the day of his arrest the entire treasure found in it had been 'a *baslotto* (jar) containing five *parpagliole* (twelve and a half *soldi*)'. Asked about the 'great person', he replied, 'Your Lordship wants the simple truth, and this I gave you when I was tortured, and in fact a bit more.'

Neither of the two abstracts of the trial mention that Mora ratified his previous confession; but if, as seems likely, they made him in fact do so, then these words of his amounted to a protest, the force of which he himself did not perhaps realize but which they must have realized. In any case it had always been the common teaching of the jurists, from Bartolo and even before him, from the authors of the Gloss, down to Farinacci, it had become a sort of axiom of jurisprudence, that 'a confession made under torture inflicted on grounds of legally insufficient evidence is null and void and remains so even if later ratified a thousand times without the use of torture': *etiam quod millies sponte sit ratificata.*[1]

After that, Mora and Piazza received the 'publication', as it was called, of the case (that is to say, its acts were communicated to them) and they were allowed two days in which to prepare their defence—why one less than the Senate had decreed is not clear. Each man was assigned an official advocate; but the one assigned to Mora declined the task. Verri suggests that this refusal was due to a cause which unfortunately would not have been unlikely in the circumstances: 'Popular fury,' he says, 'had reached such a pitch that to defend the unhappy victim was regarded as wicked and dishonourable.' However, the true cause is stated in the printed abstract which Verri could not have seen; but it is hardly less strange and, from one point of view, still more deplorable. It was on the same day, 2 July, that the lawyer Mauri was called upon to undertake Mora's defence; but he said, 'I cannot accept this responsibility, first because I am a criminal lawyer and so do not undertake defences, and also because I am neither a procurator nor a barrister: I am quite willing to go and speak with him, as a favour, but I will not undertake his defence.' So to a man who now stood in the shadow of death (and what a death! what manner of death!), a man without connexions or education, and who could turn nowhere for help except to them, who had to

[1] Farinacci, op. cit., Q. xxxvii 110.

depend on them entirely, to this man they gave a defender who lacked certain essential qualifications for the task and had some that were incompatible with it! Even supposing no malice was involved, what irresponsibility! And it was left to a subordinate to recall them to respect for the most obvious and most binding rules of procedure.

Mauri returned and said: 'I have been with Mora and he told me frankly that he had done no wrong and that he said what he did because of the tortures; and when I told him frankly that I neither wished nor was able to undertake his defence, he said that he hoped that at least the Lord President would deign to provide him with an advocate and not permit that he should die undefended.' For such favours, with such words, innocence begged from injustice! They gave him in fact another advocate.

The one assigned to Piazza 'entered and asked to be shown his client's case; they gave it him and he read it'. Was this as far as they would go to oblige the defence? Not always; for Padilla's counsel (Padilla, as we shall presently see, was to represent in flesh and blood that vaguely indicated 'great person') had the records of the whole case at his disposal; thus being able to make that copy of a substantial part of it which has survived for our information.

When the period fixed had elapsed the two poor wretches begged for more time. The Senate granted them 'the whole of the day following and no more', *et non ultra*. Padilla's defence was given three hearings: the first part, on 24 July 1631, was heard 'without prejudice to the rest being heard later'; the next was on 13 April 1632; the last on 10 May of the same year, which was about two years after Padilla's arrest. For an innocent man the slowness of this procedure must have been painful, but compared with the haste used with Piazza and Mora—no lingering for them except in the manner of their death—it represented an outrageous partiality.

However, this new product of Piazza's imagination held up the execution of the death-sentence for some days—days full of deceptive hopes but also of fresh tortures and fresh calumnies.

The Auditor of the Sanità was commissioned to hear a new deposition from Piazza, but secretly and with no notary present; and this time it was Piazza, through his counsel, who asked to be heard, giving out that he had something further to reveal about the 'great person'. Very likely he thought that if he could succeed in drawing some really big fish into this net, which was so easy to enter and so hard to get out of, the big fish, in its struggle to escape, would tear such a rent in the net that the little fish too could then slip through the hole along with it. And since among the many and various conjectures that were circulating in the city as to those responsible for that disastrous fouling of the walls on 18 May (for the angry excitement, the terrors and accusations caused by this incident were to a large extent themselves the cause of the violence employed by the judiciary, so that those who really did foul the walls were guilty of infinitely more evil than they knew) it was being rumoured that Spanish officers had done it, our miserable story-teller found something to hand that he could clutch at. Probably what caused Piazza to name Padilla in particular was (unless indeed the latter was the only Spanish officer he knew even by name) the fact that Padilla was the son of the governor of the Castle and so had a natural protector who, if he came to his son's assistance, could upset the whole trial. After the interview with the Auditor Piazza was summoned before the judges to ratify his new deposition. In his other deposition he had said that the barber refused to name the 'great person'. But now he maintained the contrary; and in order somehow or other to soften the contradiction, he said that Mora had not given him the name immediately: 'In the end, after four or five days, he said that this great man was someone or other Di Padiglia. I don't remember the Christian name although he told me it. I do know and I remember quite clearly that he said that the man was son of the Lord Governor of the Castle of Milan.' He did not, however, say that he had received money from the barber —protesting indeed that he did not even know whether the latter had had any from Padilla.

Piazza was made to sign this deposition, and then immediately the Auditor was sent off with it to the Governor. This the records tell us; and we can safely presume that the Auditor was told to ask the Governor whether, if need be, he would allow Padilla—who was a cavalry captain and at this time serving with the army near Monferrato—to be handed over to the civil authorities. The Auditor came back; Piazza was at once made to ratify his confession afresh; then off went the Auditor again, this time to the unhappy Mora, who, being pressed to say that he had promised Piazza money and told him that he (Mora) had the backing of a 'great person', whose name he had finally revealed to the Commissioner, replied: 'Before God it's all false; and if I could, I would tell him so, as my conscience bears me witness.' So a new confrontation of the two men was arranged, in which Piazza was asked if it was true that Mora had promised him money, 'declaring that he was acting entirely under the orders and direction of Padiglia, son of the Lord Governor of the Castle of Milan'. On this Padilla's counsel very rightly observes that in this way, 'under the pretext of a confrontation', they were letting Mora know 'what they wanted him to say'. Without, in fact, this or some similar device they could certainly never have got Mora to name Padilla. Torture could make him a liar all right, but not a magician.

Piazza maintained what he had said in his deposition. 'You dare to say this?' cried Mora. 'Yes, I do dare to say it, it is true,' answered the other, shamelessly; 'and it's because of you that I've got into this hole, and you know very well what you said to me at the door of your shop.' Mora, who had perhaps hoped that, with the help of his defending counsel, his innocence would be made clear to all, and who now foresaw new tortures to extort a new confession from him, had not even the strength once again to oppose lies with the truth. He only said: '*Pazienza!* It is for you that I shall die.'

And in fact, once Piazza was taken away (which was done immediately) they warned Mora that 'now at last he must tell the truth'; and as soon as he replied, 'My Lord, I have told the truth,' they threatened torture; 'to be inflicted without prejudice to whatever is already proved and confessed'. It was the usual formula; but their using it at this point shows the degree to which their intense desire to find a culprit had deprived them of the capacity to reflect. How on earth could Mora's confession that he had led Piazza into crime with the promise of money from Padilla *not* prejudice his confession that he had let himself be led into it by Piazza in the hope of making a profit from his preservative?

Put to the torture, he at once confirmed everything that the Commissioner had said; and, this not satisfying the judges, added that Padilla had in fact suggested that he make 'an unguent to smear on the doors and bolts', and promised him all the money he might ask for and given him all the money he wanted.

We for our part, of course, who have no fear of unguents or fury against their users, nor around us the fury of others demanding satisfaction, we can easily and clearly see how such a confession took place and what caused it. But if we needed light on the matter, we should have it from the lips of him who confessed. Among the many statements of witnesses which Padilla's counsel managed to collect there is one by a Captain Sebastiano Gorini, who happened at that time (we do not know why) to be imprisoned in the same building as Mora and who often spoke with one of the servants of the Auditor of the Sanità, who had been made the unhappy man's jailer. His testimony was as follows: 'This servant said to me one day, just after the barber had been brought back from an interrogation: "Sir, you don't know what the barber has said to me just now; he said that when they examined him he brought out the name of Don Giovanni, son of the Lord Governor of the Castle!" And I was amazed to hear this and said, "Is it true?" And the servant replied that it was true, but that it was also true that the barber protested that he could not remember whether he had ever even spoken to a Spaniard, and that if they had shown him this Don Giovanni he wouldn't even have recognized him. And the servant went on to say, "So I said to him, why then did you give his name?" And the barber replied that he had given it because he heard it from his examiners, and that he answered them according to whatever he heard them say or what they put into his mouth.' This, thank God, is good evidence in favour of Padilla. But are we to believe that the judges who had put Mora, or allowed him to be put, in charge of a servant of that extremely alert and inquisitive Auditor, that they only came to know what Mora had said (in words that ring so true, so desperately sincere, compared with the absurdities which pain had wrung from him only a moment before) so much later and from the accidental testimony of a witness at Padilla's trial?

And because it seemed strange even to the judges—among so much else that was strange—that a Milanese barber and a Spanish cavalier should have had such dealings with one another, they asked him who had served as the link between them; and Mora at first only said, 'one of his men', with such and such an appearance and dress: but then, they insisting on giving a name, he said, 'Don Pietro di Saragoza'. And certainly this person, at any rate, was imaginary. Later—after Mora's execution of course—a thorough and persistent inquiry was undertaken: soldiers and officers were interrogated, including even Don Francesco de Vargas, the successor to Padilla's father as Governor of the Castle of Milan. No one had ever heard of that Don Pietro. But in the end a man was found in the city prison, awaiting trial for theft, whose name was Pietro Verdeno and who had been born in Saragossa. Being questioned, he said that he had been in Naples at the time: tortured, he said the same thing. People then dropped the subject of Don Pietro of Saragossa.

Harried by more and more questions, Mora went on to say that he had then put his proposal to the Commissioner; who in his turn had received money for the same purpose 'from someone—I don't know his name'. Of course he didn't know it; but the judges wanted to know: so the poor wretch was tortured again and this time unfortunately brought out the name of a real person, a banker called Giulio Sanguinetti: 'the first name to occur to one inventing in agony'.[2]

[2] Livy, *History of Rome*, XXIV, 5.

Piazza, who had hitherto steadily denied having received any money now, being questioned again, at once said that he had received some (the reader may have a better memory than the judges had, and so be able to recall that when the police visited Piazza's house they found even less money than in Mora's, that is none at all). He had received it, he said, from a banker; and since the judges had not given him Sanguinetti's name, he gave them another: Girolamo Turcone. And Turcone and Sanguinetti and various subordinates of theirs were duly arrested, questioned, and tortured; but as they stoutly persisted in denying the charge they were finally let go.

On 21 July the supplementary acts of the trial, as from its resumption, were communicated to Piazza and Mora, and they were allowed another two days to prepare their defence. This time both chose their own advocates, probably on the advice of those originally assigned to them *ex officio*. On the 23rd Padilla was arrested; that is, as we know from the defence at his trial, Padilla was informed by the Commissioner to the cavalry that Spinola had given orders that he should go to the castle of Pomate and give himself up; which he did. His father, as we know from the same source, petitioned, through his lieutenant and his secretary, that the execution of the sentence on Piazza and Mora be suspended until they had been confronted with Don Juan. The answer sent back to him was: 'No suspension is possible because of the excited state of the public' (so for once they mention it, the *civium ardor prava jubentium*:[3] and it was only now that they could do so without confessing a vile and vicious compliancy; now that the only question was, not what their judgement would be, but when it would be carried out. But had the public only now begun to show excitement? Or had the judges only now begun to heed its clamour?) . . . 'but in any case the Lord Don Francisco need not trouble himself, for nothing said by such disreputable persons as those two could possibly cast a slur on the reputation of Don Juan.' Yet what the disreputable persons had said against each other had counted! And how often had the judges called it 'the

[3] Horace, *Odes*, III, 3.

O

truth'! And when they passed sentence they decreed that after the publication of the sentence both men should be tortured again to bring to light their accomplices! And what the pair then confessed led to further tortures, and so to more confessions and so to more executions—and, as though this were not enough, to executions where there had been no confession.

'And so,' said the above-mentioned secretary, concluding his deposition, 'we returned to the Lord Governor of the Castle and reported all that had happened: and he said no more, but was depressed and humiliated; so much so that after a few days he died.'

By the terms of the hellish sentence passed on them, Piazza and Mora were to be taken in a cart to the place of execution, being torn with red-hot pincers on the way; their right hands cut off in front of Mora's shop; their bones broken on the wheel; and, while they were still alive, their bodies twisted into the wheel and lifted from the ground; and after six hours, their throats to be cut, their corpses burned and the ashes thrown into the river. Mora's house was to be demolished and in the space where it had stood a column erected, to be called the 'Column of Infamy'; it being forbidden ever to build on that spot again. And if anything could add to the horror and indignation and pity that such a sentence arouses in us, it would be to hear the two victims, after being informed of it, renewing and even amplifying their confessions; still driven by the same forces which had extorted these: the hope, still not extinguished, of escaping death, and such a death; the violence of the tortures already suffered, which that frightful sentence no doubt made appear, by comparison, almost lenient, but also as things still present and avoidable; these motives made them not only repeat their former lies but extend them by accusing yet more people. Thus did the judges succeed, with their promise of impunity and their torture, not only in bringing innocent men to a horrible death, but also, so far as the event depended on them, in making those innocent men die guilty.

It is a relief to learn, however, from the records of the defence in Padilla's trial, that Piazza and Mora, once they were perfectly sure that they were to die and would have to answer no more questions, protested their own innocence and that of the persons accused by them. We know this through that Captain Gorini mentioned above. He deposed that, happening to find himself close to the chapel in which Piazza had been put, he heard the latter 'crying out and saying that his death was a crime, and that he was being murdered, and that they had broken their word to him'; and that he refused the ministrations of the two Capuchin friars who had come to help him to die as a Christian. 'And this,' added Gorini, 'is how I came into it—that I saw that he still had some hope that they would have to withdraw the case against him . . . and so I went to the Commissioner, thinking it would be an act of charity if I could persuade him to get ready to die well, in the grace of God; as in fact I can say that I did. Because the Fathers had not touched the point that really mattered, but I did so; which was when I assured him that I had never known or ever heard of an instance of the Senate's withdrawing a case after sentence of condemnation had been passed. . . . So at last I was able to calm him . . . and after he had calmed down, he sighed for a while and then said that he had unjustly given the names of many innocent persons.' And in fact both Piazza and Mora caused a formal retractation to be written down, by the frairs attending on them, of all the accusations which pain or hope had extorted from them. And both of them endured that long death-agony, that series and variety of agonies with a courage which—in men whom pain and the fear of death had so often overcome; in men who were dying as victims, not of some great cause, but of petty accidents and foolish errors and cheap and base deceits; in men who, even when branded with ill fame, remained lowly humble folk who had nothing to oppose to the execration of the public except the consciousness of an ordinary unheroic innocence, which no one believed in and which they themselves had repeatedly denied; in men (it hurts to think of this, but how can one put away the thought?) who had families, wives, and children—would be incomprehensible if one did not know that it sprang from resignation; from that gift, I mean, which makes one able to see in the injustice of men the justice of God, and in all punishments, whatever they may be, a pledge, not of pardon merely, but of reward. Both men continued ceaselessly, to the end, and on the wheel itself, to say that they accepted death as a punishment for their sins—their real sins. To accept what cannot be refused! Meaningless words, perhaps, for one who considers things only in their material effects; but of a deep and clear meaning for one who considers, or without considering understands, that that which may be the most difficult part of any deliberation, and is always the most important, the mind's judgement and the movement of the will, is equally difficult and equally important whether the issue depends upon it or not; whether one is assenting to something done or choosing to do it.

Those protestations of innocence might have struck fear into the consciences of the judges; they could also rouse them to anger. Unfortunately the judges succeeded in getting them in part contradicted, and this in the manner that would have been the most decisive possible had it not been the most illusory; namely, by making many of those persons whom the protestations had so authoritatively exculpated accuse themselves on their own account. Over these further trials, however, as the reader has already been notified, I will pass quickly and selectively, in order to come to that of Padilla—to the trial, that is, which, as it is the principal one in view of the eminence of the person accused, so, by reason of the form it took and of its result, it represents a touchstone by which to judge of all the others.

CHAPTER SIX

THE two scissor-grinders who had had the misfortune to be mentioned by Piazza, and later by Mora, had been in prison since 27 June, but had never been confronted with either of their accusers. Nor were they even judicially examined before the latters' execution, which was on 1 August. On the 11th of that month the father, Girolamo Migliavacca, was interrogated; and the following day tortured, on the usual pretext of having given contradictory and implausible answers. Under torture Girolamo confessed; that is, he made up a story; and did so, like Piazza, by distorting a real fact (both resembling spiders that stick the ends of their thread on to something solid and then work away in the air). Among Girolamo's things the police had found a phial containing an opiate, given him, indeed composed in his own house, by his friend Baruello; and this, he now declared, 'was an unguent intended to kill people', made of matter extracted from toads and snakes, together with 'certain powders—I don't know what *they* are'. Beside Baruello, he named another fairly well-known person; and, as the chief instigator, Padilla. The judges would have liked to connect this story with that of the two men they had murdered; so they tried to make Girolamo say that he had received 'unguent and money' from Piazza and Mora. Had he simply denied this, they had torture in reserve; but he forestalled them with these remarkable words: 'No my Lord, that is not true; but if you torture me for denying it, I shall have to say it is true, although it isn't.' This checked them: they could not, without too obviously making a farce of justice and humanity, appear to try out a means after being so solemnly assured that its effect was guaranteed in advance.

Migliavacca was condemned to the same death as his accusers. After hearing the sentence he was tortured again, and came out with fresh accusations—of another banker and of some other people. In the prison chapel and on the scaffold he retracted everything.

He was a shady character, as Piazza and Mora had said; and if this had been all they said about him, enough came out in the trial to have acquitted them of slander. But his son Gaspare they did slander, even in this respect. Gaspare was indeed, as the records show, guilty of an offence; but it was one that he himself admitted; and at a time and in a manner such as almost to constitute a proof of the purity and integrity of his entire life. To the end, under torture and face to face with death, he spoke, not just like a brave man but like a martyr. After they had failed to force him to calumniate either himself or others, they sentenced him (on what pretexts it is impossible to say) as proven guilty; and having told him of the sentence, went on to the usual questions, as to whether he had committed other crimes and as to who had been his associates in that for which he was condemned. To the first question Gaspare replied: 'I have not committed this or any other crime. And I am to die because once in anger I punched a man in the eye.' And to the second: 'I have had no associates, because I have minded my own business; and in any case, if I didn't commit the crime, I couldn't have had associates.' Threatened with torture, he said: 'Your Lordships can do as you please, because I will never say I have done what I didn't do; and I will never damn my own soul; I would far rather suffer three or four hours' pain than go to Hell to suffer eternally.' Put to the torture, he cried out at the first shock: 'Ah God! I've done nothing: you're murdering me.' Then he added: 'These pains will be over quickly, but the next world goes on forever.' The torture was intensified by degrees, up to the maximum degree; at every stage they pressed him the harder to tell the truth; and his reply was always the same: 'I have told it already. I want to save my soul. I will not have a lie on my conscience; I have done nothing.'

At this point one cannot help reflecting that if similar sentiments had inspired Piazza, poor Mora would have remained undisturbed in his shop and his home; and this young man also, more worthy of admiration than compassion, and many other innocent people would never have been troubled by even a thought of the dreadful fate they had escaped. And Piazza himself—who knows? For certainly to have condemned him when he had confessed nothing, simply on the evidence that we have seen, and when, in default of others' confessions, the crime itself would have remained the merest conjecture, to do this the judges would have had to violate even more brazenly and boldly every principle of justice and every rule of law. At all events, at least they could not have condemned him to the additional horror of making him suffer in company with one the sight of whom must have caused him continually to say to himself: I brought him to this! The root cause, then, of such horrors was the weakness. . . . But no! It was the obstinate rage and perfidy of those who, counting it as a disaster and a defeat to discover no culprits, tempted that weakness with an illegal and deceitful promise.

In an earlier chapter I quoted the official decree by which a promise similar to that made to Mora was made to Baruello; and said in passing that I wished to show how the judges' attitudes differed in the two cases. It is chiefly for this reason that the wretched Baruello's story must now be briefly told. As we have seen, he had been accused—without proof—first by Piazza, of being Mora's associate, and then by Mora, of being Piazza's; and then, by both, of having been paid to spread abroad an unguent made by Mora out of muck and worse (and on this point the two witnesses had at first protested ignorance); and then, by Girolamo Migliavacca, of having himself concocted some out of other stuff worse than muck: and now, put on trial for all these things at once, as though they constituted a single charge, Baruello denied everything and stood up stoutly to the ensuing torture. But while his case was still pending, a priest (another of the witnesses to be cited in Padilla's defence), at the request of a relative of Baruello, spoke on the latter's behalf to a barrister employed by the Senate. In due time this official informed the priest that Baruello had been sentenced to death, with all the attendant butchery, but that, at the same time, 'the Senate was prepared to obtain a promise of impunity for him from His Excellency'. The priest meanwhile must go to Baruello and try to persuade him to make a clean breast of everything, 'because the Senate wants to get to the bottom of this affair, and thinks it can obtain the truth from Baruello'. After condemning him to death! And after the execution of Piazza and Mora!

Baruello, on hearing the dire news and the accompanying proposal, said: 'Then are they going to treat me as they treated the Commissioner?' But, being assured by the priest that the promise seemed to be sincere, he launched into the following story. So-and-so (now dead) had taken him to see the barber. The latter, lifting a curtain that hung by the wall of the room and concealed a door, then led Baruello into a large chamber where many persons were seated, among whom was Padilla. The priest, who was not obliged to find culprits, thought this all rather strange; and interrupted the tale, warning Baruello that he ought to take care not to lose his soul along with his body; and then took his leave. Baruello accepted the Senate's impunity and revised his story; and, being brought before the judges on 11 September, informed them that a certain fencing-master (unfortunately alive) had told him that there was a good chance of becoming rich if one was prepared to do a service to Padilla; and that the fencing-master had then taken him to the square in front of the Castle, where they found Padilla waiting with some other men. Padilla had at once invited him to join those who worked under his orders, smearing the city walls for the purpose of avenging the insults offered to Don Gonzalez de Cordova on the occasion of his departure from Milan; and then had given Baruello money and a little jar of the deadly unguent.

To say that this story (of which I give only the beginning) was implausible would be an abuse of language; it was all a tissue of absurdities, as the reader can see from the sample offered him. However, even the judges found implausibilities in it; and, what is more, inconsistencies. Hence, after various questions followed by answers involving ever new complications, they said to him: 'You must express yourself more clearly if we are to derive any clear information from your story.' On this Baruello—whether it was that he thought of a trick to get him out of the difficulty, or really suffered a temporary derangement (understandable in the circumstances)—began to tremble and writhe, and shout for help, and roll about on the floor, and try to hide under a table. They had him exorcized and calmed down, and then bade him begin again. So he started another tale, this time bringing in witches and magic circles and incantations and the Devil, whom he said he had taken as his lord and master. Enough for us to note that he had not said these things before; and that *inter alia* he now took back what he had said about a revenge for an offence given to Don Gonzalez, asserting instead that Padilla's aim was to make himself master of Milan; and that Padilla had promised him, Baruello, a very high place in the new régime. After various questions the interrogation, if such it can be called, was declared closed. It was later followed by three more, in which, on their telling him that this assertion of his was not plausible or that one not credible, Baruello either replied that he had lied the first time or else invented some other explanation. And when at least five times they put it to him that, according to Migliavacca's deposition, he had himself given the unguent to as many people, for them to spread around the city, whereas in his own deposition these persons were not mentioned, his answer every time was that this was not true; and every time the judges changed the subject. The reader who remembers how, in Piazza's case, at the very first implausibility which the judges thought fit to find in his deposition they threatened to withdraw his impunity; and how, on Piazza's first adding a word to that deposition, when Mora made his first allegation against him and he denied it, they did in fact withdraw it; and the reader who remembers all this will at any rate now see clearly—if the point escaped him before—what an advantage it was to the judges to have played that trick on the Governor of taking it on themselves to concede the impunity without obtaining his authorization: they could make a purely verbal, and void, promise to Piazza. For he had to be the first victim sacrificed to the public's fury and their own.

Do I mean then that it would have been just to maintain that promise of impunity? God forbid! That would be as good as saying that Piazza's testimony was true. I mean only that just as the promise of impunity had been an illegality, so its withdrawal was a brutal intimidation; and that the illegality led straight to the brutality. But then, as I have said before, the judges were not capable of justice so long as they kept to the path they had chosen; their only chance would have been to turn back while there was yet time. They had had no more moral right (quite apart from legal authority) to sell that impunity to Piazza than a robber has to concede life to a man on the road, when his simple duty is to leave the man alone. That impunity was an injustice added to unjust torturing; both the one and the other being expedients which the judges deliberately adopted and applied in preference to the course of action that the law itself, let alone reason or justice or charity, required of them—namely, to ascertain the true facts of the case; have these explained to the two women who had, rightly or wrongly, called attention to them; and to the man they had, rightly or wrongly, accused; and confront the latter with his accusers.

Nothing came of the impunity promised to Baruello, because he died of the plague on 18 September; the day after he had been confronted with the fencing-master, Carlo Vedano, and had repeated, shamelessly, his accusations. But when he felt that his end was near he said to a fellow-prisoner who was nursing him (and who was to be another of Padilla's witnesses): 'Do me the kindness of telling the Lord Magistrate that all those I have accused, I accused unjustly. And it is not true that I had money from the son of the Governor of the Castle. . . . I'm going to die of this sickness, and I beg those whom I have unjustly accused to forgive me. And please tell the Lord Magistrate this; so I may die in peace.' 'And I,' added the witness, 'went and told the Lord Magistrate what Baruello had said to me.'

This retractation was able to help Padilla; but Vedano, who so far had been mentioned only by Baruello, was very fiercely tortured that same day. He had the strength to endure it without confessing anything; and was then left alone (in prison, of course) until the middle of the following January. He alone of all these little people had some acquaintance with Padilla, having fenced with him twice at the Castle—which clearly was why it occurred to Baruello to allot him a part in his story. However, Baruello had not accused Vedano of concocting or spreading or distributing deadly unguents; but only of being go-between between him and Padilla. Hence the judges could

not condemn Vedano as guilty without pre-judging that gentleman's case; which was probably what saved him. He was not
questioned again until after the first interrogation of Padilla;
and the latter's acquittal involved his own.

On 10 January 1631 Padilla, who had been transferred to
the castle of Pizzighettone, was brought thence to Milan and
put in the prison of the Chief of Police. His interrogation took
place on the same day; and if concrete proof were needed to
assure us that even those judges were capable of interrogating
without guile or lies or bullying; of not seeing implausibilities
where there were none; of being satisfied with a reasonable
answer; of allowing, even when poisonous unguents were in
question, that an accused man could tell the truth, even when
he said 'no'; the proof is to be seen in this interrogation of
Padilla and the two that followed it.

Of those who had named Padilla in their depositions, only
Mora and Baruello claimed to have spoken with him; and
both had dated their conversations, the former vaguely, the
latter more precisely. So the judges began by asking Padilla
when he had joined his regiment in the field: he told them the
day. The place from which he had gone there? Milan. Had he
returned to Milan in the meantime? Once only; and only for
one day, which Padilla specified with the same precision. It did
not agree with either of the periods invented by the unhappy
pair. Then they asked him, courteously, using no threats, 'to try
to remember' whether he had been in Milan on such-and-such
a day or another day; and each time he answered 'no', referring
back to his first reply. Then they came to persons and places.
Did he know a gunner called Fontana? (This man, who was
father-in-law to Vedano, had been named by Baruello as one
of those present at his first encounter with Padilla.) Padilla
replied that he did. Did he know Vedano? 'Yes' again. Did he
know the Via Vedra de' Cittadini and the inn of the Six Thieves
(whither Padilla had come, said Mora, accompanied by Don
Pedro of Saragossa, to put to him his proposal about spreading
poison in the city)? Padilla answered that he knew neither the
street nor the inn—not even by name. They asked him about

Don Pedro of Saragossa. Padilla did not know him; indeed he could not have known him. They asked him about two men wearing clothes of a French cut and about another dressed as a priest; persons whom Baruello had said had come with Padilla to the meeting in the square in front of the Castle. Padilla had no idea of whom they were speaking.

At the second interrogation, on the last day of January, they asked him about his relations with Mora, Migliavacca, and Baruello—the meetings, the money given, the promises; but without as yet mentioning the general plan with which these details were connected. Padilla answered that he had never had anything to do with the men in question; they were not even names to him; and repeated that he was out of Milan at the times referred to.

After more than three months spent in inquiries which, naturally, were quite fruitless, the Senate decreed that Padilla be tried for the crime of which he stood accused, be supplied with the facts of the case and an account of the trial, and given a fixed time in which to prepare his defence. This order led to a third, and last, interrogation on 22 May. After various questions touching all the points on which he was accused—questions Padilla invariably answered in the negative and, for the most part, curtly—they came to 'the facts of the case', that is to say, they threw in his face the crazy story, or rather stories, they had collected. And first, that he, the accused, had told Mora, the barber, 'near the inn called the Six Thieves, to make an unguent . . . and take the said unguent and go and smear it on the walls', and that he had paid Mora well for his trouble; and that later Don Pedro of Saragossa, acting under his orders, had sent the barber to such and such bankers to cash still more money on his account. But this tale is rational compared with the other one: namely, that the accused, having summoned Baruello to the square in front of the Castle, had said to him there: 'Good morning, Signor Baruello, I have been wanting to speak with you for a long time now'; and after various other compliments, had given Baruello twenty-five Venetian ducats and a jar of unguent, telling him that this stuff was made in Milan but that it wasn't quite suitable for its purpose, and that what was needed was to 'take some *ghezzi* and *zatti*' (lizards and toads) and 'some white wine', and put it all in a saucepan and 'boil it *a concio a concio* [very slowly] so that those animals should die in a fury'. Moreover a priest, 'called "the Frenchman" by the said Baruello' and who had come in the accused's company, had caused to appear 'one in the form of a man and dressed like *Pantalone*', and had made Baruello acknowledge the apparition as his lord; and on its vanishing, Baruello had asked the accused who it was and the accused had replied that it was the Devil. And that on another occasion the accused had given Baruello more money, and promised to make him an officer in his body-guard, on condition that he served him well.

At this point Verri (so much may exclusive attachment to one point of view cause the noblest minds to err, even about things they really know) concludes thus: 'Such was the series of charges brought against the son of the Governor of the Castle; charges which, though given the lie by all the other persons interrogated—except that unhappy trio, Mora, Piazza, and Baruello, who abandoned truth entirely under the stress of torture—were taken as evidence of an abominable crime.' But, as the reader knows and as Verri himself had related, what led two of the trio to lie was not the stress of torture but the entice-ment of impunity.

On hearing that contemptible balderdash Padilla said: 'Of all the persons your Lordship has named I know only Fontana and the *Tegnone* (a nickname for Vedano); and all that your Lordship reports as having been said in the course of the trial by those men is as completely false and untrue as anything possibly could be. It is beyond all belief that a gentleman of my rank should have done, or dreamed of doing, such infamous things. And I pray God and His Holy Mother to send me to Hell here and now if all this be true. And I am confident that God will make it known, and known to the world, that those men were lying.'

The judges replied, as a matter of form and without pressing Padilla, that he must be resolved to speak the truth; and then

P

informed him of the Senate's decree putting him on trial for the crime of making and distributing a poisonous unguent and of hiring accomplices. 'I am exceedingly astonished,' was his answer, 'that the Senate should have taken so serious a step when it is clear and proved that all this is nothing but a fraud and a lie—an insult not only to myself but to justice. What! A man of my quality, a man who has spent his life in the service of His Majesty and the defence of this State, a descendant of men who did the same—would I do or think of doing a thing that would bring me such disgrace and dishonour? I repeat: all this is a lie; the biggest fraud ever committed against a man.'

It is cheering to hear such language from outraged innocence; but horrifying to recall that, before those same judges, innocence had been terrified, bewildered, driven to despair, to lies, to calumny; and also fearless, resolute, loyal to the truth—and condemned just the same.

Padilla was acquitted: the exact date is uncertain, but it must have been more than a year later, since his defence was concluded in May 1632. And certainly the acquittal was not conceded as a favour; but in that case did it not occur to the judges that, acquitting Padilla, they declared all their previous condemnations unjust? When they admitted that Padilla had not paid a penny for those imaginary smearings, did they remember the men they had condemned for being paid by him for that very purpose? Did they remember saying to Mora that that motive (to earn money from Padilla) was 'more plausible . . . than that you would find opportunities for selling your preservative, and the Commissioner find opportunities for work'? Did they remember that in the interrogation which followed, when Mora persisted in denying that motive, they had said to him, 'nevertheless it is evidently true'? That when, confronted with Piazza, he denied it again, they had tortured him to make him confess it, and then tortured him once more to give validity to the confession so extorted? That from then on to the end the whole trial had proceeded on the supposition that that motive was the true one? That it had been expressed or implied in all their question, and confirmed by every reply, as the motive at last discovered and acknowledged, the true motive, the single and sufficient motive which led Piazza and Mora, and then the others condemned after them, into crime? Did they remember that the Lord Chancellor, at the Senate's request, had caused a proclamation to be published a few days after the execution of Piazza and Mora, declaring them 'to have fallen into so impious a state of mind as to have betrayed their own Fatherland for money'? And when, eventually, they saw that motive eliminated (for there was never any question thoughout the trial of anyone but Padilla paying anybody) did it occur to them that now there was no reason left for thinking that a crime had been committed at all, except confessions obtained in such ways as they well knew and retracted between the Last Sacraments and death? And that those confessions, already in contradiction with one another, were now in manifest contradiction with the facts? Did they, in short, realize that in acquitting the ring-leader after condemning his accomplices, they showed themselves guilty of condemning the innocent?

Quite the reverse; to judge by what appeared in public, at least. The monument was left standing, the sentence never revoked; and the families of the men it had condemned remained under the imputation of 'infamy'; and the children thus so cruelly orphaned remained legally destitute. And as for the judges' secret thoughts on the matter, who can measure the resistance to fresh evidence of which men are capable, when their error is wilful and is already toughened in the fight against evidence? Indeed, their error must have now become more dear to the judges, more precious than ever; for if previously to admit the innocence of the accused would have meant only the loss of an opportunity of finding someone guilty, now it would mean that they found themselves guilty, and dreadfully so; and all those deceits, all that flouting of the law, which they knew they had committed and which they wished to believe were justified by the discovery of criminals so depraved and so dangerous, would now not only be unveiled in their own intrinsic ugliness but would be seen by all as the means employed for committing atrocious murder. And, lastly, the

cited—provides, it seems to me, a curious example of the power which a dominant opinion can retain over the words of those whose minds it has not been able to subdue. Not only does Ripamonti never explicitly deny the guilt of those who suffered in the affair (nor, in fact, did anyone else until Verri, in any work intended for publication) but he more than once seems to want expressly to affirm it. Referring to Piazza's first interrogation, he speaks of his 'evil intentions' and of the judges' 'clearsightedness': he says that Piazza 'by so often contradicting himself, revealed his crime in the act of denying it'. So too when he comes to Mora: 'He denied his guilt as criminals usually do, so long as he could bear the torture; but gave in the end a truthful account of the whole matter (*exposuit omnia cum fide*).' And yet at the same time we find Ripamonti insinuating the contrary view—timidly hinting, in passing, at his own uncertainty as to some of the more important circumstances; dropping phrases here and there that guide the reader's reflections in the right direction; sometimes putting into the mouths of the accused words more calculated to prove their innocence than those they themselves had been able to find; lastly, evincing the sort of compassion that is only aroused by innocence. Alluding to the cooking-pot found in Mora's house, he says: 'This find made a great impression at first, though it may have been, though sordid enough, quite insignificant; but it seemed it could have a bearing on the inquiry.' Speaking of the first confrontation of Piazza and Mora, he says that Mora 'invoked the justice of God against a false and malicious fabrication, against a trap set for unwary innocence'. He calls Mora 'that unhappy father and husband who unwittingly caused his own and his family's ruin'. And all those reflections which, as the reader will remember, I made on the obvious contradiction between the acquittal of Padilla and the condemnation of the others, these and much else that one might say on the subject are all suggested by Ripamonti in a single word: 'The smearers were punished nevertheless, *unctores puniti tamen.*' What a wealth of meaning in that adverb or conjunction! And he goes on: 'The city would have been horrorstruck by the outrageous cruelty of the execution were it not that anything seemed less dreadful than the crime itself.'

But where Ripamonti's real feelings show most clearly is where he protests that he does not wish to show them. After recounting various cases of people who fell under suspicion of 'smearing' but were not in fact brought to trial, he continues:

Here I find myself at a difficult and delicate point in my discussion of the affair. Can I say that I myself am persuaded that these were the only persons mistakenly assumed to be smearers? That, in short, I believe that there were really any smearers at all? . . . Nor is my difficulty due to an uncertainty in the matter itself, but to the fact that I am not permitted the freedom to which every writer lays claim, viz. that of expressing what one really thinks. For were I to assert that in truth there were no smearers, that imagination has mis-construed as human malice what was really a punishment sent from God, the cry would at once be raised accusing History of impiety and this historian of a want of respect for a solemn judgement of the courts: so firmly rooted in men's minds is the contrary view. And the populace and the nobility, the one, as usual, credulous and the other proud, are united in eager defence of this view as of something exceedingly precious and sacred. To defy so many adversaries would be a most troublesome undertaking and in any case a futile one. Therefore, without either denying or affirming, or even inclining to one side rather than the other, I will limit myself to presenting the opinion of others.

And should it occur to the reader that, in these circumstances, it might have been more reasonable, as well as easier, to say nothing at all, he should know that Ripamonti was the city's official historiographer; that is to say, a man who could some-times be ordered to write history and sometimes forbidden.

Another historiographer (though he worked on a wider field), Battista Nani,[2] who, as a Venetian, was under no constraint in this case to say what was false for fear of giving offence, was led to believe it nevertheless on the authority of an inscription and a monument. 'It may well be true,' he wrote, 'that the terrified

[2] Nani's *Storia della Repubblica Veneta* was first printed in Venice, 1662. Manzoni quotes from Part I, Book 8, p. 473 in the ed. (Venice, Lovisa) of 1720. [Tr.]

populace imagined a great deal, but the fact remains that the crime was discovered and duly punished; witness the inscriptions that are still to be seen in Milan and the memorial marking where the houses stood in which these monsters used to congregate.' But the reader not otherwise acquainted with Nani will be greatly deceived if he bases his opinion of Nani's intelligence on this piece of reasoning. On various important embassies abroad and in public office at home Nani had abundant opportunities for observing men and things; and his historical work is there to show that he was no mean observer. But neither the sentences of criminal courts nor the fate of the poor (taken a few at a time) are regarded as a proper subject for history; so it need not surprise us that Nani, when he touched in passing on our affair, did not greatly trouble himself over details. Had anyone referred him to some other Milanese column or inscription as proof of a defeat suffered by Venice (a defeat that would be as true as the crime of 'those monsters'), Nani most certainly would have laughed.

It is more surprising and more distasteful to find the same argument and similar insults in the work of a much more famous —and very deservedly famous—man. Muratori, in his *Trattato del governo della peste*,[3] after referring to various accounts of similar cases, says:

But none is more celebrated than that which occurred in Milan during the plague of 1630, when many persons were arrested and, confessing their hideous crime, were put to death with the utmost severity. A dreadful memorial of this affair survives in the shape of the 'Column of Infamy', which I myself have seen and which stands where once was the house of those inhuman murderers; an object deserving the greatest attention lest such execrable scenes be ever re-enacted.

And it does nothing to lessen one's distaste, but only alters it, to find that Muratori was not so firmly convinced as these

[3] L. A. Muratori (1672–1750), the greatest Italian scholar of the eighteenth century. The work Manzoni refers to may be found in Vol. 47 of the Venetian edition, 1790; the words quoted being on pp. 157, 159, 160. The reference a few lines on is to *I promessi sposi*, Ch. XXXII. [Tr.]

words make him appear. For later, when he comes to discuss the horrors that can be caused by imagining and believing in such things without regard for evidence (and this, clearly, is what he is really concerned about) he writes: 'It leads to people being thrown into prison and compelled by torture to confess crimes they may never have committed, and then miserably slaughtered on the scaffold.' This looks—doesn't it?—remarkably like an allusion to our poor sufferers. And what gives substance to the suspicion is that Muratori at once continues with words which I quoted in the preceding work and which are few enough to be repeated here. 'In Milan I have met people of good judgement, and who had been well informed on the matter by their elders, who were not much convinced of the truth of that story about the contamination of the city with poisonous unguents which made such a stir during the plague of 1630.' It is, I repeat, impossible not to suspect that in his heart Muratori thought these 'scenes' which he called 'execrable' were really just stupid stories and that—and this is more serious —the men he called 'inhuman murderers' were really innocent and murdered. His case would be one of those, unhappily not infrequent, of men, by no means prone to tell lies, who, desiring to undermine the power of false and pernicious opinions, but fearing to make things worse by a frontal attack, have thought it best to start by lying so as to be able later to insinuate truth.

After Muratori we meet with a writer more famous than he as an historian and one too (which, in a matter of this kind, would make one expect his judgement to be particularly valuable) who was also a lawyer—as he himself said, 'more lawyer than politician'—, Pietro Giannone.[4] I will not, however, quote Giannone's judgement here, having too recently done so. It is Nani's; which the reader saw a little while ago and which Giannone copied word for word, this time giving the reference in a footnote.

I say 'this time' because Giannone's copying from Nani with-

---

[4] P. Giannone (1676–1748) had a European reputation as a vehement upholder of the independence of the civil power *vis-à-vis* the Church. His *Storia civile del regno di Napoli* was published in 1723. [Tr.]

out acknowledgement is a thing worth noting if, as I believe, it has hitherto passed unnoticed. His account, for example, of the rising in Catalonia and the Portuguese revolution in 1640 is a transcript of Nani's, occupying seven quarto pages, with very few omissions, additions, or alterations, the most substantial of these being that the original text, which runs on continuously, has been broken up into chapters and paragraphs. But what would be incredible if it were not true is that when our Neapolitan lawyer comes to deal, not with the risings in Barcelona or Lisbon, but with that of Palermo in 1647 and with the more famous—because it gave rise to stranger happenings and involved Masaniello—rebellion of Naples in the same year, he can think of no better, of no more detailed way of describing those events than to lift his entire account of them—not just the materials but the complete narrative—from the work of the Knight and Procurator of St. Mark! And this too after the following words introducing this section of his book:

The unhappy events which these revolutions involved have been described by a number of writers, some trying to present them as quasi-miraculous exceptions to the ordinary course of Nature, while others confuse the reader with too much petty detail, and so fail to bring out clearly the true causes of what happened and its aims and development and conclusion. Therefore I shall make it my business, guided by the weightiest and most discerning authorities, to present an account of the matter reduced to its just proportions.

Yet, as anyone can see who takes the trouble to compare text with text, Giannone had no sooner written these words than he laid hands on Nani's narrative, mixing a little of his own with it now and then, especially near the beginning, altering a little here and there, sometimes because he really had no choice, just as if you buy second-hand linen you must substitute your own markings for the original owner's. Thus where the Venetian has 'in that kingdom', the Neapolitan writes 'in this kingdom'; where the contemporary writer wrote 'the factions remain almost as they were', the later one says 'the residue of those old factions remained'. True, we do find, in this lengthy section,

besides such small additions and alterations, sundry longer
pieces in the patchwork that are not from Nani. But, believe it
or not, they are almost all lifted, and almost word for word,
from someone else—from Domenico Parrino, a writer who
(reversing the fate of so many) is now forgotten but still much
read, perhaps indeed more than he himself had ever hoped, if
people read as much as they praise, both in Italy and abroad,
the *Storia civile del regno di Napoli* which bears the name of
Pietro Giannone. For—still keeping to the two periods just
mentioned—if, having transcribed from Nani a description of
the Catalan and Portuguese rebellions, Giannone goes to Nani
again for his account of the fall of the favourite Olivares, it is
from Parrino that he copies out his account of the consequent
recall of the Viceroy of Naples, the Duke of Medina, and the
latter's dodges for putting off as long as possible the surrender
of his post to his successor Enriquez de Cabrera. From Parrino
too is copied out most of Giannone's account of Cabrera's
government; after which bits from Parrino and Nani are fitted
together like inlaid work when we come to the government of
the Duke of Arcos and through the rest of the period preceding
the risings in Palermo and Naples; and, as I have said, throughout the progress of these to their conclusion under the government of Don John of Austria and of the Count of Oñatte. Then
it is Parrino alone who is used, still in long pieces or a lot of
little ones, for this last Viceroy's expedition against Piombino
and Portolongone; as also for the Duke of Guise's attempt on
Naples; as also for the plague of 1656. Then it is Nani for the
Peace of the Pyrenees; and then Parrino, finally, for a short
appendix on the effects of this peace on the kingdom of Naples.

Voltaire, in his *Siècle de Louis XIV*,[5] speaking of the tribunals
set up by that king at Metz and Brisac in order to adjudicate
his claims to the territories of neighbouring States, has a footnote
mentioning Giannone with high praise, as was to be expected,
but also with a rebuke. Here is the footnote translated:
'Giannone, so celebrated for his valuable history of Naples, says
that the tribunals were set up at Tournai. He is often wrong

[5] Ch. 17.

on matters that do not concern his own country. He says, for example, that at Nimeguen Louis XIV made peace with Sweden; which was in fact his ally already.' But, leaving aside the praise, the rebuke was not this time deserved by Giannone, who, as on so many other occasions, had not even gone to the trouble of making a mistake. It is true that in this 'so celebrated' author's work occur these words: 'Peace followed between France, Sweden, the Empire, and the Emperor' (which, after all, may be ambiguous rather than wrong); and also the following:

They [the French] then set up two tribunals, one at Tournai and the other at Metz; and arrogating to themselves a jurisdiction such as the world had never seen over neighbouring sovereigns, they did not merely make over to France, as 'dependencies', every country to which they took a fancy along the frontiers of Flanders and the Empire, but actually and in fact took possession of those territories, constraining the inhabitants to acknowledge the Most Christian King as their sovereign, drawing the frontiers where they pleased and exercising in fact all those rights of overlordship which Princes are accustomed to claim over their subjects.

But it was poor unknown Parrino who penned these words; and Giannone has not even excised them from the narrative where they occurred but has carried them off context and all; because often Giannone cannot wait to pluck a fruit here and a fruit there, but must dig up the whole tree for transplanting in his own garden. His entire account, one may say, of the Peace of Nimeguen is the work of Parrino; and likewise, in great part, with much left out and a few additions, his account of the viceroyalty in Naples of the Marquis de los Veles, during which that Peace was concluded and with which Parrino ends his narrative and Giannone the penultimate book of his. And probably (I had almost said certainly) anyone who cared to amuse himself by completing these comparisons would find that what has been observed with regard to some decades of the Spanish dominion in Naples held good for the entire preceding period back to the beginning of that régime, which is also the point at which Parrino begins his narrative; nor, if I am not very much deceived, would he ever find this much-plundered author mentioned by name. From Sarpi too (as a kind and learned friend has pointed out to me) Giannone lifted many passages without acknowledgement and the whole plan and order of one of his digressions. And who knows what other un-noticed thefts would come to light if one cared to look for them; but so much as we have seen—appropriations, not merely of other writers' choice and arrangement of materials, or of their judgements and comments and general spirit, but of entire pages and chapters and books—this, in a famous and highly com-mended author, is surely something of a phenomenon. Whether due to sterility or to sloth, the result is certainly a rarity, as the audacity was rare that brought it about: but more than rare, but unique, was Giannone's good fortune—that, for all this, he re-mains (while he does remain) a great man. And let this circum-stance, together with the occasion for pointing it out which our theme supplied, be my excuse to the gentle reader for taking him on so long a *détour* in what is, after all, only a supplementary chapter of a small book.

Who does not know Parini's unfinished poem on the Column of Infamy? Yet who would not be surprised to find no mention of it here?

Here then are the few lines of this fragment, in which the celebrated poet echoes only too faithfully what the common people and the inscription said:

> Quando, tra vili case e in mezzo a poche
> rovine, i' vidi ignobil piazza aprirsi.
> Quivi romita una colonna sorge
> in fra l'erbe infeconde e i sassi e il lezzo,
> ov'uom mai non penetra, però ch'indi
> genio propizio all'insubre cittade
> ognun rimove, alto gridando: lungi,
> o buoni cittadin, lungi, che il suolo
> miserabile infame non v'infetti.[6]

---

[6] '. . . when I saw before me an ignoble square between mean houses and scattered ruins. Here a solitary column stands among sterile grass and stones

Was this opinion really Parini's? We do not know: and his
having expressed it so affirmatively—but in verse—is no argument; because at that time it was a rule commonly accepted
that poets had the privilege of making use of any belief, true
or false, that was likely to produce a powerful or pleasing impression. The privilege! A privilege to uphold falsehood and
make it exciting! But then the answer given was that this did
not matter because . . . well, poets, nobody believed what *they*
said. To which answer there is no answer; except that it may
seem odd that poets were satisfied with either the permission or
the excuse.

Then at last came Pietro Verri, the first writer after one
hundred and forty-seven years who saw and said who had been
the real murderers; the first to speak up for the innocent who
had been butchered with such barbarity and abhorred so
obtusely; to claim for them a compassion the more due for being
so long delayed. And yet Verri's *Osservazioni*, written in 1777,
were not published until 1804, when they came out with other
works of his, some already printed and some not, in a collection
of 'Italian Classics of Political Economy'.[7] And in his preface
the editor explained the delay. 'It was thought,' he said, 'that
the good name of the Senate might suffer from the disrepute
that would attach to the Senate of former times.' A very usual
kind of sentiment, this, in those days; an effect of that *esprit de
corps* which made each member of an institution, rather than
ever admit that his predecessors had made mistakes, assume
responsibility even for follies not committed by himself. In our
day this kind of loyalty to institutions has less chance of extending so far back into the past, because almost everywhere in
Europe institutions are of recent origin—with a few exceptions,

---

and smells. It is approached by no one, for the guardian Spirit of the
Lombard city turns all men from this place, crying: Away, good citizens,
away, lest the wretched infamous ground infect you!' These last words
render the Latin inscription on the Column: *Procul hinc, procul ergo boni cives,
ne vos infelix infame solum commaculet.* Giuseppe Parini (1729–1799), like
Manzoni a Milanese, is one of the finest Italian satirical poets. [Tr.]

[7] Milan, 1804: Verri's *Osservazioni sulla tortura* is in Vol. 17, pp. 193–312.

to be sure, and one in particular which, since it does not draw its origin from man, can be neither abolished nor replaced. In addition, such institutional loyalty is, now more than ever before, resisted and undermined by individualism: the 'I' thinks itself too rich to beg from a 'We'. And in this respect individualism is beneficial; God forbid I should say in every respect.

In any case, Pietro Verri was not the man to sacrifice truth-telling to human respect of this kind, when the truth to be told was important both because of the credit enjoyed by the contrary falsehood and still more because of the purpose he had in mind in telling it. But there was a circumstance which rendered human respect, in this case, just: the President of the Senate was the illustrious writer's father. And so it happens quite often; good reasons come to the aid of bad ones, and then the combined effect of both is that a truth which has taken a long while to come to birth has still to remain for a while concealed.